OTHER BOOKS BY HERBERT FEIS

The Road to Pearl Harbor: The Coming of the War Between the United States and Japan

The China Tangle: The American Effort in China from Pearl Harbor to the Marshall Mission

Churchill-Roosevelt-Stalin: The War They Waged and the Peace They Sought

Between War and Peace: The Potsdam Conference

The
Atomic Bomb
and the
End of World War II

BY HERBERT FEIS

Originally published in 1961
under the title *Japan Subdued:
The Atomic Bomb and the End
of the War in the Pacific*, now
revised and made more complete
and revealing.

PRINCETON NEW JERSEY
PRINCETON UNIVERSITY PRESS

Preface

This volume is the complement of *Between War and Peace: The Potsdam Conference*. In that book I told how after the defeat of Germany the Allied governments strove to dispose of the unsettled situations in and around the rim of Europe. In this narrative I relate the plans and acts of the Allied and Japanese governments during this climactic period of 1945, of the events leading to the end of the war in the Pacific, of the discussion about future arrangements in the Far East, and of the course pursued and orders issued by the American government.

The effort to achieve atomic fission culminated at this time, and atomic weapons were introduced into war. Because of the enduring interest and import of these developments I have gone outside the rigorous narrative boundaries and ventured on some analytical reflections about two connected decisions which are still the focus of dispute—the timing of the explanation of the Allied demand upon Japan for unconditional surrender and the decision to use the atomic bomb to compel surrender most quickly.

My impulse was to have a different subtitle from the one which the book bears—to call it "Japan Subdued: Eternity Imperiled." But this was adjudged puzzling and sensational. Too sensational it would not have been, nor excessive in import. But I was reconciled to the more matter-of-fact subtitle by the thought that the events narrated will, in themselves, imprint the conclusion which I had wanted to epitomize.

As in the preceding studies, I have been much aided by others—in and out of government. It is in order to repeat the acknowledgement made in *Between War and Peace* of the opportunity to consult the collection of papers regarding the Potsdam Conference which have been assembled by the State Department, and to express thanks for assistance in their use to members of the Historical Division, particularly Dr. J. Bernard Noble, Dr. E. Taylor Parks, and Dr. G. M. R. Dougall. I am also indebted to the Department of the Army, which permitted me to consult various records, including segments of the file on the Manhattan Project (the atomic bomb), and for guidance in their use to members of the Military Records Branch in the Federal Records Center, particularly Sherrod East, Wilbur Nigh, and Edward Reese.

Again the records which the Honorable W. Averell Harriman, former American Ambassador to the Soviet Union, with steadfast generosity, allowed me to draw on were of much value. So were the papers of the Honorable Joseph C. Grew, then Under-Secretary of State. The Honorable Eugene H. Dooman, who was closely associated with Grew in formulation of our Far Eastern policy, was kind enough to read the manuscript; his dissent from the conclusions in the two last chapters of the book did not deter him from helping me to improve the others.

Several of the chief directors of and contributors to the Manhattan Project were obliging enough to read and comment on those sections concerned with the development and use of the atomic bomb—notably General Leslie H. Groves, Director of the Manhattan Project, Dr. Vannevar Bush, Dr. James B. Conant, and Dr. J. Robert Oppenheimer. General Groves, moreover, responded to the demands I made upon his memory and knowledge in talk. Thanks are due also Dr. Rudolph Winnacker, distinguished historian in the Office of the Secretary of Defense, for reviewing these chapters, correctively.

Mrs. Margaret Gowing and Lord Sherwell (formerly Roger Makins) reviewed with me the course of discussion within British official circles about the decision to use the atomic bomb against Japan.

Mrs. Arlene Van B. Pratt strove to see that my facts and citations were correct, and my reasoning defensible. Miss Rebecca Fuller carried out with good natured patience the tasks of typing and custodianship of sources and manuscripts.

My wife, Ruth Stanley-Brown Feis, edited, read, and corrected the proofs, and despite all earlier vows and experience did most of the work on the index.

I am grateful to the Rockefeller Foundation for its supporting grant and to the Institute for Advanced Study for its appointment to membership and generous working facilities.

I wish again to repeat the statement in the prefaces to my other studies of this wartime era, "The aid given by persons in the government should not be construed as an indication of official sponsorship or approval, nor should that given by persons outside the government be taken to mean that they share responsibility for the contents of the pages that follow."

HERBERT FEIS

York, Maine

Several reasons impelled me to write this revised edition. New and important information has enabled me to give a more complete and authoritative narrative. The lapse of time has revealed more clearly the significance of the events recounted; and interest in the decision to use the bomb has become more critical and resounding.

July, 1965   HERBERT FEIS
York, Maine

Contents

PART ONE

May 1945 – Japan Alone

1. How Could the War Best Be Ended?

MAY 1945. The war in Europe was over. The members of the coalition were about to enter upon joint occupation and control of Germany. The Charter of the United Nations was being conceived at San Francisco. Truman, Churchill, and Stalin had agreed to confer about the many unsettled European situations.

Japan, all alone, was fighting on. The United States was assembling ever larger forces—army, navy, and air—for the next great actions in the Pacific. The Soviet government was transporting divisions to the Far East for deployment along the Manchurian frontier. The British Commonwealth was planning the expulsion of the Japanese from the south Pacific and southeast Asia. The Chinese were getting ready to start a march toward the coast in the Canton-Hong Kong area, to be their first offensive since their country was invaded.

The structure of Japanese life and production was being smashed and burned. The Japanese Navy and Air Force were but remnants of what they had been. But the spirit of defiance was still alive in the armed services and among the people—unwavering in their acceptance of suffering and the sad stroke of death. In Okinawa over one hundred thousand Japanese, hunted with mortar and fire, shelled from the sea and bombed from the air, were refusing to give up. Japanese suicide planes were flinging themselves in exalted desperation against the off-shore American fleet—with frightening effect. These grim experiences were taken as proof that the ordeal still ahead might be long and agonizing.

How could it be ended surely and quickly? The American managers of the war were giving thought to three sets of measures, all of which were being shaped for use.

The obvious and perhaps most certain way was to beat down the Japanese until they could no longer fight on—by enlarging the assaults on Japan and Japanese armed forces wherever they could be reached, by air and sea and on land, culminating in the invasion of the Japanese home islands.

Another was by inducement. The Japanese might agree to submit before they were utterly crushed if the coalition (including perhaps the Soviet Union, not yet at war with Japan) informed them how they would be regarded in defeat. Might not even this hardy nation, if assured of tolerable treatment after surrender, be brought to give up before it was reduced to the last extreme of misery? Might not the elements who

[3]

knew the war was lost prevail, if a promise was given the Japanese people that after their means of making war were broken, they would be allowed to re-engage in peaceful pursuits, determine their own political forms and future, and that their fighting men would not be kept in long captivity?

The third, most secret, was by shock. The Japanese might be awed into surrender when they found out that a refusal could lead only to utter destruction—because their enemies had an irresistible new weapon and the Soviet Union was joining them.

Each of these routes could lead to the end of the war; or two or three of them could do so, in combination or in succession. Within the American government each had its own group of activators who nursed their plans and evolved their policies more or less separately from the others. The three were conjoined only in fitful and irregular consultation between the men in the small circle of ultimate decision-makers, and with the President.

The ideas of the heads of the military organization—the Joint Chiefs of Staff and top commanders of our forces—were centered on strategic plans for the advancement of the assaults by sea, land, and air on going lines, and in preparations for the next greater operations. Although not opposed to trying, they thought it unlikely that promises of leniency could induce surrender until the Japanese armed forces were thoroughly subdued. Some officials in the State Department had long been advocating an appeal to the preservative sense of the Japanese people before the struggle reached its portended climax. Secretary of War Stimson joined them in June. However, he conceived the exposition of our intentions as an accompaniment to an ultimate warning of destruction, fused by the atomic bomb. He was Chairman of the small group (known as the Interim Committee) who knew most about the progress and potentialities of this emergent secret weapon, and hoped that its burst would bring the war to an almost instant end.

This narrative will follow each of these three sets of means and measures separately toward their convergence.

2. By Combined Assault

THE end of the war in Europe released American, British, and Russian forces for use in the Pacific. The amplitude of their combat resources enabled the members of the coalition to agree easily upon their respective parts in the assault upon Japan; they were great enough to enable each to engage in those operations upon which it was most intent.

After many months of discussion, several differences of judgment within the American government were still unresolved.

Some senior naval and air force officers, including the Commanding Admiral of the United States Fleet, Admiral King, and the President's representative on the Joint Chiefs of Staff, Admiral Leahy, believed that Japan could be forced to accept our terms merely by our suffocating naval blockade and our devastating air assaults.[1] To assure the utmost effect for these measures they favored the acquisition of several more bases nearer to and around Japan. If that were done, they believed that the Japanese would be forced to give up before long, without having to engage in land battles on the Japanese home islands, and even if the Russians should refrain from entering the war.

However, the proponents of this belief did not challenge the opinion prevailing in the Army that it was essential to prepare for, and if need be undertake, the invasion of the home islands. Two reflections made it easier for them to go along with plans for this venture. Enlarging naval and air attacks were to be continued anyway, to break down resistance to the invasion; these might be so damaging that Japan would quit before great scheduled land battles were fought. And, in any case, the losses suffered in the air and naval services would be less.

But as late as April General Marshall and Admiral King had variant ideas about the range and schedule of the operations for which we ought to be getting ready. The differences between them had been summarized in a message which Marshall sent to General MacArthur on April 12th, asking for his judgment. Marshall related that one group (mainly Navy) thought that much more preparation would be needed for the invasion program than was possible with the target dates then in mind, November 1945, for the landing in Kyushu, southernmost of the four main islands, and March 1, 1946, for the surge onto the Tokyo plain. Hence they favored a preliminary campaign not only of air and sea assault, but

---

[1] *Fleet Admiral King*, by Admiral Ernest J. King and W. M. Whitehill, page 605, and William D. Leahy, *I Was There*, pages 384-385.

also an operation in the Ningpo-Chusan area of the China Coast, south of Shanghai and north of Formosa, and perhaps also a lodgment on Shantung or Korea, and seizure of islands in the Tsushima Strait area.[2] The advocates of these measures were saying that before the invasion was launched it was essential to be sure that Japanese air power was destroyed and that the Japanese troops could not be moved from the mainland of China to the defense of the home islands. But they were not concealing an ardent hope that if these actions were taken the surrender might be effected without a major landing on Japan proper, for they predicted that on their own soil the Japanese would fight more desperately than ever.

The proponents (mainly Army) of the more frontal strategy were maintaining that the landing in Kyushu ought to be begun as soon as the assault forces could be well organized in the Philippines and adequate bases established in the Ryuykus and elsewhere for land-based air operations; and in any event not later than November. They were confident that the programmed American naval actions and air attacks would have reduced by then Japanese air and sea power vitally, that we would be able to prevent any movement of Japanese forces from the mainland to Japan, and that our air assault would have devastated such large areas in the home islands that the Japanese ability to resist invasion would have been greatly weakened. The experience in the Philippines and even in Okinawa was deemed to show that the losses that would be suffered in the invasion were acceptable. Moreover, they argued that a series of operations against other islands (Formosa or in the Tsushima Strait) or other limited objectives (in Shantung or Korea) would result in higher losses, and might lead to engagement of large numbers of troops while not assuring the early termination of the war.

MacArthur's response to this query could have been anticipated. As early as February (1945) he had elaborated his ideas to a member of the Operations Division of the War Department who had made them of full record on his return to Washington. The future Supreme Allied Commander had then said he was sure that the only means of defeating Japan was by the invasion of the industrial heart of the country. He believed that the Tokyo Plain was the proper place to invade Japan,

[2] A directive of April 3, 1945, on Pacific operations, had said this about a possible Ningpo-Chusan operation: "Continue planning for seizing positions in the Chusan Archipelago and the eastern portion of the Ningpo Peninsula. Plans should include the possibility and desirability of confining objective to the Chusan Archipelago."

The Tsushima Strait area is the passage between the island of Kyushu and the island of Tsushima, half way to Korea.

and that it would be best to aim straight at it without a previous landing either in the island of Kyushu in the south, or Hokkaido in the north. For he thought that proper timing, in conjunction with a movement by the Russians and the strategic surprise to be gained, would bring the greater advantage.[3]

The answer that MacArthur had returned to Marshall on April 20th was consonant with this earlier exposition of his ideas, except he agreed now that the invasion might well be in two stages. After analyzing the several possible strategic routes, he said he thought that the best course was to proceed as soon as possible with the assault on the southern island of Kyushu to be followed with utmost speed by the decisive landing on the Tokyo Plain. His opinion, corroborating the judgment of the Army staff organization, had shaped the further study of the Joint Staff Planners and the conclusions of the Joint Chiefs of Staff.

On May 16th Secretary Stimson gave President Truman a preview of the recommendations to which the Joint Chiefs were giving precision. In connection with his report, Stimson pointed out that it was probable that the deployment of American forces from Europe to the Pacific would require so much time that the President would have the chance he wanted to pursue his diplomatic purposes with our allies before the start of invasion of Japan. The Secretary of War meant that there would be time to revise or abandon this program of invasion as the outcome and import of the several other initiatives—of which we shall be telling— became known.

On May 25th, less than three weeks after the German surrender, the Joint Chiefs dispatched a formal directive to MacArthur, Nimitz and Arnold, the first paragraph of which stated:

"The Joint Chiefs of Staff direct the invasion of Kyushu (operation OLYMPIC) target date 1 November 1945, in order to:

(1) Intensify the blockade and aerial bombardment of Japan.

(2) Contain and destroy major enemy forces.

(3) Support further advances for the purpose of establishing the conditions favorable to the decisive invasion of the industrial heart of Japan."

The President was not sure that this program of bold and direct invasion of Japan was essential and sound. Quite possibly he was dis-

---

[3] The main sections of the memo of this talk made by Col. Paul L. Freeman, Jr., are printed in the publication (in mimeograph) issued by the Department of Defense in September 1955, entitled "The Entry of the Soviet Union into the War Against Japan: Military Plans, 1941-1945," pages 51-52 footnote.

turbed by Admiral Leahy's sustained opinion that we could win the war without invading the home islands and incurring excessive loss of lives. In any case he asked Leahy to inform the Chiefs of Staff that he wished to discuss the proposed strategy with them again, explaining tactfully that he wanted to prepare for the talks with Churchill and Stalin, scheduled for the middle of July. In particular, the President wanted to know how many men and ships would be needed for an invasion of the home islands; and how long the consequent land battle would go on; and what losses we would incur if we attempted the invasion, and what they would be if we relied solely on sea and air blockade and attack; and what we wanted the Russians and other allies to do. "It is his [the President's] intention," Leahy informed the Chiefs of Staff on June 14th, "to make his decisions on the campaign with the purpose of economizing to the maximum extent possible the loss of American lives."

The Joint Chiefs wrote out a thorough and defensive exposition for use in talking with the President. The purport of this was that it would not be advisable to wait and see whether the Japanese could be forced to surrender unconditionally merely by the prolongation of air and naval assault and blockade. It reaffirmed the expectation that before OLYMPIC operation was started the movement of Japanese shipping south of Korea would have been reduced to almost nothing and the Japanese navy would be without power, so there would be no need to capture other positions close to Japan in order to prevent transfer of Japanese from the mainland to the home islands. A preliminary attempt to land in Korea was judged unnecessary, harder and more dangerous than the planned entry into Kyushu. A lodgment on that southernmost of the main islands was deemed essential to tighten our blockade of the whole of Japan, to make our bombardment overwhelming, and to force surrender by invasion of the Tokyo Plain.

In the writing of this paper, uncertainties were encountered in the attempt to forecast the number of casualties that might be suffered. Marshall hustled off an urgent message to MacArthur telling him that the President was much concerned about this matter, and asking whether he held by his earlier estimate that about 50,800 casualties were likely to be incurred in the first thirty days of the landing at Kyushu. MacArthur answered at once that he had made that earlier estimate for routine purposes of planning for medical care and replacements. He did not anticipate that losses would be so high. He thought that of any plan of operations that had been proposed, this would mean the smallest loss of lives in the end. Then, repeating what he had said before, he pointed out that the risk and losses would be greatly lessened if a Soviet attack were launched from Siberia sufficiently ahead of the U.S. target date. Marshall was just as desirous to have the Russians do so before the Americans tried to invade Japan. He thought the Japanese armies in Manchuria much stronger than they were.

Secretaries Stimson, Forrestal, and Assistant Secretary of War John J. McCloy were present when the Joint Chiefs of Staff met with Truman on June 18th, but although Under Secretary of State Joseph C. Grew had been told by the President a few days before that his presence at this conference was also desired, when it came about neither he nor anyone else of the State Department was asked to attend. Marshall, following closely the line of reasoning in the briefing paper, took the lead in explaining the described program.[4] He said that the fight against Germany indicated that the hope that air power alone would be able to drive Japan out of the war was unjustified; and that the task would be the more difficult there since the Japanese were scattered through mountainous country. As for the number of casualties that would be suffered in the invasion of Kyushu, experience in the Pacific war was so diverse as to make it hard to give any estimate; but there was reason to believe that losses in the first thirty days of Kyushu should not exceed those suffered in Luzon (31,000 killed, wounded, and missing) and they would almost certainly be less than would be incurred in any attempt to gain entry into Korea. In sum, he "felt that the plan offered the only way the Japanese could be forced into a feeling of utter helplessness."

This opinion about the limitations of what could be achieved by air power alone was confirmed by General Ira Eaker, speaking for General Henry H. ("Hap") Arnold, Commanding General, Army Air Force. Eaker went on to observe that those who advocated reliance on air power alone overlooked the impressive fact, revealed by our experience in Europe, that air casualties are always much heavier when air faces the enemy alone. In the ensuing discussion no one tried to reconcile this opinion with the expectation that Japanese air power would soon be so maimed and reduced that it would be able to do hardly anything to ward off our air assault, though perhaps still able to send out suicide planes. Nor was the possibility of starving out the Japanese discussed.

Admiral King's comments were in concordance with those of his

---

[4] The main sections of minutes of this meeting are contained in the publication cited in footnote 3, "The Entry of the Soviet Union into the War Against Japan: Military Plans, 1941-1945." A slightly censored version is contained in Potsdam Papers, Document 598. Still another account, with somewhat different selective emphasis is in the Forrestal Diaries for June 18, 1945.

colleagues. He said that he had become more and more impressed with the strategic location of Kyushu as the key to the success of any major campaign. When and as Kyushu was won, there would be time to judge the effect of possible operations by the Russians and the Chinese. He agreed it was sound to prepare now for the Tokyo Plain; the invasion could always be stopped if desired. Marshall concurred in the idea that reckoning in regard to action beyond Kyushu could be deferred. When the President asked if the ultimate decision would not depend on what the Russians did, it was agreed that this would have influence; perhaps it would not be necessary to invade the Tokyo Plain (operation CORONET).

Leahy turned the discussion back to the question of casualties. Thirty-five per cent of the troops engaged in Okinawa were casualties (killed, wounded, missing); would they not, he asked, range as high when Kyushu was assaulted? Marshall thought it improbable.[5] Admitting that all predictions were dubious, King said he did not think so, since in Okinawa the landing forces had to make a straight frontal attack, but that the assault on Kyushu was to be on three sides simultaneously and there would be much more room for maneuver.

Here the narrative may be interrupted to call attention to two perplexities which the available incomplete record does not clear up.

In none of the memos or directives about these strategic plans is there any mention of the atomic bomb as a *tactical weapon* to be used in connection with the landings. There were several reasons for the abstention, some avowed, some conjectural. Primary was the rule of secrecy. Some of the senior military leaders may have found it hard to contemplate that the great forces under their command might be displaced by this new weapon in the final achievement of victory. Then they underestimated the power of the bomb, as did Marshall. In any case, Assistant Secretary of War John McCloy was hushed up when, as this meeting was about to disperse, he spoke of the chance that invasion might be staved off by the bomb.

Nor did the assembled company, then or later, formally discuss the bomb as a tactical weapon. But General Marshall had given thought to it.

[5] At this meeting on June 18th Marshall estimated that the assault on Kyushu would be carried out by 767,000 troops and opposed by about 350,000 Japanese. This did not include naval or air forces. He said that in view of the diversity of experience in other engagements, it was not sensible to give an estimate of numbers of casualties, *but in the first thirty days* of combat on Kyushu they should not exceed those suffered in Luzon—31,000. (My italics.) Potsdam Papers, Document 598.

As he recalled later, "One of the things that appalled me was the cost in casualties of an invasion. . . . To get to the plains would have been a very costly operation in lives. We knew the Japanese were determined and fanatical like the Morros and we would have to exterminate them, almost man by man. So we thought the bomb would be a wonderful weapon as a protection and preparation for landings. But we didn't realize its value to give the Japanese such a shock that they could surrender without loss of face."[6]

To revert to the account of this meeting of June 18th—the President, after hearing these several reassuring statements, said that he gathered the Joint Chiefs were now unanimously of the opinion that the Kyushu operation was the best course. All members of that group affirmed that such was their belief. Stimson and Forrestal concurred, Stimson however saying that he did so since there was no other choice, but he ". . . still hoped for some fruitful accomplishment through other means."[7] Of what he had in mind more will soon be told. "The President said he considered that the Kyushu plan was all right from the military standpoint and . . . the Joint Chiefs could go ahead with it; that we can do this operation and then decide as to the final action later. . . . He had hoped there was a possibility of preventing an Okinawa from one end of Japan to the other. He was clear on the situation now and was quite sure that the Joint Chiefs of Staff should proceed with the Kyushu operation."

Marshall let MacArthur know that his answer to the inquiry regarding the advisability of the OLYMPIC operation, and his estimate of possible casualties that might be incurred in capturing Kyushu, had had a determining influence in bringing the President to authorize that enterprise.

The course of the discussion revealed that each of the chief participants could find enough reasons to acquiesce in the vast plan for the invasion of Kyushu; but this fused assent was permeated by a variety of hopes that we would not have to go further and force our way upon the Tokyo

---

[6] Talk with Lilienthal, June 12, 1947. *Journals of David E. Lilienthal, Volume Two, The Atomic Energy Years*, page 198. Lilienthal noted that Marshall does not seem to have taken into account the possible effect of radioactivity upon our landing forces. Marshall told him that the invasion plans called for a total of twelve bombs. But in a later interview he spoke of wanting nine bombs. John P. Sutherland, "The Story General Marshall Told Me," *U.S. News and World Report*, November 2, 1959, page 53.

However, the prospect of having this tactical weapon does not seem to have been considered in the forecast of casualties probably because, as explained by Marshall, "At the time we didn't know the real potential of the bomb."

[7] Potsdam Papers, Document 598.

Plain. It was clearly understood that plans and preparations to execute this ultimate operation would be subject to constant review.

No attempt was made on this occasion to estimate the number of casualties that might be suffered if the *whole* strategic plan, ending in a great landing on the plains near Tokyo, was carried through. With any that may have been made by the Joint Chiefs in other talks or papers I am not acquainted. However, Truman, in connection with his account of his decision to use the atomic bomb, wrote, "General Marshall told me that it might cost one half million lives to force the enemy's surrender on his home grounds."[8] And Stimson in the same connection has recorded that he was informed that American forces alone might suffer a million casualties.[9] It is clear that there was much leeway in the several estimates, so much leeway that in reality they were only surmises derived from differing assumptions.[10]

The approved plans were discussed with the British Chiefs of Staff during the next fortnight, and their concurrence was obtained. This was to expedite the more complete program for the coordination of operations that the two groups expected to work out when they met at Potsdam.

Even before the war against Germany ended, British Commonwealth forces had started to try to wrest segments of their former empire from the Japanese. They had expelled the Japanese from Central Burma and secured control of the port of Rangoon. Australian troops had landed in Dutch Borneo.

A strong element of the British fleet had aided in the capture of Okinawa and was taking part in the bombardment of the Japanese home islands. Churchill and the British Chiefs of Staff did not wish to have future British military effort confined to the liberation of colonial possessions in the Far East; they wanted to prove by deed their will to share actively in the invasion of Japan. But the Joint Chiefs of Staff were not eager to have the British do so. Perhaps they were influenced by fear that if they did, the British Chiefs might insist upon being consulted about operational strategy. They were reluctant to complicate the arrangements for command and the assignments for action. The smoke of

[8] Harry S. Truman, *Year of Decisions*, page 417.

[9] Henry L. Stimson, "The Decision to Use the Atomic Bomb," *Harper's Magazine*, February 1947. Elting Morison in his biography of Stimson states that his estimate in the spring of 1945 of casualties was a half million to a million.

[10] The difference in these two estimates may be due to the fact that Marshall was talking of lives lost while Stimson was referring not only to lives lost but to men wounded or taken prisoners.

past arguments in the European and China-India-Burma theaters of war hung heavily over their thoughts. Would the British be willing to fit their operations into the American plans; would they refrain from arguing about the selection of tasks allotted to them, and from asking excessive equipment and a more important place in the command organization than they ought to have? Pending assurances about these matters, the U.S. Joint Chiefs postponed decision until they could talk them over with the British Chiefs.

The strategic plans that were adopted by the Joint Chiefs on May 25th and approved by the President on June 18th were conceived to be effective even if the Soviet Union should not enter the war. But the wish to have Russian forces join with ours in the final assault remained an integral element of our plans.

In the draft of the message of inquiry which Marshall sent MacArthur asking his views about the several proposed strategies, Marshall inserted by his own hand a sentence reading, "Russia's entry into the war would be a pre-requisite to a landing in the Japanese homeland in December." Marshall presumably knew that MacArthur attached importance to such conjoined aid. For he had emphatically stated to the visitor from the War Department who had solicited his opinions in February that *no* attempt ought to be made to invade Japan proper unless and until the Russian army had been previously committed to action in Manchuria; that he thought this was essential, and should be brought about without the delay of three months after the conclusion of the defeat of Germany which he understood was the date of which Stalin had advised the President. MacArthur had gone on to say that he understood what Russia would want: to wit, all of Manchuria, Korea, and possibly part of North China. But he thought this seizure of territory by the Soviet Union was inevitable, and since this was so, the American government ought to insist that Russia earn these rewards by invading Manchuria at the earliest possible time after the defeat of Germany.[11] His later answer to Marshall indicated no amendment of his judgment.

Marshall in his exposition at the White House Conference of June 18th had stated that our aim should be to have the Russians and the Chinese "clean up" the situation on the mainland of Asia; to get the

[11] Freeman memo of talk with MacArthur in February 1945. See "The Entry of the Soviet Union into the War Against Japan: Military Plans, 1941-1945," cited in footnote 3.

Russians to deal with the Japanese forces in Manchuria, and those in Korea also, if necessary. He thought that the Russian entry might so affect the already hopeless Japanese that it might be the decisive action in causing them to surrender ". . . at that time or shortly thereafter if we land in Japan."[12] He then quoted MacArthur as observing, "The hazard and loss [of the landing on Kyushu] will be greatly lessened if an attack is launched from Siberia sufficiently ahead of our target date to commit the enemy to major combat. . . ."

The prospectus of action presented to the President retained the stipulations that the Soviet Union was to be encouraged to enter the war against Japan, and was to be given all needed and practicable aid in doing so. The President approved the purpose. Toward the end of the discussion on June 18th, he said "one of his objectives in connection with the coming conference [with Stalin and Churchill] would be to get from Russia all the assistance in the war that was possible." Admiral King said that "he wished to emphasize the point that, regardless of the desirability of the Russians entering the war, they were not indispensable and he did not think we should go so far as to beg them to come in. While the cost of defeating Japan would be greater, there was no question in his mind but that we could handle it alone. He thought that the realization of this fact should greatly strengthen the President's hand in the forthcoming conference."[18] Perhaps it did. But the surviving wish to have Russian cooperation in the war continued to constrain American officials in their differences with the Soviet Union over various European situations. And it moderated our protests to Stalin when in the fortnight before the conference at Potsdam he tried to exact excessive concessions from the Chinese government in return for a promise of Soviet friendship.

[12] *Ibid.*
[18] *Ibid.*

3. By Inducement

If it should prove necessary to carry out the invasion plans, the resultant loss of life would be tragic. The chaos and suffering of a war fought to the most bitter end, as it had been in Germany, might be irremediable. There would be ruined countries and broken people on both sides of the expanding Communist realm, appealing to the miserable. These anxieties had aroused a wish to find a way to induce Japan to give up before it was compelled abjectly to do so.

Acting Secretary of State Grew had been Ambassador in Japan during the ten years that had ended mournfully in 1941. He believed that the war could have been averted and had not ceased to regret what he regarded as the failure not only of Japanese but also of American diplomacy. Encouraged by him, informed experts on the Far East attached to the State Department had been for many months working on a statement of policies toward Japan which might serve as a basis for an arranged surrender.[1]

Late in April the aged Admiral Kantaro Suzuki was named Prime Minister. He had been regarded as a "moderate," and had been wounded in the military uprising of 1936. His selection evoked a hope in the State Department that the Emperor was bent on finding a way to end the war.[2]

On May 1st, at his regular meeting with the Secretaries of War and Navy, Grew found support for an attempt to bring about a salvaging and reconciling peace. Secretary of the Navy Forrestal raised the question, "How far and how thoroughly do we want to beat Japan?"[2] Grew and Stimson had said that they shared his belief that it would be regrettable if we had to lay Japan in ruins before it would submit, and that for many reasons the American government would be well advised to try to secure the end before the damage was complete. The three Cabinet officers agreed to propose to the President that he let the Japanese know that if they submitted to our demand for "unconditional

---

[1] The State-War-Navy Coordinating Committee (SWNCC) had approved a paper prepared by Dr. George H. Blakeslee and Dr. Hugh Borton as early as the summer of 1944. See F. C. Jones, H. Borton, B. R. Pearn, *Survey of International Relations, 1939-1944, The Far East, 1942-46*, page 316n.

[2] What has since become known of the circumstances of his selection indicates that this hope was justified. The Army had another candidate. Suzuki was proposed by the group of former Prime Ministers known as the Jushin. A characteristic Japanese deal was made whereby promises were given that Suzuki would comply with the judgment of the Army if it would cease its opposition. However, at the instance of the Emperor's brother, Prince Takamatsu, Suzuki assured the Emperor that as Prime Minister he would implicitly carry out the Emperor's wishes.

surrender" they would not be destroyed as a nation nor condemned to prolonged suffering. The President, having ascertained that the Chiefs of Staff had no objection, on May 8th, the day after the German surrender, had given a statement to the press intended to intimate the nature of our policy.

The tone was stern. For the President shared the feeling of most Americans that the Japanese aggression against China, the Japanese assault upon us, and the Japanese cruelties during the war warranted severity. Moreover, inside the State Department an excited argument was going on between those officials who thought that the American government ought to relax its rigorous attitude in order to hasten the peace and those who feared that if it did so the Japanese leaders and organizations who had brought about the war would survive.

Truman's statement reaffirmed the intention to carry on the war "until the Japanese military and naval forces lay down their arms in unconditional surrender." Then it went on to aver that while such a surrender would mean "the termination of the influence of the military leaders who have brought Japan to the present brink of disaster," it would not mean "the extermination or enslavement of the Japanese people" and it would provide "for the return of soldiers and sailors to their families, their farms, their jobs."

Whether due to his own inclination or out of deference to presumed American opinion, or because of the objections of some senior members of the State Department, the President had not adopted Grew's advice to include in this statement a promise that unconditional surrender would not mean the forced elimination of the existing imperial dynasty. Grew believed that such an affirmation was not only helpful to induce surrender but essential. He thought that the Japanese, in reverent devotion, would fight to the death against no matter what odds to retain their imperial institutions, while if these were not threatened they would accept other penalties. Moreover, he was convinced that it would be greatly to our advantage to allow the Emperor to remain and issue orders to his subjects. Unless he did so it was uncertain whether, even if our troops got to Tokyo, the millions of Japanese soldiers in East Asia would stop fighting, and we might have to engage in a weary and costly fight to overcome them; but if the Emperor were kept in office he could be prevailed upon to issue a rescript ordering the Japanese forces to surrender which would be obeyed. Nor, he contended, need the American government have qualms about so using the Emperor, since by doing so it would not be hindered in the resolve to destroy and control the war-making capacity of Japan.[3]

Truman's statement had been dismissed by the Japanese censors as obnoxious propaganda, a stupid and dire response. This exposition of American intentions, not forgiving but not vengeful, would have been used by a less proud and overwrought governing group as a chance to find out what forbearance they might be shown if they yielded before the compelled end. But those who still ruled Japan, headstrong, turned down this chance.

Grew and his associates were downcast. Still they clung to the belief that a more explicit explanation of our intentions might lead to a surrender, as it became clearer that Japan was at our mercy. On May 26th and 27th American superfortresses almost wiped out Tokyo. Strong winds whipped fires which engulfed the area of government offices and damaged buildings within the compound of the Imperial Palace. The time had come, the advocates of moderation thought, to grasp the chance to end the ordeal.

On the morning of the 28th, Grew once more urged the President to try to induce Japan to surrender by dispelling the worst fears of the consequences. He shared without reserve the intent to carry on the war until the Japanese military organization was wholly destroyed and the cult of militarism extinguished. But our aim, he stressed, surely was to achieve this and our other purposes with the smallest cost in American lives. Thus were we not called on to consider any step which, without renouncing our aims, might lead quickly to the capitulation we wanted? He believed that their alarm lest the revered imperial institution would be destroyed would deter the Japanese from giving up the struggle, and that unless this was quieted and they were able to "save face" they would fight on until the bitter end. But they might be influenced by an indication that they would be allowed to determine their own political structure. If, after victory, we should ban the imperial institution, the Japanese would try to restore it, and the effort would prevent resignation to defeat and reconciliation with the United States. Moreover, Grew concluded, for the Japanese a constitutional monarchy might be the most suitable form of government.

Having made his plea, the Acting Secretary submitted a written statement for possible inclusion in an address which the President was

---

[3] Grew's thoughts were well expressed in a letter he wrote on April 14, 1945, to Randall Gould, who was editor of the American edition of the *Shanghai Evening Post and Mercury*, to be found in his book *Turbulent Era*, Vol. II, pages 1420-1421.

scheduled to make within the next few days.[4] The main points in the text submitted by Grew survived in later versions of which we shall be telling.

Truman told Grew he was thinking along similar lines. He suggested a meeting with the Secretaries of War and Navy and General Marshall and Admiral King to discuss this realm of policy, and said that thereafter the whole group might go over it again with him.

By accident on this same evening Hopkins, in Moscow, was querying Stalin about the policies to be pursued toward Japan. Stalin said that he thought it best to maintain the policy of unconditional surrender and to occupy the country. But, he added, the treatment of the Japanese people might be somewhat softer than in the case of Germany, and they should be left something to live on. However, he went on, there was another possibility, and that would be to accept a conditional surrender and then subsequently to impose in stages successively harsher terms which would cope with the Japanese military potential.[5] Or, as Hopkins expressed it in his report to the President, "In other words, it seemed to us that he proposes under this heading to agree to milder peace terms but once we get into Japan to give them the works."[6]

Hopkins sent the President that same night (May 28th, Moscow time) a report of this talk. But it is improbable that the officials who met in the office of the Secretary of War on the morning of the 29th had seen it. Grew read aloud the draft of the statement which he had submitted to the President the day before. Stimson, Forrestal, and Marshall

---

[4] Some time before, Douglas Fairbanks, Jr., then in the Navy, had consulted officials in the State Department about a text of another statement that might be issued by the President; its dominant note was threatening: in effect, "surrender or we will blow you to Hell." It was set aside, but some of its language reemerged in the preamble and last paragraph of the Potsdam Declaration.

Grew had then asked Eugene Dooman to prepare a more adequate statement of our policy. He accepted this despite strong objections by other members of the State Department, especially to a clause that indicated that the Japanese might be allowed to retain a constitutional monarchy.

Grew, in his memo of this conference, has written that he then submitted "to the President a rough draft of a statement which he might wish to consider including in his proposed address on May 31." He then goes on to tell that Judge Samuel Rosenman, Special Counsel to the President, who had been present at this talk with the President, looking forward to a prospective meeting with the Secretaries of War and Navy on the following day, suggested three or four points that might be included in "the statement." *Turbulent Era*, Vol. II, pages 1428-1431.

But the text which Grew prints in his memoirs immediately after the memo of this talk is not the one which he gave to the President on May 28th, but a much later draft, intended to serve as a Declaration by the Heads of the Allied Powers, not merely by the President alone.

[5] Potsdam Papers, Document 26. Memo of Hopkins-Stalin conversation, May 28th.
[6] Robert Sherwood, *Roosevelt and Hopkins*, pages 903-904.

all expressed favor for the proposal and for its main features. Stimson said also that he thought the Japanese might be allowed a little more latitude in effecting reforms, as Japan had in the past produced statesmen as enlightened as any in the West. Elmer Davis, Head of the Office of War Information, protested against the leniency of the proposed statement and argued that it would allow Japanese militarism to survive. Memories and records differ as to the subsequent course of the talk. All agree that General Marshall said that in his opinion publication of the statement "at this time would be premature." Stimson may have, probably did, speak to the same effect; in any case he confided in his diary his belief that it would not be advisable for the President to make such a statement *at this time*; and that the question of *when* to make it was the nub of the matter. This judgment prevailed.[7]

Stimson concluded, and Marshall seems to have been thinking similarly, that the question of what to say to the Japanese, and when to say it, should be governed by whether and when the United States had the atomic bomb. For while the Secretary of War was in accord with the exposition of our intentions in the statement composed in the State Department, he did not believe that it would be heeded until Japan was still more thoroughly beaten; and he conceived that the really decisive note in the statement, when it was issued, would be an impressive warning of utter destruction. As he told Marshall after the meeting, he thought that the decision to postpone issuance of the statement was sound but he would have to consider it again preparatory to the use of the atomic bomb.[8] Perhaps he was at this time inclined to let the Japanese know the nature of the atomic weapon before its use, and changed his mind later.

Grew, downhearted, informed the President that it was the sense of the Cabinet group that it was advisable to defer the issuance of a fuller public explanation of our intentions. Truman said he also thought so.

But the period of waiting was not a quiescent one. On June 12th at one of the weekly conferences of the Secretaries of State, War, and Navy, Forrestal took up the cause where Grew had left it.[9] He remarked that we ought not to cling to a frozen position and so lose the chance to take advantage of developments in Japan; he had in mind particu-

[7] Grew later wrote that he inferred that the unexplained military reason was that since the fighting in Okinawa was still going on it might be construed as a confession of weakness. *Turbulent Era*, page 1424. Grew knew of the progress of the work on the atomic bomb, but Elmer Davis, Eugene Dooman, Judge Rosenman, and some of the military officers who were present at this meeting knew nothing of it.

[8] Memo of talk, Stimson-Marshall-McCloy, May 29, 1945.

[9] Minutes of Meeting of the Committee of Three, June 12th, Stimson-Forrestal-Grew, with McCloy as recorder.

larly the mystical relation of the Japanese people to the Emperor and the general religious background of some of the Japanese. Stimson said that he also thought that if we could effect our aims without using the phrase "unconditional surrender," we ought not to hesitate to give it up. In any event we would have to occupy Japan in order really to demilitarize it. Grew agreed that occupation was necessary, but he emphasized the chance of enlisting the better elements of Japan toward the adoption of more peaceful and democratic policies.

During the next week Grew tried twice again to get the President to "clarify" our policies toward the Japanese people and the Emperor. The Joint Chiefs of Staff had been suggesting that a communication be sent at once demanding immediate unconditional surrender, since they were afraid that the Japanese government might propose a negotiated peace at the very time when a large number of troops returned from Europe would be in the United States awaiting transfer to the Pacific. Grew advised the President that he thought this would be futile unless there was a "clarification" of what we would do if they yielded. In pursuit of this opinion, he submitted another expository statement designed to persuade the Japanese that it was better to survive in defeat instead of dying in resolve and glory. In this, the section bearing on the crucial question of the disposition of the Emperor was introduced by an extract from an address that had been made by Chiang Kai-shek on New Year's Day, 1944. "One important problem . . . concerns Japan's form of government. When President Roosevelt asked my views, I frankly replied 'It is my opinion that all the Japanese militarists must be wiped out and the Japanese political system must be purged of every vestige of aggressive elements. As to what form of government Japan should adopt, that question can better be left to the awakened and repentant Japanese people to decide for themselves.' " This quotation was followed by circumambient language which could be read by the Japanese to mean that they might keep their Emperor, and by opposed Americans to mean that they might be forbidden to do so.

On the 15th, after once more adverting to the reasons for his advice, Grew urged the President to issue this statement when he announced the fall of Okinawa. Truman said he would think it over. He was going to meet with the Joint Chiefs of Staff on Monday next (the 18th) to discuss "this whole problem," but he supposed this would be mainly a military discussion. When Assistant Secretary of State Julius Holmes, who accompanied Grew, remarked that in these matters military and political elements were inseparable, the President assented. He thereupon not only asked Grew to be present at the conference with the Joint Chiefs on the 18th but also agreed that Eugene Dooman, whom Grew named as "our outstanding expert on Japan," might come along with him.

Grew had been keeping the Secretary of State, Edward Stettinius, who was still at the United Nations Conference in San Francisco, informed of the initiatives, and he had forwarded to Stettinius a copy of the text of the demand for surrender which had been written by the staff of the Joint Chiefs. In his response to Grew, Stettinius suggested that it might be well to consider turning the statement into a *three or four power demand* to be issued when the President met with Churchill and Stalin at Potsdam; and asked whether it would be useful to couple such a call for surrender with assurances to the Japanese regarding their future.

On the next morning (the 16th) Grew showed the President this message from Stettinius. The Acting Secretary was surprised by being told if he had any further recommendations *along the line of Stettinius' message*, to send them along at once so that they could be considered before the meeting with the Joint Chiefs. Only the day before, Grew reminded, he had left a statement of his ideas with the President. It was his conviction that the President should not put off its issuance either because of military reasons or in order to discuss it with Churchill and Stalin. Why not, he asked, act as soon as Okinawa fell? For then all sensible Japanese would recognize that thereafter their country was doomed to defeat. Let us make our intentions clear, and thus try to save ourselves and the Japanese more needless strain and suffering.[10]

When next the President saw Grew, on the morning of the 18th just before the scheduled conference with the Joint Chiefs about Pacific strategy—of which we have told—Truman said that he had carefully considered the most recent statement Grew had submitted for release after the fall of Okinawa. While he liked the idea, he decided to wait until he could discuss it with Churchill and Stalin.[11] That meant that at least another month would go by before it was issued.

The closing sentences of Grew's memo of his talk with the President on the morning of June 18th read: "The President having ruled against the step at this time, there was of course nothing to be done, but I felt that this question should be kept prominently in mind. The President

[10] Grew's line of reasoning is well stated in a letter which he sent to Rosenman after leaving the President, which is printed in *Turbulent Era*, Vol. II, pages 1435-1436.
[11] Potsdam Papers, Document 159.

asked me to have the subject entered on the agenda of the Big Four meeting. . . ."[12] Although Grew had been invited by the President a few days previously to be present at the conference with the Joint Chiefs of Staff which was about to begin, he was not asked to stay on for this other gathering.

Truman has since explained that he deferred action because he wished to demonstrate to Japan that the allies were united in their purpose, and the postponement would enable us to learn more about Russian intentions and the atomic bomb.[13] But might not the first purpose have been served by consulting at once Churchill and Chiang Kai-shek (and perhaps Stalin) through our ambassadors? And might not the second purpose have been served by direct inquiry of Stalin? The Chiefs of Staff were advising him not to present our demands and explain our intentions until the results of air and naval assaults were more conclusive and we were ready to follow a Japanese refusal with the assault of our invasion forces. Stimson was advising him to keep this declaration in reserve until the atomic bomb was tested. Moreover, the President may well have reckoned that contrasting risks would be minimized by waiting: one was that any exposition of surrender terms that might be deemed softer than earlier punitive statements would arouse popular or Congressional opposition at home; the other was that the Japanese government might manage to involve us in a prolonged and demoralizing discussion about terms.

Stimson, though advising the President to postpone his explanatory address to the Japanese, was not reconciled to the need to invade the home islands of Japan. On the morning after the meeting with the Joint Chiefs, at which the military plans were approved by the President, Stimson told Grew and Artemus L. Gates, Under Secretary of the Navy, it would be deplorable if we had to go through with the contemplated operations, routing out the Japanese cave by cave, utterly destroying their country, and with great loss of life.[14] He indicated a belief that the desire professed before the war by substantial elements in Japan to cooperate with the West was genuine. Grew took up the cause; he said that he thought that despite their outer show of defiance, the Japanese rulers might be having a change of mind and heart of which we did not

[12] This memo is also in *Turbulent Era*, Vol. II, page 1437.
[13] *Year of Decisions*, page 417.
[14] Stimson Diary. Forrestal was not present at this State-War-Navy meeting, but his Diary contains an entry for June 19th recording the talk. Presumably, it was derived from a report by Gates. This may explain why the account given is divergent in detail from Stimson's, assigning the lead to Grew rather than to Stimson.

know. Thus, while continuing to insist on unconditional surrender and to plan on occupying the Tokyo Plain, it seemed to him that the American government could and ought to explain its intentions toward them in a way that might cause the Japanese to seek peace at once. He then read the recent report he had made to the President. Some of his associates in the State Department, he confided to his Cabinet colleagues, did not agree with him, particularly that we should state our willingness to allow the Japanese people to determine for themselves their future political structure, provided it did not include hostile or warlike elements. Then he ruefully reported that the President had told him that an immediate announcement would not fit with plans for the coming meeting with Churchill and Stalin.

Stimson, recording the course of this discussion in his diary, noted that his [Stimson's] only fixed date for the "last chance warning" was that it must be given before the actual landing of the ground forces in Japan, and that fortunately the plans provided for enough time to bring in "the sanctions" to our warning by the heavy ordinary bombing attacks and an attack of S-1 (the atomic bomb). When Stimson went over the same ground with Marshall later in the day, the Chief of Staff reminded him that there was another prospective sanction—the entry of the Russians into the war.

During the fortnight remaining before the President and his advisers left for Potsdam, the initiative in the composition of the statement to be addressed to the Japanese (a combination of a warning and an exposition of the meaning of unconditional surrender) passed from the State to the War Department.[15]

A State-War-Navy subcommittee, to which the three Cabinet officers consigned the task, strove to compose a "short form" of what had become thought of as a Proclamation or Declaration and was called sometimes by one and sometimes by the other of these names. Assistant Secretary

[15] The officials of the State Department were at this time also completing analytical statements of policy toward Japan for inclusion in the Briefing Book which was to be taken to Potsdam. These advocated that the American government let the Japanese know definitely what treatment they would receive if they made an "unconditional" surrender. They thought such a statement would tend to dissipate Japanese fears of the unknown, combat Japanese domestic propaganda to the effect that unconditional surrender meant the extinction of the Japanese state and enslavement of the Japanese people, create a conflict in Japan between the Japanese die-hard militarists and those who wanted to end the war before the country was ruined, alleviate Japanese anxiety over the fate of the throne, and satisfy a growing body of opinion in the United States which was demanding that we try to hasten the end of the war in the Pacific by stating our war aims clearly. Potsdam Papers, Document 589.

of War McCloy dominated the discussions. But many elements of the resultant draft were derived from the longer State Department texts.

On July 2nd Stimson went over to the White House in the same energized mood with which he used to take his great law cases into court. He took with him a memo summing up the arguments for issuance of the warning proclamation, as well as the latest version of that document. Grew and Forrestal had approved the tenor of the memo and subscribed to its recommendations.[16] The main features of both may be briefly summarized.

The struggle for the conquest of Japan following our landing might be "very long, costly and arduous." Therefore before beginning it, the Americans ought to try to secure an equivalent result by giving the Japanese a warning of what was to come and a definite opportunity to capitulate. Some elements in the Japanese situation and certain traits of the Japanese people, as reflected in their history, indicated that there was enough chance that they might accept such a proffer to warrant making it. Therefore, let the three (or four) great allies call upon the Japanese to surrender and permit the occupation of their country in order to insure its complete demilitarization. Let them be told of the overwhelming force they face and the inevitable and complete destruction. Let them be made to understand that however the war ends, the allies are determined to limit Japanese sovereignty to the four main islands and render them powerless to mount and support another war. But let them be told also (1) that they would not be extirpated as a race or destroyed as a nation (2) that they would be permitted to maintain industries needed to sustain a reasonable standard of peacetime living (3) that as soon as allied objectives were accomplished, and a peacefully inclined government, truly representative of the people, was constituted, the forces of occupation would be withdrawn, and (4) "I personally think that if in saying this we should add that we do not exclude a constitutional monarchy under her present dynasty, it would substantially add to the chance of acceptance."

Stimson in conclusion again stressed that the action ought to be carefully timed in view of the extremely sensitive national pride of the Japanese, observing that ". . . the warning must be tendered before the actual invasion has occurred and while the impending destruction, though clear beyond peradventure, has not yet reduced her to fanatical despair.

---

[16] As stated in the letter which Stimson gave to the President along with the memorandum. The texts of both are in the Potsdam Papers, Document 592.

If Russia is a part of the threat, the Russian attack, if actual, must not have progressed too far. . . ."[17]

"You will note," he wrote in his covering letter and repeated in his ensuing talk with the President, that the Four-Power Proclamation ". . . is written without specific relation to the employment of any new weapon. Of course it would have to be revamped to conform to the efficacy of such a weapon if the warning were to be delivered, as would almost certainly be the case, in conjunction with its use."[18] We are left to decipher this ambiguous note in his thought. Perhaps at this time he still believed that in the warning Proclamation we might inform the Japanese explicitly of the nature and destructive power of the weapon after testing but before its use. Or to the contrary, and more probably, he thought our aim would be most effectively served ". . . by giving her a warning after she had been sufficiently pounded, possibly with S-1 [the atomic bomb]";[18a] and at once thereafter to address the summons to surrender to a smitten and awed people.

On the next morning (July 3rd) James F. Byrnes took office as Secretary of State. As representative of the President on the Interim Committee he had been a firm proponent of its conclusions in regard to the use of the atomic bomb. But he had not taken part in the discussions about the Proclamation which was to explain our intentions toward Japan and serve as an ultimate warning. During the last three days before the President and Byrnes left for Germany, Grew and McCloy and their associates strove to perfect the provisional text of the Proclamation. The great remaining undecided question was what, if anything, was to be said about the Emperor. Stimson and McCloy both favored an avowal that the Japanese would be allowed to have a constitutional monarchy under the present dynasty, if they so wished, and if the allies were convinced that Japan would live in peace. Opinion in the State Department was still divided. Those who were opposed to the advice proffered by Grew and Dooman were maintaining that the cult of emperor worship had enabled the coalition of aggressive groups, military and civil, to control the Japanese people, and hence that if the imperial institution were allowed to survive it would endanger the future. Moreover, they thought it unjust and illogical to eliminate and punish all other elements responsible for leading Japan into the war and to spare the Emperor.

[17] *Ibid.*
[18] *Ibid.*
[18a] Stimson Diary, June 26, 1945, following a meeting with Forrestal and Grew.

While this difference of opinion remained, a text was completed and turned over by Grew to Byrnes on July 6th just before the Secretary of State left for Potsdam. The paragraph which related to the future of the imperial institutions read: "The occupying forces of the Allies shall be withdrawn from Japan as soon as these objectives [designated in other sections] have been accomplished and there has been established a peacefully inclined, responsible government of a character representative of the Japanese people. This may include a constitutional monarchy under the present dynasty if the peaceloving nations can be convinced of the genuine determination of such a government to follow policies of peace which will render impossible the future development of aggressive militarism in Japan."[19]

The new Secretary of State was still not committed on this issue and after his departure for Potsdam the opponents of this course continued to maintain that it was wrong.[20] According to Forrestal, Grew told him on the evening after Byrnes left that he was pleased that "we had finally whipped into shape" this contemplated statement of what would follow "unconditional surrender" but that he was afraid that the draft "would be ditched on the way over [to the Potsdam Conference] by people who accompany the President . . . who reflect the view that we cannot afford to hold out any clarification of terms to Japan which could be construed as a desire to get the Japanese war over with before Russia had an opportunity to enter."[21] But this may be Forrestal's rather than Grew's rendition of the reasoning of those who wanted to eliminate this element in the statement, and who were causing Grew to fear that the text would suffer change.

[19] Paragraph 12 of Potsdam Papers, Document 594. This was approved by Grew, Stimson, Forrestal, King, and probably by Marshall. A footnote to this document states that the compilers of the Potsdam Papers have not definitely established that this is the draft given to Byrnes on July 6th, but that it was clearly a revision of the draft which Stimson had submitted to Truman on July 2nd (see Enclosure 2 to Document 592).

In a Briefing Book Paper entitled "Military Government and Occupation of Japan, Attitude toward the Emperor," the State Department recorded its recommendations regarding the treatment of the Emperor in its more immediate aspects among which were (1) that the constitutional powers of the Emperor should be suspended, and (2) that if politically practicable and physically possible the Emperor and his family should be placed under protective custody in a detached palace outside Tokyo, and (3) that the Emperor should proclaim that Japan has surrendered unconditionally and should command all armed forces and people of Japan to cease hostilities and comply with all the requirements imposed by the designated commander for Japan [MacArthur]. Potsdam Papers, Document 590.

[20] See Potsdam Papers, Document 593. Memo of Assistant Secretary of State Archibald MacLeish to Secretary of State. Subject: Interpretation of Japanese Unconditional Surrender, July 6th; and Document 595, Extract from Minutes of 133rd meeting of the Staff Committee of the Secretary of State, July 7th; and Document 596, Memo of Legal Adviser, Green H. Hackworth, July 9th.

[21] Forrestal Diaries, July 6, 1945.

It was understood that the President would choose the time to issue the Declaration after learning when the Russians were going to enter the Pacific war, and the outcome of the test in New Mexico. While the text taken to Potsdam was ominous in tone, it did not tell of these two impending events which were the thunder and lightning hidden in the cloud of somber words.

4. By Shock: The Atom Bomb

THE prime incentive of the effort to make an atomic bomb had been to assure and hasten the defeat of Germany. But as the great dimensions of the task became apparent and as hard and baffling problems were encountered, its creators had been compelled to face the fact that the war against Germany might be over before the bomb was achieved. Yet they decided that it was imperative to carry on with undiminished vigor, because of the wish to have the bomb for use against Japan, if need be.

All this time the group who knew most about the progress in the making of the atomic bomb nursed the thought that this weapon, climaxing other destructive assaults, might do what they did not think a promise of fair treatment alone would do—cause the Japanese to surrender even before the expeditionary force set out for the invasion of Japan.

As early as October 1943, Vannevar Bush, one of the two scientists (James Conant was the other) who were the President's advisers and informants about the project, had foretold that there was a "good chance" that the atomic bombs might enter our arsenal in the first part of 1945. This had been confirmed by General Leslie R. Groves, the Commanding General of the Manhattan District Project, in a memo to the President in April 1944. By August he had become more precise, telling Marshall that current expectations were that several bombs of one type would be available between March and June 1945, but if further work on this type did not come up to this mark, he was confident that another and more powerful type would be ready by the first of August. The import of these prognostications had been stressed in a memo which Bush and Conant sent to the Secretary of War in September 1944. In this, which was intended primarily to stimulate thought about the policy to be pursued when the American government became possessed of this new weapon, the authors predicted that the blast damage of the type in production would be equivalent to from one to ten thousand tons of high explosive. More awesome still was their statement that on the not too distant scientific horizon was the hydrogen bomb, many times more powerful. These super-bombs, they explained, would release energy akin to that given out by the sun, and single ones would destroy great areas. They surmised that it might be possible to make them within a year or so after the first plutonium bomb was perfected.

Then on December 30, 1944, Groves had still more confidently predicted that the enormous secret effort to make an explosive weapon which would use the energy of fissured atoms would succeed. But he again corrected the prospective schedule of production. The first paragraph read:

"It is now reasonably certain that our operation plans should be based on the gun type bomb, which, it is estimated, will produce the equivalent of a ten thousand ton TNT explosion. The first bomb, without previous full scale test which we do not believe will be necessary, should be ready about 1 August 1945. The second one should be ready by the end of the year and succeeding ones at . . . intervals thereafter."[1]

Groves had then gone on to state, "Our previous hopes that an implosion (compression) type of bomb might be developed in the late spring have now been dissipated by scientific difficulties which we have not as yet been able to solve. The present effects of these difficulties are that more material will be required and that the material will be less efficiently used." But he believed that "We should have sufficient material for the first implosion type bomb sometime in the latter part of July" and more during the rest of 1945. He anticipated that the explosive force of the first specimen of this implosion type would be equivalent to about 500 tons of TNT, and that the effectiveness of those to follow should increase toward 1000 tons and, if some problems were solved, to as much as 2500 tons.[2]

On the morning of December 30th, Stimson had given Roosevelt a copy of this report. It so commanded Roosevelt's interest that he had Stimson come again the next day, Sunday, to continue their talk. Of the ensuing conversation we shall tell as we pursue the quest for the answers to the political and military questions begat by the bomb.

Work upon it had gone apace; and on March 15, 1945, Stimson had given the President the most recent forecast of when specimens of the new weapon would be in hand. A week later Sir James Chadwick, the British technical adviser to the Combined (U.S.-British) Policy Committee on Atomic Affairs which had been formed in Washington, had been impressed enough by what he learned, to inform Sir John Anderson, the Cabinet Minister in charge of the British part in the project, that it was

---

[1] Underlining and excision in the original, as in State Department Publication, *The Conference at Malta and Yalta*, pages 383-384. The underlining was done by the Secretary of War for emphasis in presentation to President Roosevelt.

[2] ". . . as late as the middle of May 1945 the responsible heads of Los Alamos felt that the explosive force of the first implosion type bombs would fall somewhere between 700 and 1500 tons." Letter of General Groves in *Science Magazine*, December 1959.

"as certain as such things can be that the weapon would be ready in the late summer."[3]

Stimson had continued to follow each advance intently, noting in his Diary after a visit to the works in Tennessee in early April that although "success is ninety-nine percent assured, yet only by the first actual war trial of the weapon can the actual certainty be fixed." About this time reports that the Germans had an active establishment for making atomic weapons in an area located in the zone of occupation to be assigned to France caused a tremor of alarm to run through the American government. But this turned out to be false.

Thus Roosevelt, in his last months in office, knew it was virtually certain that the United States would soon be the exclusive possessor of a tremendously more destructive weapon than had ever been known. This must have lessened his anxieties about the outcome and duration of the war in the Pacific, and caused him to anticipate that the prime wishes of the United States about post-war arrangements would be respected. But the task of deciding whether to use the weapon, how to assure that it could not in the future destroy mankind but rather serve it well, worried him "terribly." On these gravest of decisions neither history nor past experience gave reliable guidance.

These enigmas had been anxiously thrashed over by official and scientific circles in the United States and Great Britain.

The focal issues had been first defined and stirred up by an eminent Danish physicist, Niels Bohr, whose cognizance of the meaning of the force which was about to be loosed would not let him rest. He felt an intense responsibility for what might occur. He had elucidated the basic theory of atomic structure and had been one of the joint authors of that article published just before the war which had set off the initiatives of the American and British governments in this field. In December 1943, he had been smuggled by the British government out of Denmark—where he was in imminent danger of arrest because of the haven he had provided for refugee scientists from Fascist countries.[4]

Early in 1944, Bohr had gone out to Los Alamos and shortly thereafter he had written to Sir John Anderson that he was convinced that there could be no real safety for any country without a universal agreement

---

[3] John Ehrman, *Grand Strategy*, Vol. VI, page 275.

[4] A detailed account—superior to any paperback thriller—of how messages were gotten to and from him and how he was brought out of Denmark is told in the first segment of the official history of the United Kingdom atomic energy project—*Britain and Atomic Energy 1939-1945* by Margaret Gowing, pages 245 *et seq.*

based on mutual confidence. As reported in the British official account of his thoughts, "Effective control [of this new source of energy] would involve the most intricate administrative problems and would demand concessions over exchange of information and openness about industrial efforts and military preparations that were hardly conceivable in terms of pre-war international relationships. But Bohr felt that the invention of atomic bombs was something so climacteric that it would facilitate a whole new approach to these relationships. A unique danger presented a unique opportunity. An early initiative from the side which had obtained a lead in an effort to master these forces of nature hitherto beyond human reach might turn the bomb to lasting benefit to mankind."[5]

In other words, Bohr was hopeful that the bomb might nurture confidence and cooperation between nations if candidly revealed and justly controlled. But, to the contrary, he was convinced that it would lead to great tension between Russia and the Western Allies if Russia were left to learn about it illicitly. He was certain that it would not take the Russians long to construct a bomb since their scientists were competent and the Germans would help them in order to cause trouble.

Bohr had confided his ideas and anxieties to Justice Felix Frankfurter, who had conveyed them to Roosevelt. The President had authorized Frankfurter to tell Bohr he was most eager to explore with Churchill "the proper safeguards in relation to the bomb."[6] Frankfurter had passed this message on to Bohr.

In April, Bohr had returned to England at the request of Lord Halifax, the British Ambassador in Washington, and Sir John Anderson, who were converts to his ideas. On his arrival he received, six months after it had been written, a letter from Professor Peter Kapitza, the Russian physicist, who along with several of the British physicists engaged in the project, had worked with Lord Rutherford at the Cavendish Laboratory in Cambridge. Kapitza invited Bohr to settle in Russia and promised all help needed to carry his work forward. There could be little doubt that the Soviet government favored this invitation, and Bohr had a definite impression that the Russians knew what the Americans were doing.

Anderson had told Churchill that if an attempt was to be made to effectuate international control, it would be advisable to inform the Russians of the fact that the Americans expected to have this devastating weapon and to invite them to collaborate in the preparation of a plan for interna-

[5] *Ibid.*, pages 347-348.
[6] *Ibid.*, page 350.

tional control. But Churchill had answered that he did not believe this step urgent and that he was "adamantly" opposed to an extension of the circles of those who knew of the project. By the entreaties of intimate advisers, the Prime Minister had, however, been persuaded to see Bohr—that was in May 1944—only to repulse him. For Churchill had been annoyed and upset by Bohr's muffled and discursive way of speaking. Their talk had not reached, and certainly had not penetrated, the intricacies of the dilemmas of secrecy or free exchange of information, international control or atomic arms race.

Bohr had returned to the United States. There he wrote out a fuller exposition of his view of the scientific aspects of the project, the problems of policy it introduced and his ideas about them. After reading it—on August 26th—Roosevelt had had a long and amiable talk with Bohr. The President had said that an approach to Russia must be tried, opening a new era or vista of human history. He seems to have buoyed up Bohr by allowing him to infer that by his, Roosevelt's, intermediation, Churchill and Stalin might be brought around. He agreed the matter was urgent and had told Bohr that he would be meeting Churchill shortly and would talk over with him the possibility of inviting the Russians to join soon thereafter in consideration of the subject. Bohr took these statements without any discount for Roosevelt's affability and wish to put off, while pleasing, so ardent and unworldly a visitor.[7]

Offsetting suspicions were rampant. Churchill remained mistrustful of Bohr. French scientists who had been working on the project at Montreal resigned and had returned to London. In July they told General de Gaulle about the bomb. One of them, with British assent, had gone to France, and several others were trying to get permission to do so. It was deemed quite possible that information was being leaked to Professor J. Joliot-Curie in Paris, a professed Communist, and perhaps directly to the Soviet government.[7a] American officials, particularly Groves, were sure that the

---

[7] This account of the Roosevelt-Bohr talk is based on Gowing, *Britain and Atomic Energy*, pages 356-357, which is probably derived from messages sent by Bohr to Anderson and the account which Bohr gave Frankfurter subsequently. Bohr could easily have been, and probably was, misled by Roosevelt's affability, responsiveness and broad assurances, as well as by his own hopes.

[7a] The British authorities had allowed several French scientists to visit France after they returned to London from Canada. The British had entered into an agreement with the French scientists and French government during the very early stage of the attempt to develop atomic energy in return for the assignment of important patents in this realm. By this agreement the British government may have obligated itself to keep the French government informed of the further course of the effort and an ultimate share in the benefits. When the French scientists wished to visit France, the British authorities had to deal with the assertion that this was within the original understanding. They may have

Russians were trying to obtain knowledge through espionage. These combined suspicions probably influenced the tone, if not the main elements of the agreement reached by Roosevelt and Churchill when, on September 18th, they met at Hyde Park.

For then and there they had signed an *aide-mémoire* with import wholly different from that of the views which Roosevelt had let Bohr believe he was inclined to adopt. Incisively it was stated that "The suggestion that the world should be informed regarding Tube Alloys, with a view to an international agreement regarding its control and use, is not accepted. The matter should continue to be regarded as of the utmost secrecy."[8]

The belief that knowledge needed to make the new weapon could be long confined, and that during the period of confinement the United States and Britain might secure advantage—or at least be more assuredly able to prevent the Soviet Union from being too pushful—had prevailed.

We are left to surmise why Roosevelt so completely subscribed to Churchill's judgments. At this time the Russians were acting ruthlessly toward the Poles and showing themselves determined to replace the Polish Government-in-Exile with one dominated by Communists who took orders from Moscow. That may well have caused the supposition that the Russian leaders might be turned into trustworthy cooperators by an offer to share knowledge and control to seem visionary; and to have been regarded as indicative proof that when the Russians knew how to produce this new weapon, they could not be dissuaded from doing so regardless of the resultant intensification of the struggle for mastery. Moreover, a great flare-up of opposition to revelation could be foreseen; most military officers, as exemplified by Groves, would protest. And it was deemed doubtful whether the American people could be brought to approve disclosure of the weapon before its actual use. The traditional national attitude would, Roosevelt probably thought, yield only to proof of the danger to all contained in its destructive power, and then only gradually.

---

feared also that if they forbade the visits, the French scientists might make their knowledge public, or find other ways of passing it on to Joliot or directly to the Soviet government.

[8] A brief third paragraph stipulated that "Enquiries should be made regarding the activities of Professor Bohr and steps taken to ensure that he is responsible for no leakage of information particularly to the Russians." What inept language for a document signed by Churchill! For he was in all probability responsible for this paragraph. Churchill questioned not only Bohr's discretion but his integrity. Lord Cherwell, Churchill's adviser on technical matters, Anderson, Halifax and others stoutly told Churchill he was making a grave, almost nonsensical misjudgment. Cherwell and Bush argued similarly with Roosevelt. *Ibid.*, pages 358-359.

The two signatories of this agreement kept its very existence secret. Roosevelt did not let even those who were directing the production of the bomb know of it, not even Frankfurter who had brought him to listen to Bohr's pleading. Stimson, himself, did not learn of it until after Roosevelt's death.[9]

The President was thereby spared the embarrassing task of defending to them the resolve to maintain secrecy. Moreover, he probably regarded the Hyde Park Agreement as provisional and reversible. Whatever his reasons, he made it possible for the discussion of these questions to proceed on the supposition that the doors to decisions were still open.

Thus before a fortnight had passed, Bush and Conant, in the memo sent to Stimson previously noted, again thrust forward views and recommendations similar to those which Bohr had advocated. After describing the ominous destructive power of the weapons coming into being, they predicted that all peoples would be at the mercy of any that used them first. It was impossible to foretell, they averred, which nations might produce them since knowledge essential for the purpose was widely diffused. Hence the advantage of the United States and Great Britain should be regarded as temporary; any other country with good technical and scientific knowledge might overtake them in three or four years, and perhaps by accident of research surge ahead of them.

Bush and Conant had boldly gone on to recommend the course that seemed to them dictated by these probabilities. It would be foolhardy to try to maintain American supremacy by preserving secrecy. The American government should therefore disclose the facts about the new weapon as soon as it was demonstrated. It should take the lead in advocating free exchange of information under the auspices of the international association of nations that was to be formed to maintain peace after the war. This association should be enabled to inform itself of all activities in this realm anywhere in the world. The Soviet Union, they predicted, would be more reluctant to agree to this arrangement than any other country but could be persuaded of its advantages. To these two ardent minds it did not seem paradoxical to make it easier for every nation to inform itself how it might make these weapons—in an attempt to avert a frenzied competition. For they hoped that appreciation of that dangerous prospect would act as a

---

[9] Even then, when it was brought to Truman's and Stimson's attention, no actual text of it could be found, and they had to ask the British government to supply a copy. Roosevelt's own had been deposited in the files of his Naval Aide. Whether because the heading "Tube Alloy" !misled whoever handled it, or intentionally, it was placed among the papers concerning naval supplies.

restraint on all nations in pursuit of this goal, and decrease chances of another and utterly disastrous war.[10]

Stimson had been much impressed by this presentation which was more coherent than any of Bohr's. When borne upward by his wishes, he glimpsed the possibility of a redeeming spiritual revival among the nations which would cause them to use the new discovery for good rather than for hostile opposition. When borne down by somber observations, he found it hard to subdue the impression that this was unlikely, and that nations were so poorly qualified to manage their affairs that the new weapon might doom their future.

He was in one of his more downcast moods in the talk he had with Roosevelt on December 31st after passing on to him the report from Groves, to which I have adverted. This trend in Russian diplomacy caused Stimson to say that he thought it advisable to require the Soviet government to accede to our wishes in some other regard in return for any information that was given it about the atomic bomb. Even though the secret could not be kept, he added, it seemed to him that we ought to wait before sharing our information. Roosevelt, without mentioning the understanding he had with Churchill, said he was of the same mind.[11]

But Stimson kept hoping that our relations with the Soviet government would take a turn for the better. And Roosevelt apparently had the same bright expectation when he set off for Yalta in February. If it was dimmer when he returned, he did not acknowledge it. Stimson, stressing the need to prepare for the coming climax had, during the remaining month of Roosevelt's life, tried to arouse him to think more decisively about the problems that would befall the United States. That he did in their last talk on March 15th, once again stressing how urgent it was to decide whether our knowledge about the bomb should be kept secret or shared if agreement could be reached on acceptable conditions; and what were these? But although Roosevelt had responded to Stimson's exposition in his customary outgoing way, he had continued to keep his counsel. Even if well and buoyant, would he have dared to strike out on an unmapped and untested path? Who is to know? The hammer of actualities was chipping hard at his hopes that the allies could continue to work in unison after the war. Stimson did not realize how tired the President's body and mind were, how tried his spirit. Stalin was grasping and unyielding.

[10] The main points in the Bush-Conant memo of September 30th are summarized in *The New World*, pages 329-330.
[11] Stimson Diary, December 29, 30 and 31, 1944.

Churchill was repulsing all proposals that knowledge about atomic weapons be disclosed to anyone.

Up to the end, Roosevelt seemed to be waiting for the answers to come to him. Thus the few men in Roosevelt's and Churchill's circle who believed that the world could be saved only if international consultations were begun at once, could do no more than propound queries to each other as to how and on what terms these could be initiated. Halifax and Frankfurter were so engaged on the morning of April 12th as they walked in Rock Creek Park along the path between the British Embassy and Georgetown. While they were pooling their forebodings, the church bells began to toll. Roosevelt was dead. His successor was going to inherit the crucial decisions which so perplexed him, and which were to trouble still more deeply some of the progenitors of the bomb.

Within an hour of Truman's induction into office, Stimson had lingered after the first Cabinet meeting to tell him briefly of the immense undertaking. Byrnes, who had been Director of War Mobilization, on the next day had said to him in quiet tones which did not disguise his feeling of awe, that the explosive emerging from American laboratories and plants might be powerful enough to destroy the whole world.

On the evening of April 23rd, a scant and crowded ten days afterwards, Truman received Molotov. The Soviet Commissar for Foreign Affairs had been defending every bastion of his interpretation of the accords made at Yalta and justifying Soviet elevation of its subservient Communist group to be the Provisional Government of Poland. Truman tried to budge the unbudgeable. It may be that what he had learned of the new weapon in the making sharpened his tongue. For after expressing the opinion that the Soviet government was not carrying out the agreement about Poland fairly, he said he wanted it clearly understood that our friendship with Russia could only be on a basis of mutual observances of agreements, not on the basis—as he phrased it—"of a one way street." Molotov, if Truman's memory is exact, blurted out, "I have never been talked to like that in my life."[12]

Stimson and Marshall had both been disturbed by the fractious outcome of this talk. Stimson was worried by its connotation for both political and military cooperation. Marshall was cognizant that the Russians might, as they could, delay their entry into the Pacific war "until we had done all the dirty work."

[12] Harry S Truman, *Year of Decisions*, page 82.

Groves had just turned out a special report for the purpose of briefing Truman adequately about the new weapon. Stimson determined to use it as the occasion for making the President think hard about the ways in which the bomb might affect our relations with Russia for better or worse; and in that connection to realize how urgent it was to decide whether to disclose the weapon before use with the intention of placing it under international control. Stimulated by Groves' memo, his thoughts about the surmounting set of questions surged out. Marshall approved his statement of facts and their meaning. With the portrayal of the paramount importance of the new form of force, and the crucial dilemmas it posed, readers of this narrative will have been already well acquainted. Stimson was pondering the same questions over and over, and would continue to as long as he was in office.

Truman asked Stimson to come to the White House Executive Office at noon on the 25th. The budget of news that morning was exciting. The Conference at San Francisco was about to open.[13] The American and Russian troops were shaking hands on the Elbe. Our soldiers had at last broken the impasse in Okinawa. And in front of Truman was another message from Stalin about the quarrel over Poland ". . . which showed plainly that Churchill and I were going to have persistent, calculated resistance from Stalin in our dealings with the Russians."[14]

Stimson entered the Executive Office by the front door while Groves used the side door and an underground passage. Stimson gave his own memo to the President. Its first sentence was intentionally startling. "Within four months we shall in all probability have completed the most terrible weapon ever known in human history, one bomb of which could destroy a whole city."[15]

The question of whether or not this foreknowledge might assist us in our diplomatic relations with other countries, particularly the Soviet Union, he left to the consideration of the President and the State Department. But Stimson and his military associates felt main responsibility under the President for the decision whether, when and how the new weapon should be used in the war against Japan, and in connection with what strategy.

---

[13] This event was certainly in Stimson's mind as he wrote; Bohr and those who thought alike were saying whatever might be attempted at San Francisco would prove empty unless an atomic arms race was averted. Similarly Sir John Anderson had written Churchill "No plans for world organization which ignore Tube Alloys can be worth the paper on which they are written."

[14] *Year of Decisions*, page 85.

[15] This memorandum is printed in Stimson's article "The Decision to use the Atomic Bomb" in *Harper's Magazine* of February 1947.

And beyond these urgent questions still loomed a cluster of still greater ones. What would the command of controlled atomic force mean in the future to mankind, to the nature of international society and the question of war and peace? "The world," Stimson predicted, ". . . would be eventually at the mercy of such a weapon. . . ." Its control "will undoubtedly be a matter of the greatest difficulty and would involve such thorough going rights of inspection and internal controls as we have never heretofore contemplated. Furthermore, in the light of our present position with reference to this weapon, the question of sharing it with other nations and, if so shared, upon what terms, becomes a primary question of our foreign relations. Also our leadership in the war and in the development of this weapon has placed a certain moral responsibility upon us which we cannot shirk without very serious responsibility for any disaster to civilization which it would further. On the other hand, if the problem of the proper use of this weapon can be solved we would have the opportunity to bring the world into a pattern in which the peace of the world and our civilization can be saved."

President Truman appeared to accept without demur the reasoning and inferences in this statement; he did not question any of them. So the three went on to read simultaneously copies of the twenty-four page Groves report which re-told the history of the project, its current status, the anticipated schedule of production—the first specimen ready for testing in July, the second of a different type for which further testing was not required by August 1—and anticipated estimates of their explosive force. The President interrupted his reading of this report several times, saying: "You know I don't like reading papers." When Stimson and Groves rejoined, "Well, we can't tell you this in more concise language," he persisted to the end. To his visitors Truman seemed impressed but not astounded. It is to be wondered whether he really grasped the huge difference in impact and effect between this new kind of weapon and the powerful kinds of artillery which had been fired upon a populace. Many years later he told an interviewer that a comparison with the shells Big Bertha had sent into Paris in the First World War came into his mind.[16]

After this exercise in exposition ended, Stimson had sought the President's approval for the formation of a committee to consider the whole range of questions—political, military and scientific—which he had set forth. The Secretary of War conceived that this group would make recommendations to both the Executive and Legislative branches of our government.

[16] Interview with representative of the National Broadcasting Company for TV.

The Committee, which became known as the Interim Committee, was constituted quickly. The President and Stimson decided that the better to assure and indicate that all aspects of the development would be considered, this group should be entirely civilian. For this reason not even General Groves was included. Stimson was the Chairman. Byrnes was chosen by the President to represent him. The other members were the Under-Secretary of the Navy, Ralph A. Bard, Assistant Secretary of State, William L. Clayton, a specialist in international trade, who was quite vocative in the Committee discussions, and three scientists who had played significant parts in the development of the project, Vannevar Bush, James B. Conant and Karl T. Compton, Chief of the Office of Field Service in the Office of Scientific Research and Development. George Harrison, President of the New York Insurance Company was appointed Secretary, appropriately or ironically as may be found; he filled in as Chairman when Stimson could not be present, and as intermediary with individual members. The Secretary of War kept in close and constant touch with the Committee, almost every day talking over the same questions which it was considering with his able Assistant Secretary John McCloy, his confidential Special Assistant, Harvey Bundy, and General Marshall.

Conant had had misgivings about whether he and Bush should serve on this Committee. He told Stimson he did not think that they should represent the scientists actively working on the project. Among some of them, he advised the Secretary, there was unrest and anxiety about the international impact of the bomb. For they sought to know what the ultimate outcome for humanity of their labors would be, wanting the comfort of serving peace and not other and more frightful wars and, fearing that a deadly armament race with the United States would ensue, particularly if the United States flung the bomb against Japan before informing the Soviet Union. Conant asked Stimson therefore whether, in order to allay these apprehensions, he could be permitted to show the memo which he and Bush had written months before to some of the agitated scientists, and also let them know that Stimson had acquainted Truman with its arguments. He also expressed hopes that Stimson would have the Interim Committee ask a few of the most eminent scientists to present their views on the international aspects either through the Interim Committee or directly to the President. Stimson, in response, suggested that Conant defer circulation of the memorandum because thought was being given to the formation of a Scientific Advisory Panel to the Interim Committee. Thereupon, Conant, in consultation with Bush, recommended four scientists for appointment to the Panel. On doing so, he said that he thought the Interim Committee would be well advised to ask other scientists also for their views on the political and social questions which were coming to the fore, since the panelists, chosen for their technical abilities, might not be the best qualified to judge matters outside their professional sphere.[17]

Soon after the Advisory Panel of Scientists was formed. On it were J. Robert Oppenheimer, Director of the Los Alamos Laboratory, Arthur H. Compton of the cover-named Metallurgical Laboratory of Chicago, Ernest O. Lawrence, Director of the Berkeley Radiation Laboratory and Enrico Fermi who had been in charge of the first controlled chain reaction experiment, all physicists who had made and were making great theoretical contributions to the conception and production of the new weapon.

The Interim Committee conferred several times during May. On the 16th, Bush distributed to the other members copies of the memo in which he and Conant had advocated a wide exchange of scientific information and the prompt inauguration of a program of international control of the production of atomic weapons. This seems to have been too momentous a proposal for the Committee to examine with care at this meeting. The discussion then and at the next session a few days later became hung up on the question of how long it would take the Soviet Union to produce an atomic weapon. The reason why, as remembered by Gordon Arneson, Recording Secretary of the Committee, was that several members of the Committee thought as did Byrnes, the President's representative, who was a novice in this realm, that ". . . the estimate of how long it would take the Soviet Union to produce an atomic weapon . . . would have a bearing on the subject of how we should try to deal with the subject in relation to the Soviet Union; whether we should try at an early stage to bring about collaboration with them or outdistance them in the race."[18] Later events have indicated that this should *not* have been a leading consideration in determining our policy.

During the weeks of May, while the members of the Interim Committee were trying to sort out their thoughts, the scientists engaged in the design of the bomb were striving their utmost to make sure that it

[17] This account of the discussion of the advisability of seeking the opinion of the scientists is derived from Hewett and Anderson, *The New World*, pages 345-346, who give the substance of correspondence between Conant, Stimson and Harrison, May 5-9, 1945.

[18] As recalled in 1965 by Arneson in a TV interview with a representative of the National Broadcasting Company.

would be in hand by summer. As recalled by Robert Oppenheimer, "The deadline never changed. It was as soon as possible"; and "After the collapse of Germany, we [the scientists] understood that it was important to get this ready for the war in Japan. We were told that it would be very important to know the state of affairs before the meeting at Potsdam at which the future conduct of the war in the Far East would be discussed."[19] Haste was decided more important than perfection. Again as remembered by Oppenheimer, ". . . I did suggest to General Groves some changes in bomb design which would make more efficient use of the material. . . . He turned them down as jeopardizing the promptness of the availability of bombs."[20]

Concurrently Stimson was keeping the British well informed. On April 30th Field Marshal Sir H. M. Wilson, Head of the British Joint Staff Mission in Washington and a member of the Combined Policy Committee on the Atomic Bomb, had let Anderson know that "the Americans propose to drop a bomb sometime in August."[21] Wilson had gone on to raise two connected questions: "Do we agree that the weapon should be used against the Japanese. If for any reason we did not, the matter would presumably have to be raised by the Prime Minister with the President. If we do agree, various points still arise on which it would be desirable to have consultation with the Americans . . . whether any warnings should be given to the Japanese."[22]

On May 14th Stimson had brought Anthony Eden, the Secretary of State for Foreign Affairs, who was in Washington, up to date, telling him of the then current time-table for the production and testing of the bomb. But the ensuing ministerial discussions in London were cursory. Churchill loitered in his response and his instructions to Wilson.[23] Was he skeptical about the scientists' predictions? Or, and that is much more probable, having stated his ideas and judgments clearly and firmly, was he willing to have the Americans exercise the predominate right to decide these issues, being sure how they would decide them? For whatever reasons, Churchill, who was communicating with Truman every day about the unsettled situations in Europe, did not enter into direct personal

[19] *In the Matter of J. Robert Oppenheimer. Transcript of Hearing before Personnel Security Board, U.S. Atomic Energy Commission, Washington, D.C.—April 12, 1954 through May 6, 1954*, page 31. This will be hereinafter cited as "Oppenheimer Hearings."
[20] *Ibid.*
[21] *Grand Strategy*, Vol. VI, pages 275-276.
[22] *Ibid.*, page 298.
[23] *Ibid.*, page 297.

discussion with him about these issues until they met in Potsdam in July. By then the bomb had been tested.

To revert to that interrupted tale of the deliberations of the Interim Committee.

It came together again in a critical two-day meeting on May 31-June 1.[24] By then, it will be remembered, the Joint Chiefs of Staff had settled on their plans for invasion of Japan and the President had decided to wait until he met with Churchill and Stalin before making a more extensive and explicit statement of our intentions toward Japan.

Stimson opened the day's discussions by expressing his ideas about the nature and meaning of the new achievement. He was intent on making the scientists understand that he and Marshall did not regard it merely as a new weapon; that they realized it would bring about a revolutionary change in the relation of man to the universe, with more effect on human destiny than the theory of Copernicus and the law of gravity, and of the utmost consequence in the relation of nation to nation. Thus success in utilizing the energy of the atom could mean either the doom of or great advancement in human civilization. It might turn into a Frankenstein's monster that would devour all, or a blessing that would make the world secure. How, under the ruling conditions of our own and international society could it best be developed, used, and controlled? Marshall spoke with similar seriousness.

The Committee then listened to the scientists explain the work under way and its imminent and predictable potentialities. All four members of the Scientific Panel and Conant contributed to this exposition. They outlined three stages in the development of atomic weapons. The first was the production of enough Uranium-235 for the type of bomb already mastered—the given type that was to be used at Hiroshima. Boosting previous estimates, they variably reckoned that this type would have an explosive force equivalent to anywhere between 2,000 and 20,000 tons of TNT. The second stage was the production of enriched materials from which plutonium or new kinds of uranium could be developed, the first specimen of which was to be tested in New Mexico in the middle of July. A bomb containing these materials, they estimated, could develop an explosive

[24] The account of the course of discussion during these two days is based on study of the summary minutes available to me, the information contained in *The New World*, particularly pages 356-360, which in turn were largely based on these minutes, though probably a more complete version of them than the one which was made available to me, and Gordon Arneson's interview with representatives of National Broadcasting Company for TV.

force equivalent to between 50,000 and 100,000 tons of TNT. In the third, and more remote stage, in which the product of the second would be used as a detonator of heavy water, it was considered possible that the resulting weapon might produce an explosive force equal to 10 million and even up to 100 million tons of TNT. Oppenheimer estimated that it would require a minimum of three years more to develop this superbomb, which was to become known as the thermo-nuclear bomb.

After these explications the Committee and the Advisory Panel of Scientists discussed the whole range of problems posed by the prospect of possession of the bomb.

One was the still unsettled question—or so it was regarded for the consultants did not know of the Hyde Park Agreement—of how the new source of explosive power and energy was to be controlled internationally; and in that connection how much should be revealed to the world, especially to the Russians, about the nature and method of production of the new weapon, and when the disclosure should be made.

As noted, the answers to these questions were thought by some of its members to be largely dependent on how long it would take the Soviet government to produce a bomb if we maintained secrecy; how long, in other words, we might have exclusive control of atomic energy, and how much of a lead we could count on and maintain over rival efforts. The wish to have expert opinion on this question had been one of the reasons why the Interim Committee had asked the Scientific Panel to meet with it that day, and another advisory panel of industrialists to meet with it the next day. The four members of that panel were executives of companies which were doing the main engineering and operating jobs at the great plants at Oak Ridge and Hanford (W. S. Carpenter, Jr. of Dupont, George M. Bucher of Westinghouse Electric, James White of Tennessee Eastman and James Rafferty of Union Carbide).

The surmises of the members of the Scientific Panel on May 31st scattered cautiously. But all tended to agree that the period that would be needed by the Soviet government to develop the weapon would not exceed greatly, if at all, the Bush-Conant forecast of three to five years. Those ventured by the industrialists the next day ranged from five to ten years if the Soviet Union had to rely on its own talent and resources; a shorter period if it benefited by knowledge gained through espionage and/or was assisted by German scientists and production experts. General Groves, deeply impressed by the continual and novel difficulties that the Americans had had to overcome in the manufacture of the weapon, and perhaps skeptical of Soviet knowledge of the theoretical fundamentals, thought it would take the Soviet Union much longer—perhaps as long as twenty years. The President's representative, Byrnes, was more impressed by the longer estimates—subsequently recalling that "I concluded that any other government would need from seven to ten years, at least, to produce a bomb."[25]

When the talk traveled from this particular question into the broader realm of policy, it became diffused. The members of the Scientific Panel, particularly Oppenheimer, spoke up in favor of the general policy of free exchange of basic information and cooperation with other nations that had been advocated in the Bush-Conant memorandum and endorsed in the one which Stimson had given Truman. They were confident that if a free exchange of information were permitted under a system of international control, the democracies would fare well.

But as the Committee attempted to assess the possibilities and problems of international control, uncertainty set in. Conant said he believed adequate inspection would be requisite to assure the reliability of any system of international control. Clayton seemed dubious about the desirability of a policy of international control involving, as it would, a system of inspection. Oppenheimer suggested that we ought not to prejudge the Russian attitude and response to any proposals for cooperation. Marshall, though dubious whether we could rely on the efficacy of inspection in view of the excessive secrecy of the Stalinist state, still seemed inclined to favor a test of the Soviet response to proposals we put forward; perhaps if we built up a combination of like-minded powers in support of our proposals, their coalesced influence might bring the Soviet government into line. The scientists thought that if governments agreed to permit free exchange of information, this would improve the possibility of knowing what the Soviet Government was doing. But they refrained from pressing the point that it would make little difference in the end whether inspection worked satisfactorily or not, if the Soviet by its own initiative could develop atomic weapons in a few years.

Byrnes, at this point in the discussion, the official history informs us, "intervened decisively." He said he was afraid ". . . that if we gave information to the Russians, even in general terms, Stalin would ask to come into the partnership. . . . He concluded that the best policy was to push production and research and make certain that the United States

[25] James F. Byrnes, *Speaking Frankly*, page 261. This book was published in 1947 before the Russians exploded their first bomb. Interesting comment on this subject is to be found in Caryl P. Haskins' "Atomic Energy and American Foreign Policy," *Foreign Affairs*, July 1946.

stayed ahead. At the same time he favored making every effort to improve political relations with Russia."[26] Then according to the same source, "All present indicated their concurrence."[27] This is perplexing in view of what several members of the Committee had just been saying. The concurrence, if it was positive or mere abstention from objection, may be explained by the fact that it was thought the efforts to improve relations with Russia could include an invitation to join in an international system of control. Certainly the recapitulation of the morning's discussion which Arthur Compton made for Stimson, for he had left the meeting for awhile, was general enough to permit all to assent. "First, the United States should permit as much freedom of research as was consistent with national security and military necessity. Second, it should establish a combination of democratic powers for cooperation in atomic energy. Third, it should seek an understanding with Russia."[28] Had Stimson sighed and wondered about the value of having the Committee—and I am conjuring up the thought—it would have been understandable.

The talk was then directed to the other major question: how was the bomb to be used against Japan? The Committee was told that this must be decided without delay, since complicated and exact preparations would have to be made.

That very morning, before the Interim Committee met, Stimson had once again talked over with Marshall, Groves, Harrison and Bundy ". . . how we should use this implement in respect of Japan."[29] *How* not *whether*, the reader will note; and it was about how and not whether that the Committee and the Scientific Panel were consulted in the discussions that began the next day. As recalled by one of the members of the Scientific Panel: "Throughout the morning's discussions it seemed a foregone conclusion that the bomb would be used."[30]

This had been the impelling purpose from the start. Stimson was counting on the new weapon to bring the war to a quick end. This is evidenced by several entries in his Diary, among them one on May 10th which recorded that he and General Marshall had talked ". . . on rather deep matters—the coming progress of strategy for the operations in the Pacific where I wanted to find out whether or not we couldn't hold matters off from very heavy involvement in casualties until we had tried out S-1. I

[26] *The New World*, page 357.
[27] *Ibid.*
[28] *Ibid.*, page 358.
[29] Stimson Diary, May 30.
[30] A. H. Compton, *Atomic Quest: A Personal Narrative*, pages 238-239.

found that probably we could get the trial before the locking of arms and much bloodshed."

To all engaged in the final stage of the bomb's development, this was the greatest incentive. Thus no one of the participants in this meeting disputed the view that the bomb should be used without warning against a populated target in Japan if that was clearly the only and best way to achieve this commanding purpose. However, were there not more sparing ways?

Two were mentioned and discussed. One was to give a fully informative warning notice to the Japanese people of the nature and destructive power of the new weapon that would be used if they did not surrender. The other was to give a demonstrative detonation of it in some unpopulated area. The two became coupled in the drift of the discussion. That was regrettable, I believe, because when the proposal that the bomb be demonstrated before use was discarded—as will be told—the idea of giving adequate advance notice to Japan of another sort was also cast away.

The records of what was said about some form of demonstration are meager and in a degree divergent, as are the memories of those present during the discussion.[31] The idea had been mentioned in passing during the morning's meeting. At luncheon the group sat at several tables and thus several conversations took place concurrently; which may explain the two different stories of who brought up the question again at lunch. According to one, Stimson asked Compton whether some sort of demonstration might serve our purpose. According to another, Byrnes enlisted the attention of the group to the suggestion by asking Lawrence for his opinion. That scientist was skeptical. So was Oppenheimer, who said he doubted whether any sufficiently startling demonstration could be devised that would convince the Japanese that they ought to throw in the sponge; since the Japanese had gone through the ghastly fire raids of Tokyo, were they likely to be impressed enough by any display of the weapon? Byrnes mentioned that the Japanese might bring American prisoners in the demonstration area. Then, the query was asked, what if the test should fail, if the bomb should be a "dud"? Byrnes' fears of the effect of a failure were grave. Almost twenty years later, he seemed still to shudder

[31] The sources known to me are 1) The summary minutes of the meeting. 2) A. H. Compton's statements in his book, *Atomic Quest*, pages 238-239. 3) James Byrnes, *All in One Lifetime*, page 285. 4) The account in *The New World*, page 358, derived from the foregoing and from an exchange of letters between E. O. Lawrence and K. K. Darrow in August 1945. 5) Henry Stimson and McGeorge Bundy, *On Active Service in Peace and War*. 6) The retrospective comments of Conant, Arneson and Byrnes in 1964 in interviews with representatives of National Broadcasting Company for TV.

at the thought of what they might have been—saying to a TV audience, "The President would have had to take the responsibility of telling the world that we had this atomic bomb and how terrific it was . . . and if it didn't prove out what would have happened to the way the war went God only knows."

Because of the various doubts and objections expressed, the idea of having a prior demonstration was passed by, and after luncheon the talk turned to the most efficacious use of the bomb as a weapon. Oppenheimer stressed the fact that the effects produced by an atomic bomb would differ from those produced by air attacks with other explosives; its visual display would be stupendous, and it would spread radiation dangerous to life for a radius of at least two-thirds of a mile. These foreglimpses of what an atomic burst would look like, and do, seem astounding in their correctness to this baffled historian.

The consideration of *how* to use the bomb was led to its end by Stimson's summary of the several general conclusions which seemed to him to have emerged from the discussion: that we should not give the Japanese any informative warning; that we ought not to concentrate on a civilian area but we should seek to make a deep psychological impression—to shock as many Japanese as possible. When Conant remarked that for this purpose the bomb should be aimed at a vital war plant surrounded by houses, Stimson agreed. No one objected. Not Marshall, who the day before had told Stimson that he wondered whether we might first use the bomb against a military target that was wholly military, as for example, a naval installation. Nor any member of the Scientific Panel; if some had qualms, they kept quiet about them at this critical juncture. The accepted demands of war downed uneasy thoughts about the future effects of revealing the bomb to the world this way.

These conclusions were made more definite after consultation with the panel of industrialists on the next day, June 1st. On that afternoon Byrnes submitted three recommendations which the members unanimously adopted.[32]

1) The bomb should be used against Japan as soon as possible. The wish to cast the bomb into the scale of war as quickly as could be was stimulated by the hope of suspending the transfer of American youth to the Pacific and by the wish to dispel the vision of an embattled landing in small boats on the shores of Japan. Whether it was also animated by a desire to end the war before the Soviet armies had swarmed far

[32] Under-Secretary of the Navy Ralph Bard subsequently changed his mind and wrote a letter of dissent on June 27th to George Harrison.

over Manchuria remains a matter of conjecture. Probably so, although the American government was then counting on Soviet entry into the war to supplement the impact of the atomic bomb—in combination to compel the Japanese to recognize that instant surrender was the only way to avert the ruin, if not the extinction of their nation.

2) The bomb should be used on a dual target—that is, on a military installation or war plant surrounded by or adjacent to houses and other buildings most susceptible to damage.

It was thought that the effects of the bomb on such a target would make the maximum impression on the military and civilian rulers of Japan. Any more sparing course was deemed by Stimson and his associates on the Interim Committee to involve a ". . . serious danger to the major objective of obtaining a prompt surrender from the Japanese."[33]

3) It should be used without explicit prior warning of the nature of the weapon by which we meant to enforce the call to surrender.

The responsible group was influenced by the opinion to which I shall revert, that divulgence to the Japanese in advance of the nature and power of the new weapon would hinder rather than serve our wish to end the war at once. For it was deemed that the Japanese would not be impressed or frightened enough to surrender; and that it might diminish the impact of the bomb when it was dropped; unexplained, it would be the more fearsome.

The Committee, having set the American course in the atomic field for the time being, dispersed. Before doing so, it agreed to ask the members of the Scientific Panel for their views about what sort of organization should be established to direct and control atomic energy, and to write them out in a memorandum. It is notable that the Committee, however, did not enter into the question of whether the American government should or should not elucidate or ease the surrender terms for Japan. That question the group no doubt thought was outside its assignment, as it was.

Byrnes acquainted the President at once with the recommendations of the Committee. He explained that they had taken into account the plans sponsored by the Joint Chiefs of Staff, which contemplated the invasion and its many, many casualties. At the end of this talk the President ". . . expressed the opinion that, regrettable as it might be, so far as he could see, the only reasonable conclusion was to use the bomb."[34]

[33] Stimson and Bundy, *On Active Service in Peace and War*, page 617.
[34] In the narrative of his official activities which he published later, the President's liai-

On June 6th Stimson gave the President a more comprehensive account of the conclusions arrived at by the Interim Committee.[35] He said that the Interim Committee had decided that the work on the bomb should *not* be disclosed to any other country until the bomb had been successfully used against Japan. Truman remarked that he had secured more time for the United States to guard its secret since he had deferred his conference with Churchill and Stalin until July 15th.

But the dilemma of whether the American government should merely wait on events or should seek to devise some international system of control, Stimson told the President, was still before them. The only suggestion proffered by the Interim Committee, he related, was that the United States should take the lead in securing an international agreement whereby each country obligated itself to make·public all work done on atomic energy. The responsibility of ascertaining whether this pledge was being observed should be placed on an international committee, empowered to inspect and patrol the whole realm. To interject—it will be noted that this proposal did not stipulate that countries should desist from making atomic weapons. It would permit the United States, and presumably other countries, to accumulate enough fissionable material or weapons "as insurance against being caught helpless."[36] Whether because of the provision for inspection, or because it would not have completely curbed the United States, or for some other reason, Stimson said that he thought that Russia might not assent. Certainly, Stimson repeated, the United States should not disclose what it was doing until a system of control was developed; until we were reasonably sure that it would not assist a hostile rival.

Together they wondered whether it might be possible to secure satisfaction from the Soviet government in some currently disputed issues, such as those of Poland and Eastern Europe in connection with a cooperative agreement on atomic energy. But no such suggestion was ever put before the Soviet rulers; the bomb was left to make its own impress. Again, to transgress outside the boundaries of this narrative, while it probably did restrain the Communist thrust, it did not cause Stalin to lessen

---

son representative on the Interim Committee, however, erroneously dates this talk with Truman as July 1. Byrnes, *Speaking Frankly*, pages 261-262. But he dated it correctly in his later book, *All in One Lifetime*, page 285.

[35] I believe that the recommendations of the Interim Committee were revised or at least reworded in another recorded statement by them on June 7th. The differences were not significant. Presumably Stimson used the first version when talking with the President on June 6th.

[36] Stimson Diary, June 6, 1945.

or relax those territorial claims he had staked out soon after Russia entered the war.

While discussions within the American government of our policies settled and subsided after this May 31-June 1 meeting of the Interim Committee, it flared up higher among some of the scientists who were well acquainted with the problems of atomic fission and who foresaw the enormous destructive power that could be conjured out of atoms. From what they learned of the program endorsed by the Interim Committee they were convinced that it was shortsighted, and morally and perhaps mortally wrong.

The asseverations of Bohr—and of Stimson when he wrote and spoke as preacher-statesman rather than as soldier—that the new discovery made it compulsory for nations to behave differently to each other than ever in the past, were flaming gospel in the studies and laboratories of many scientists. As the momentous event, the birth of the weapon, neared, they resounded louder and louder.

A group who had achieved much at the laboratories in Chicago, known by its cover name as the Metallurgical Institute, were among those most upset by what they learned about the trend of official planning, so disturbed that they might have been openly mutinous except for the clamps of secrecy and security. The group abhorred the thought that their work might destroy nations and envisioned the possibility that it might draw them together at last.

Knowing of the stew they were in and their clamorous wish to have their views considered, Arthur Compton had stepped forward and acted as liaison between them and officialdom.[37] On his return from Washington after the May 31-June 1 meeting, he assured the laboratory leaders that the Interim Committee was receptive to suggestions about all aspects of the future of atomic energy, and would be glad to be fully advised of them before its next meeting.[38] The Chicago scientists had thereupon formed several committees, each of which was to be concerned with an aspect or area of the field. One of these was the Committee on Social and Political Implications. Its chairman was an eminent chemist, Professor James O. Franck; its catalytic member was Professor Leo Szilard.[39]

One of the main authors of the memo presented by this committee

---

[37] *The New World*, pages 365-367.
[38] *Ibid.*, page 365.
[39] *Ibid.*
The seven members of this Committee were: James O. Franck as Chairman, Leo Szilard, T. R. Hogness, Donald Hughes, J. J. Nixon, E. Rabinowitch, Glenn Seaborg and J. C. Stearns.

to the government, Professor E. Rabinowitch, has recalled its origins and the flow of feeling that penetrated it. "I remember many hours spent walking up and down the Midway with Leo Szilard arguing about these questions [and] sleepless nights when I asked myself whether perhaps we should break through the walls of secrecy and get to the American people the feeling of what was to be done by their government and whether we approve it. . . . Franck started drafting the report but had difficulty because of the language, and turned over his notes to me. . . . The report was prepared essentially by me with the important contribution of Leo Szilard. . . . [He] was responsible for the whole emphasis on the problem of the use of the bomb which really gave the report its historical significance—the attempt to prevent the use of the bomb on Japan. While the authorship of the whole report was mine, the fundamental orientation was due above all to Leo Szilard and James Franck. . . ."[40]

Their eloquent charge still reverberates today. But the main features of its supporting argument are essentially the same as those in previous presentations of which we have told. The notion that the United States could protect itself for an indefinite time was dismissed as mistaken. For the basic facts and implications of nuclear power were common knowledge, and the experience of Russian scientists in nuclear research was sufficient

---

Just before the San Francisco conference convened, Arthur Compton had taken Professor Franck of Chicago to see Vice President Henry Wallace. They expounded their views to Wallace and gave him a memo stating them, "Scientists found themselves in an intolerable situation. Military restrictions were tearing them between loyalty to their oaths of secrecy and their conscience as men and citizens. Statesmen who did not realize the atom had changed the world were laying futile plans for peace while scientists who knew the facts stood helplessly by."

Szilard, while working with Fermi at Columbia University in 1939-40, had been one of the persons who had persuaded Einstein that the American government ought to be examining the adaptation of atomic fission for military purposes, and induced Einstein to write a letter to President Roosevelt which, by calling attention to the military significance of recent scientific progress in fissuring the atom, helped to focus official interest on the field, which resulted in the Manhattan Project.

By the time that the bomb had been created and Germany was defeated and all danger that it might acquire this weapon was past, Szilard and his colleagues began to have misgivings about the introduction of this new and greater destructive force into warfare. So, before the meeting of the Interim Committee (May 31-June 1), he had gone down to South Carolina to see Byrnes who was Presidential representative on the Committee. He had spoken critically of the three scientist members of the Committee (Bush, Conant and Karl Compton) but well of the Scientific Panel. About this visit Byrnes subsequently wrote, "Szilard complained that he and some of his associates did not know enough about the policy of the government with regard to the use of the bomb. He felt that scientists, including himself, should discuss the matter with the Cabinet, which I did not feel desirable. His general demeanor and his desire to participate in policy making made an unfavorable impression on me. . . ." *All in One Lifetime*, page 284.

[40] Interview with a representative of the National Broadcasting Company for TV.

to enable them to retrace our steps within a few years, even if we should make every attempt to conceal them. The idea that the country could assure its security by increasing its nuclear armaments greatly was deemed invalid, since even if we maintained quantitative superiority we would not be safe, since "In no other type of warfare does the advantage lie so heavily in favor of the aggressor, and the United States would be the more vulnerable because of the concentration of its people and industry." Safety for one and all nations henceforth could be achieved only if they agreed to subject their activities in atomic energy to international control. However, the chance of bringing about such an agreement would be greatly lessened by the sudden and unannounced use of the weapon against Japan, because of ". . . the ensuing loss of confidence and by a wave of horror and repulsion sweeping the rest of the world and perhaps even dividing public opinion at home."

Therefore before hurling the bomb, the Committee pleaded, we ought to demonstrate it in a place and way that would not cause loss of life. This we should do in the presence of representatives of other countries including Japan—addressing ourselves to them somewhat to the following effect, "Say, look here: this is the kind of power which we have discovered, which we could use and legitimately as a method of warfare in a world where power politics will continue, wars will be a repeated phenomenon and a terrible danger to other nations. Therefore we want to call on you for the foundation of the United Nations on the basis of this new knowledge which requires a world system which would really prevent wars. If that is done the United States is willing to be the first to sacrifice some of its national sovereignty in order to do whatever must be done to make atomic war impossible. . . ."

If Japan did not heed this demonstration, and if the sanction of the United Nations were obtained, we might then use the bomb with better conscience and to better effect. For the Committee believed that in any case the procedure proposed would not prejudice the chance that the Soviet Union would cooperate in the creation of a system of international control.[41] The memo did not probe deeply into the problems that would present themselves in any attempt to do so. Its plea rested on the hope that nations would find terms of agreement and accept the necessary restraints when they recognized that only by doing so could they be freed from the peril of atomic weapons.

[41] The published text from which these quoted paragraphs and summaries are extracted is not complete, but is adequate.

To be sure that this statement would receive attention while decision might still be influenced, Compton met Franck in Washington on June 12th. Stimson was not available, so they left an unsigned copy of the memo with Arneson along with a letter signed by Compton addressed to Stimson.[42] Presumably Stimson was informed of the letter and the memo; but whether he read them, the record does not inform us. Almost certainly, Harrison consulted Stimson before telephoning Compton in Los Alamos on June 16th to tell him that the Interim Committee would like to know what the Scientific Panel thought of the recommendations made in the memo.

The reasons why four days were allowed to elapse before that message was sent to the Scientific Panel is conjectural. Perhaps Harrison could not secure Stimson's attention quickly. Perhaps it was because he knew that the Scientific Panel was about to meet, or was meeting, to consider among other matters, a previous request by the Interim Committee for "a report as to whether [it] could devise any kind of demonstration that would seem likely to bring the war to an end without using the bomb against a living target."

It also remains undetermined whether the Panel had in hand a complete copy of the Franck memo when they met, or merely knew of its reasoning and proposals.[43] It would hardly have mattered, because the members were thoroughly familiar with them, and had often talked them over among themselves and with other scientists. We may be sure that the consideration of them was as conscientious as time allowed.[44]

On the 16th their report to the Interim Committee was completed and forwarded by Oppenheimer to Harrison with a covering letter. In this he explained that the report of the Panel covered only the matters on which all its members could agree. The first two of the four paragraphs of its report read:

"Introductory: You have asked us to comment on the initial use of the new weapon. This use, in our opinion, should be such as to promote a satisfactory adjustment of our international relations. At the same time, we recognize our obligations to our nation to use the weapons to help save American lives in the Japanese War.

"To accomplish these ends we recommend that before the weapons are

[42] Compton's letter, after summarizing the memo, observed that it did not mention the possible consequences of a failure of the demonstration, which notation may have suggested that he had doubts about the recommendations in the memo.

[43] Oppenheimer has denied that the Panel had a copy when they met to talk about it.

[44] Inquirers have not been able to ascertain whether they met during the weekend of June 10-11 as well as later, or only communicated with each other by telephone before the meeting on June 16.

used not only Britain, but also Russia, France and China be advised that we would welcome suggestions as to how we can cooperate in making this development contribute to improved international relations."[45]

When in *Harper's Magazine* for February 1947, Stimson published a summary history of the decision to drop the atomic bomb these two paragraphs were omitted. Why? It will be noticed that this recommendation of the Panel is akin to that in the Franck memo and contrary to that made by Stimson and Byrnes to Truman. This has been overlooked in the strictures of the Panel for taking, in the other two paragraphs of its reply, an adverse view of the proposal of a demonstration, and it has given rise to the idea that the Panel's views were entirely opposed to those in the Franck memo.

The rest of the Panel report read:

"The opinions of our scientific colleagues on the initial use of these weapons are not unanimous; they range from the proposal of a purely technical demonstration to that of military application best designed to induce surrender. Those who advocate a purely technical demonstration would wish to outlaw the use of atomic weapons, and have feared that if we use the weapons now our position in future negotiations will be prejudiced. Others emphasize the opportunity of saving American lives by immediate military use, and believe that such use will improve the international prospects, in that they are more concerned with the prevention of war than with the elimination of this special weapon.

"We find ourselves closer to these latter views; we can propose no technical demonstration likely to bring an end to the war; we can see no acceptable alternative to direct military use."[46]

Here we may pause in our narrative to comment on the nature of some of the issues raised by the Franck Committee and some of the comments in the report of the Scientific Panel related to these issues.

Some of the matters reviewed in the Franck memo were within the professional knowledge of its sponsors; notably how long it might take other countries, particularly the Soviet Union, to produce the bomb; and what would be the effect, if measured in comparison to the effect of tons of TNT, of the detonation of the bomb (20,000 tons, it was forecast). Their conclusion about these matters turned out to be correct, remarkably so. On other matters, however, the opinions of the authors could be only venturesome guesses.

The supporting exposition in the Franck memo roamed far beyond the

---

[45] Author's underlining.
[46] This sentence is in italics in Stimson's article in *Harper's Magazine*.

realm of scientific authority. The advice proffered was supported by conjectures concerning human behavior about which neither the Franck group nor the Scientific Panel were especially informed or qualified. They ranged over the whole political and military landscape and beyond the visible horizon.

Might any demonstration that could be devised have so forceful an impact on the Japanese ruling group as to cause them to submit to our demand for unconditional surrender? Could it have made a difference in the response of the Soviet government to our later proposal that other countries not enter into a competitive effort to produce atomic weapons and that all agree to confine this new force by a reliable international accord? Would it convince nations that in order to survive they would genuinely have to renounce war? Or to achieve these imperative purposes would it prove necessary to give undeniable proof, in the brutal ledger of life and death, of the tremendous destructive power that men could now command and use against each other? About these interrelated elements of the problem of decision, the opinion of the members of both the Franck Committee and the Scientific Panel could be no more than personal intuitions, influenced to an unknown degree by pertinent facts about physical components of the problem.

That the members of the Scientific Panel were aware this was so is evidenced in another section of their report.

"With regard to these general aspects of the use of atomic energy it is clear that we, as scientific men, have no proprietary rights. . . . We have . . . no claim to special competence in solving the political, social and military problems which are presented by the advent of atomic power."

Oppenheimer, the chief drafter of the Report of the Panel, reminiscently testified, "We didn't know beans about the military situation in Japan. We didn't know whether they could be caused to surrender by other means or whether the invasion was really inevitable. But in back of our minds was the notion that the invasion was inevitable because we had been told that. . . . We thought the two overriding considerations were the saving of lives in the war and the effect of our actions on the stability, on the strength and the stability, of the postwar world. We did say that we did not think exploding one of these things as a firecracker over a desert was likely to be very impressive. This was before we had actually done that. The destruction on the desert is zero."[47] Probably the Panel had in mind the fact that although the illumination effect would be as-

[47] Oppenheimer Hearings, page 34.

tounding, the blast and radiation effects would not be startlingly evidenced in a demonstration area.

Rather than break the narrative, we will postpone further explanation and examination of the variety of reasons advanced against taking the risks of a demonstration.

Stimson was still at his home on Long Island a few days later when the Interim Committee took cognizance of the reply of the Scientific Panel. It was unswayed by the Franck Committee's exhortation that the bomb be demonstrated before use, unconvinced that it would serve our purposes. Thus it confirmed its previous recommendations that the weapon should be used as soon as could be, without warning, against a military-industrial complex near homes or other vulnerable structures. But in a rather restrained way it took up with the proposal that the American government notify its main allies before using the bomb in combat. It was obligated to confer with the British government before doing so. No good or necessary reason for informing France or China was perceived. But what about the oft-repeated proposal that Russia be given advance notice, in connection with a bid for future cooperation? After an animated discussion the Interim Committee on June 21 unanimously agreed that the President should tell Stalin that the American government was working on the project with excellent chances of success and expected to use the bomb against Japan—remarking also that he hoped to discuss later ways of insuring that this would be a force for peace, not war. Stimson was informed of these conclusions, noting in his Diary that "The Committee had strong recommendations in regard to relations with Russia" and that he had asked the "two leaders of the proposal [presumably Bush and Conant] to draft their ideas and submit them to me."[48] Before their departure for Potsdam Stimson informed the President of these conclusions, saying that he agreed with them.

Stimson also gave thought to a reversal in the judgment of Under-Secretary of the Navy, Bard. He had come to the conclusion that Japan was so badly beaten that its government might be searching for a chance to surrender on terms acceptable to us. He advocated that we strive to find out whether it would or not. Why not, he urged, ask envoys of Britain, the Soviet Union, China and France to join with us in arranging a meeting with Japanese representatives somewhere on the coast of China, after the Potsdam Conference? Then and there Japan might be told of the new weapon and its impending use, and that the Soviet Union intended to en-

[48] Stimson Diary, June 21-22.

ter the war. At the same time the Allied spokesmen might convey whatever assurances the President might be willing to give in regard to the Emperor and the treatment of Japan after surrender. But, also, Bard's proposal did not seem realistic to Stimson, nor realizable.

To foretell, the ultimatum issued during the Potsdam Conference did not divulge the nature of the new weapon by which we meant to compel the Japanese to yield, nor clearly indicate whether the Emperor could be retained.

This narrative will have shown that it would be erroneous to attribute the use of the bomb against Japan primarily to the advice of the Interim Committee or the Scientific Panel. Their opinions were merely confirmatory. For, as tersely recalled by Stimson, "The conclusions of the Committee were similar to my own, although I reached mine independently. I felt that to extract a genuine surrender from the Emperor and his military advisers, they must be administered a tremendous shock which would carry convincing proof of our power to destroy the Empire. Such an effective shock would save many times the number of lives, both American and Japanese, than it would cost."[49]

Neither did Churchill have any doubt about what should be done. His concern at this juncture was to arrange that the decision should be taken in a way that validated the Quebec agreement which contemplated American-British partnership. Field Marshal Wilson informed him that Stimson and Marshall intended to consult the British government "as to the best means of recording concurrence by His Majesty's Government to the operational employment of an atomic weapon."[50] Churchill decided that "the most satisfactory procedure" would be to record the decision in a Minute of the Combined Policy Committee rather than through the Combined Chiefs of Staff.[51]

On July 2nd, two days before the Combined Policy Committee met, Anderson advised Wilson that the "Prime Minister has approved my proposal that agreement to decision to use Weapon should be recorded at next meeting of [the Combined Policy] Committee. Prime Minister mentioned that he would naturally wish to discuss this matter with President at 'TERMINAL' [the Potsdam Conference] and that it would be as well that Committee should take note of this."[52]

[49] *Harper's Magazine*, February 1947.
[50] *Grand Strategy*, Vol. VI, page 298.
[51] *Ibid.*, and *Britain and Atomic Energy*, pages 372-373.
[52] *Grand Strategy*, Vol. VI, pages 298.

The Combined Policy Committee met on July 4th. Besides the members of the Committee—Stimson, Field Marshal Wilson, the Honorable C. D. Howe (Canadian Minister of Munitions) and Vannevar Bush—the Earl of Halifax, Sir James Chadwick, General Groves, George Harrison, and the Joint Secretaries, Harvey Bundy and Roger Makins were present.

Field Marshal Wilson, as authorized, stated that the British Government concurred in the use of the atomic bomb against Japan. Then he added that the Prime Minister might wish to discuss this subject with the President at the forthcoming meeting in Berlin. The Minutes record that: "The Committee: Took note that the Governments of the United Kingdom and the United States had agreed that T.A. [for the code designation Tube Alloys] weapons should be used by the United States against Japan. . . ."[53]

British acquiescence in the American decision seems to have been almost a matter of course. The reasons why are plain. 1) Churchill's firm agreement with the decision; 2) the sense of the fact that the United States had borne the main burden of the war in the Pacific entitled it to have the conclusive say on the subject; 3) the tendency to regard the decision as a military matter, and 4) because the British share in the partnership which led to the production of the bomb was the smaller one. As summed up by an informed British historian: "The balance of power, both in the atomic project and in the Pacific, lay too heavily with the United States for the British to be able, or to wish, to participate in this decision. They therefore preferred to acquiesce in it without more ado, relying on talks between the President and the Prime Minister at Potsdam to learn the reasons for it and to influence if need be, the manner of its execution."[54]

The British conferees were in fact well acquainted with the reasons which governed the American decision. Churchill had previously made known that he was firmly of the same mind. Military considerations were as foremost in his thoughts as they were in those of the Americans. However, he and some of his advisers were also swayed by other reflections. The Prime Minister was as expectant as Secretary of State Byrnes that the same bombs which were to upset the Japanese rulers and bring the

[53] Potsdam Papers, Document 619. Still other subjects discussed at this meeting were 1) how and how much to disclose about the new weapon and its use. The British participants, following Churchill's bent, favored caution, partly on the score that if other countries were fully informed they might be less likely to assent to plans for international control. Stimson said that he thought that if Truman said nothing when he saw Stalin, it would hurt relations between the allies; and 2) reports that a great quantity of uranium oxide had been discovered in Sweden.
[54] Grand Strategy, Vol. VI, page 299. The account given in the official history Britain and Atomic Energy is conformable.

PART TWO

Fateful Days at Potsdam

I will show you fear
in a handful of dust

—T. S. ELIOT

war to a swift end would also impress the Soviet government and cause it to be more conciliatory. Moreover, the British authorities thought it imperative that the war in the Pacific should be ended as soon as possible so that both Great Britain and the United States could give primary attention to the impending misery and chaos in Europe. As recalled by Roger Makins, the British Secretary of the Combined Policy Committee, "The British were poised to invade Malaya at the end of August, and it would certainly have involved heavy casualties, and while these massive resources were being mobilized in the Far East, Europe and the European countries were sinking slowly into an economic decline and the task of reconstruction was clearly going to be more difficult the longer the war in the East continued."[55]

In sum, the British decision-makers believed, as did the Americans, that conjectural anxieties about the future effects of using the bomb against Japan should not deter them from taking the measure which could bring the war to an end much sooner than any other, as well as with less loss of life.

The American delegation to the Potsdam Conference, headed by Truman and Byrnes, was scheduled to leave by ship two days later after this meeting of the Combined Policy Committee. Stimson asked the President whether it might not be a good idea if he flew over, so as to be on the spot when the bomb was tested. The President said he would be pleased if he did. By that time it was known with virtual certainty that the test would be made a day or so before or after the delegation arrived at the conference site in Germany.

The Chiefs of Staff were the mentors of military plans to compel surrender by combined assault. The Secretary of State was custodian of the text of a Proclamation to be addressed to the Japanese people, telling them how they would fare if they surrendered, and warning them that they would be destroyed if they refused to heed the warning. The Secretary of War was the guardian of the knowledge that if the Japanese government disregarded this summons to surrender, we would be able to smite Japan so astounding a blow that it would have to yield at once. Never was a group so triply armed.

Of how the news of the test was received at Potsdam, of what was told to Stalin, and of how the decision to drop the bomb was riveted by a definite order to do so, the narrative will tell as it follows Truman, Stimson and Byrnes abroad.

[55] Interview for television by the representatives of the NBC.

5. The Two Faces of Policy

DURING the ten days that the President was traveling to Potsdam our planes and ships spread havoc over Japan. Great fleets of what were then called superfortresses were smashing and burning the industrial centers, railroad yards, docks, oil and steel plants, and nearby crowded residential areas on the main island of Honshu. Carrier planes were swooping at will over Japanese airfields and installations. The ships of our Pacific Fleet, standing close to shore, were sending their heavy shells into coastal targets and towns within range. The wish to conserve the small remaining reserve of combat planes against the awaited invasion of the homeland, the scarcity of skilled pilots, lack of gasoline and parts were so disabling that the defending Japanese air force was almost inactive. The whole country and its people were at our mercy although their military leaders did not dare admit that it was so. Readers of the press in the United States were almost as well informed of each of our blows as the officials who received the secret battle and intelligence reports.[1]

The American people were determined to continue and extend their assaults until the Japanese submitted to our will. Some were ruled by vengeful fury—by a wish to make the Japanese suffer because of the suffering they had caused—in recall of the attack on Pearl Harbor, the march of the American captives at Bataan, the fighting in the jungles of Guadalcanal, the death of comrades under suicide attacks. But this was not the prevalent or dominating American state of feeling. Most Americans did not want to kill for the satisfaction of killing, or punish just in order to even up the resentful score. When they thought ahead to victory they were set upon seeing to it that Japan would never again be able to start a great war, and they were determined to suppress those Japanese leaders and elements who had led Japan in aggression. But toward the Japanese people they were relenting. They detested some Japanese ways and they feared some dark and devious turns of the Japanese spirit. But they were not vindictive.

Thus the officials in Washington who were striving to compose a statement which would tell the Japanese how we intended to treat them could count on popular approval of a regime of control which was strict

---

[1] The damage being done by the air and naval assaults was widely and fully reported in the American press and radio each day. Frequent summaries of the results of the attacks were given out by General George F. Kenney, Commander of the Far Eastern Air Force, by Admiral William F. Halsey in command of the U.S. Third Fleet which was cruising off Japan, and by Admiral Chester W. Nimitz, Commander of the Pacific Fleet with headquarters at Guam.

but unsickened by hate. The Japanese, after they had cast aside their arms and reformed their institutions, were to be enabled to regain a tolerable way of life. The defeated veterans were to be permitted to return to their homes, the Japanese people were to be encouraged to let their sorrows fade into the past, to rebuild their houses and factories, and resume their peaceful activities in production, trade, studies, and the arts.

Thus there is irony in the contrast between the two edges or faces of the fate prepared for the Japanese at Potsdam. Seldom has so crushing and relentless a combination of forces been arrayed against an enemy; seldom, at the end of so awful a war, has so large a residue of toleration remained.

In the formal sessions of the Heads of Government and the Foreign Ministers at Potsdam, the discussions focused on the situations in and around the rim of Europe which they had not been able to settle by more usual diplomatic efforts.

The Far Eastern questions, some urgent, some imminent, in which the three allies had a converging interest, were neither listed in the work sheet of the conference nor treated in the ordinary order of business. For this there were several reasons. The Soviet Union was not yet in the war against Japan. The American government, although eager to settle plans for concerted military operations with the British and Soviet allies, did not wish to subject to negotiation its ideas about the management of the surrender of Japan and the occupation of the country. Then also some main issues were of vital interest to China, and the Chinese government was not represented at the conference.

Thus the only regulated consultations about Far Eastern questions were those between the military authorities. Talks about all other contemplated policies, plans, and activities in the Far East took place on the margin of the conference, when one or another of the chief figures sought the opportunity. Moreover, these occasional private chats were à deux; Truman with Churchill or Stalin separately, Byrnes with Eden, Bevin, or Molotov separately. As a consequence, understandings reached about such matters as the issuance of the last call to the Japanese to surrender (the Potsdam Declaration), the terms of the Sino-Soviet accords that were to clear the way to Soviet entry into the war with Japan, the plans for the use of the atomic bomb, the arrangements for the occupation and control of Japan, were neither jointly conceived nor conclusive.

Every day at Potsdam—every forenoon, afternoon and night—decisions were made which impinged upon each other, either as activating cause or affecting circumstance. So the meaning of each can be grasped only as part of the flow of all together, and can be justified in the afterlight of history only when related to the concurrent activity within the Japanese government. To conform to reality, we should tell what was thought and done hour by hour by both friend and foe. But as a compromise with the reader's patience, a selective day by day recital will serve.

6. The Calendar of Days at Potsdam

JULY 16

THE opening of the conference was delayed a day[1] because Stalin had suffered a slight heart attack. Truman used this free time to drive to Berlin from his quarters at Babelsberg. He was deeply impressed; in his own later words, "In that two-hour drive, I saw evidence of a great world tragedy. . . ."

The Emperor of Japan was leaving his isolated seclusion and making an active effort to arrange a peace. Despite Soviet indifference to Japanese proposals for a new treaty and confirmed reports of concentration of Soviet troops on the Soviet frontier, the Japanese government had clung to the belief that the Soviet government might mediate between itself and its enemies, and in return for favors granted, help Japan get peace on acceptable terms.[2] Advised by Marquis Kido, the Lord Keeper of the Privy Seal, on July 7th, the Emperor had urged the Prime Minister to let the Soviet government know openly that the Japanese government would like it to mediate; the Emperor was ready to send a special envoy to Moscow with a personal message from him and authority to explain the wishes of the Japanese government.

The Japanese Ambassador in Moscow, Naotaki Sato, had been waiting for the Soviet government to respond to the previous Japanese overtures for a new treaty, waiting despondently because he was sure they would be rejected. Now before venturing on its appeal for mediation, the Japanese government had besought him to try once again to get an answer before Molotov left for Potsdam. But all that Molotov told him on the morning of the 11th was that the question would require more careful study. This reply was all the more deceiving because during these same days Stalin and Molotov were spending many hours in talks with Soong about

---

[1] In the day-by-day chronicle of events during the period of the Potsdam Conference, I have divided the days according to the time calendar in use at Potsdam (German Summer Time which was one hour advanced from Standard Time). However, when events occurred in close or causal sequence, I have designated in the text the day and hour as recorded on the local time calendar in use at the point of occurrence.

The actual differentials in July 1945 were: London and Berlin (Potsdam) 6 hours later than Washington, D.C. Moscow 7 hours later, Tokyo 13 hours later. For example, when clocks in Potsdam struck midnight on August 5-6, 1945, it was 6 p.m. August 5 in Washington and 7 a.m. August 6 in Tokyo.

[2] The Soviet government had on April 5, 1945, notified the Japanese government that it was not going to renew their Neutrality Pact, which was due to expire a year later.

the terms of a Sino-Soviet accord which was to clear the way for Russian entry into the war.

On the 11th (Tokyo time) Togo had sent new instructions to Sato. The first of his two messages began:

"The foreign and domestic situation for the Empire is very serious, and even the termination of the war is now being considered privately. Therefore the conversations [in Tokyo between former Premier Koki Hirota and Soviet Ambassador Jacob A. Malik] are not being limited solely to the objective of closer relations between Japan and the USSR, but we are also sounding out the extent to which we might employ the USSR in connection with the termination of the war. . . .

"Therefore, although we of course wish the completion of a [Japanese-Soviet] agreement from the Malik-Hirota negotiations, on the other hand, sounding out the Soviets as to the manner in which they might be used to terminate the war is also desired. We would like to learn quickly the intentions of the Soviet Government regarding the above. As this point is a matter with which the Imperial Court is also greatly concerned, meet with Molotov immediately whether or not T. V. Soong is present in the USSR."[3]

However, this order to find out whether the Soviet government might act as mediator was accompanied by a caution which exemplifies the tragic nature of Japanese diplomacy.

"As you are skilled in matters such as this, I need not mention this, but in your meetings with the Soviets on this matter please bear in mind not to give them the impression that we wish to use the Soviet Union to terminate the war."

The Ambassador has been left to interpret what his government had in mind from one vaporous passage which he was told to use in explaining to Molotov the attitude of the Japanese government:

"We consider the maintenance of peace in Asia as one aspect of maintaining world peace. We have no intention of annexing or taking possession of the areas which we have been occupying as a result of the war; we hope to terminate the war with a view to establishing and maintaining lasting world peace."[4]

In the meantime, the Supreme War Direction Council had agreed, in obeisance to the Emperor's wish, that steps should be taken at once to send a special envoy to Moscow in pursuit of a mediated peace. Accordingly, on the 12th Sato had been sent a transformed instruction

---

[3] Potsdam Papers, Document 580.
[4] Ibid., Document 581.

which informed him that ". . . it is His Majesty's heart's desire to see the swift termination of the war. In the Greater East Asia War, however, as long as America and England insist on unconditional surrender our country has no alternative but to see it through in an all-out effort for the sake of survival and the honor of the homeland." Therefore, he was to inform Molotov that the Emperor ". . . intends to dispatch Prince Fumimaro Konoye as special envoy to the Soviet Union, bearing his personal letter . . . and promptly obtain from the Soviet Government admission into that country for the special envoy and his suite."[5]

Sato had tried to present this message to Molotov personally, but the Soviet Minister would not receive him, and he was compelled to leave it with one of the Deputy Ministers for Foreign Affairs, Alexander Lozovsky.[6] That official said he was doubtful whether an answer could be had before Stalin and Molotov departed for Potsdam. Sato reported his rebuff to Tokyo. Togo, the Foreign Minister, has since told that even then he did not appreciate the Soviet attitude and intentions. "I thought it very strange that, on the ground of being occupied with preparations for a trip, the high Russian authorities should refuse to receive our Ambassador and should delay their reply to an address so portentous. Stupidly, I failed to imagine the truth: now that three months had elapsed since the defeat of Germany, the Russians were due, in accordance with their promise given at Yalta, to attack Japan; hence, they had no intention of seeing our Ambassador or of receiving Prince Konoye in their country."[7]

Sato, however, was more realistic; he had advised his government that if Konoye was coming merely to enumerate "previous abstractions, lacking in concreteness" he might better not take the trouble.[8] This admonition, even if received before the Supreme Council for the Direction of the War met again on the 14th, did not have a decisive effect. For in the apparent belief that the Russians would receive Prince Konoye, it was agreed that he should be accompanied not only by the Vice Minister of Foreign Affairs but also by a general and an admiral representing the High Command. Whether it was conceived that the presence of

---

[5] *Ibid.*, Document 582.

[6] In an effort to make sure that Stalin and Molotov would be advised of the Japanese initiative on the 13th, Foreign Secretary Togo informed Malik, the Soviet Ambassador in Tokyo, that the Emperor wanted to send Konoye as a special envoy with a personal message expressing the Imperial wish to end the war.

[7] Shigenori Togo, *The Cause of Japan*, page 306.

[8] The Potsdam Papers, Document 587: Telegram from Sato sent July 13th, 10:40 p.m. Moscow time (July 14th, 5:40 a.m. Tokyo time).

these two uniformed figures would increase the impressiveness of what Konoye was to propose, or whether they were being sent along to make sure that Konoye would not propose anything that the High Command did not approve, is not clear. But almost certainly the Army leaders regarded themselves as Konoye's guardians. For the War Minister, again directing attention to the number of places on the map which Japanese soldiers still held, had continued to argue that the terms of peace ought to be based on the fact that Japan was far from defeated. In vain the Foreign Minister, Shigenori Togo, and the Navy Minister, Admiral Mitsumasa Yonai, had argued that imminent future developments of the military situation ought to be taken into account. No agreement had been reached about what Konoye was to say about peace terms if and when the Soviet government received him.

On the next day the members of the Supreme Council had learned from the Ambassador in Moscow that Stalin and Molotov had left for Potsdam without answering the request to receive Konoye. Sato thought that among the probable reasons were uncertainty as to what the Japanese government was proposing and a wish to ascertain the attitudes of American and British leaders. However, Sato then bluntly told his self-deceiving superiors at home that in his opinion ". . . a peace treaty by negotiation is something which cannot win the support of the Soviet Union. In the final analysis, if our country truly desires to terminate the war, we have no alternative but to accept unconditional surrender or something very close to it." He urged that if Konoye was sent the Cabinet and Supreme Council should resolve to have him bring along a concrete proposal for the termination of the war.[9]

It is almost certain that the essential features of these messages were known to Stimson, and to Truman and Byrnes—and my surmise is to the Joint Chiefs of Staff also—before the conference opened.[10]

[9] This message was sent July 15th, Moscow time. No hour indicated. Potsdam Papers, Document 588.

[10] The intercepted messages, from which the extracts and summaries given in this review of Japanese peace feelers in the pre-conference period were taken, are contained in the Potsdam Papers in the section entitled "JAPAN: Peace Feelers Through the Soviet Union." They were intercepted by American military agencies. But the State Department historians who collected and edited the Potsdam Papers have not found it possible to establish precisely which of the messages (in translation) were read by Stimson and other members of the American civilian and military groups while they were in Potsdam, nor precisely when they were informed of the contents of particular messages.

Entries in the diaries of Secretary of Navy Forrestal for July 13th and 15th and in Stimson's diary, show, however, that the contents of the main messages that had been exchanged between the Japanese Foreign Office and the Japanese Ambassador in Moscow during the week preceding the Potsdam Conference were transmitted to Stimson and

Stimson had their import in mind when on the afternoon of the 16th he completed a memorandum for the President the first sections of which were called "The Conduct of the War" and "The Warning to Japan."

This summary of his views started with a statement of his belief that in the event of an invasion the Japanese would fight to the last limits of their lives and endurance in defense of their homeland, and that it was imperative that the American government seek to avoid the need for such action. In his opinion, the time had come to explain our intentions to the Japanese and to warn them that they faced utter destruction if they did not surrender; he thought our massive air and naval assault on Japan and the prospect of Soviet intervention must be causing even the reckless Japanese military leaders to become aware of the plight of their country and the fate it would meet. His judgment was that it was better that this warning be given too soon rather than too late. The hidden vein of his reasoning may be traced from his sequential statement that if the Japanese ignored this warning ". . . the full force of our newer weapons should be brought to bear in the course of what a renewed and even heavier warning, backed by the power of the new forces and possibly the actual entrance of the Russians in the war should be delivered."[11]

Secretary of State Byrnes also was reconsidering the contents and timing of the proposed declaration. Before leaving Washington he had consulted former Secretary of State Cordell Hull about the advisability of issuing the proposed Declaration. Hull, in his circuitously and cautiously phrased answer sent to Byrnes on the 16th, pointed out that the paragraph which intimated that the Japanese would be allowed to preserve the Emperor and the Monarchy would create serious differences if issued "now" and asked whether it would not be well to await the climax of allied bombing and Russia's entry into the war.[12]

The same subject arose in the course of the first meeting of the American and British Staffs, that afternoon in Potsdam. The two groups began their discussion by considering an estimate of the enemy situation which

---

passed on by him to Truman and Byrnes soon after their arrival. Potsdam Papers, Document 1236, Footnote 4.

The texts of the messages printed in the Potsdam Papers are not the English translations made at the time by the intercepting agents. They are transcripts made in the State Department from microfilm copies now on deposit in the Library of Congress of portions of the Archives of the Japanese Ministry of Foreign Affairs.

[11] Stimson's Diary, July 16th, Memo for the President.

[12] Hull underlined the word "now" in this message. *Memoirs of Cordell Hull*, Volume II, page 1594.

had been made by the Combined Intelligence Committee. The main points can be briefly summarized: the Japanese ruling groups were thought to be already aware of the desperate military situation; the reducing consequences of the sea blockade and the devastation caused by the bombing would deepen their realization of their plight; and the entry of the Soviet Union would finally convince them that defeat was inevitable. However, at present they would not surrender unconditionally since many believed that would be equivalent to national extinction, and they found revolting the prospect of foreign occupation and foreign custody of the person of the Emperor; so they were playing for time in the hope that war weariness would cause allied disunity or some miracle would bring them the chance to arrange a compromise peace. The Committee ventured the conjecture that "to avoid these conditions, if possible, and, in any event, to insure survival of the institution of the Emperor, the Japanese might well be willing to withdraw from all the territory they have seized on the Asiatic continent and in the southern Pacific, and even to agree to the independence of Korea and to the practical disarmament of their military forces."

Referring to the surmise about how far the Japanese government might go to get surcease from the war, Field Marshal Sir Alan Brooke (now Lord Alanbrooke) asked whether the U.S. Chiefs of Staff had considered the question of interpreting the demand for unconditional surrender. He said British Chiefs of Staff thought there might be advantage in trying to explain the terms in a way which would insure that the war would not be unduly prolonged in outlying areas. If a version could be found which preserved the Imperial Institution, the Emperor might order fighting to stop in all outlying areas, while if the dynasty was destroyed the outlying garrisons might continue to fight on for months or years. The U.S. Chiefs of Staff volunteered the information that such an initiative had been thoroughly considered "on a political level"—one proposal being that some form of agreed ultimatum be issued at the correct psychological moment, which might be, as Alan Brooke had remarked, right after the Russian entry into the war. The idea was to explain what "unconditional surrender" *did not* mean rather than what it *did* mean. Admiral Leahy said that as this matter was primarily political, the Prime Minister should give his views and suggestions about the interpretation of the surrender formula to the President. It was agreed that the British Chiefs should consider asking Churchill to do so.[13]

[13] Potsdam Papers, Minutes of the Combined Chiefs of Staff, July 16th.

At 7:30 in the evening Stimson received the first report about the detonation of an atomic bomb in New Mexico from George Harrison who, in Stimson's absence, was acting as Chairman of the Interim Committee. In clinical code it read: "Operated on this morning. Diagnosis not yet complete but results seem satisfactory and already exceed expectations. Local press release necessary as interest extends great distance. Dr. Groves pleased. He returns [to Washington] tomorrow. I will keep you posted."

The type of bomb tested was called by its makers and attendants the Fat Boy. It contained plutonium, a material derived from uranium, and was of the implosion type (the explosion was caused by a bursting inward as the density of the fissionable material was increased to the point of explosion by sudden and equal pressure at all points of the mass).

The test had been deemed necessary for two reasons: the fusing mechanism was complicated and delicate, and definite knowledge of the explosive power of this type bomb was needed in order to determine the altitude at which it should be detonated over Japan to get the desired results.

As soon as the President returned from Berlin Stimson hurried over to tell him of this arousing bulletin. It is probable that at the same time he gave the President his memo on "The Conduct of the War with Japan."[14]

We do not know what visions or ideas may have coursed through the night-thoughts of those American figures in their unreal and temporary dwellings in devastated Germany. We do not know whether or not they billowed brilliantly yet somberly as did the mushroom cloud over Alamagordo.

JULY 17

Stalin called on Truman at noon and stayed for lunch. Byrnes, Molotov, and Vyshinski listened.

The talk touched on various subjects which were on the conference program. When it turned to the Far Eastern situation, Stalin told Truman he had not yet succeeded in reaching an accord with the Chinese government, which he regarded as a prerequisite to the Soviet declaration of war against Japan. Truman, of course, knew that full well. Soong, who had been conducting the negotiations with Stalin and Molotov, had made Harriman, the American Ambassador in Moscow, his confidant. He had reviewed each talk with Harriman, and sometimes

[14] *Ibid.*, Document 1236.

read to him detailed notes of the discussion. Harriman had reported frequently and fully to the State Department about the way in which Stalin was distorting the meaning of the Yalta accord and of Soong's refusal to accede to some of the Soviet conditions. The Ambassador had concluded that there would not be an agreement unless the American government exerted itself to bridge the differences. So he had suggested to the President and Byrnes in a message sent on July 9th and relayed to the U.S.S. *Augusta* that an official American interpretation of the Yalta accord (especially what we thought China should grant in regard to ports and railways of Manchuria and the status of Outer Mongolia) be prepared, and that President Truman should discuss the disputed issues with Stalin when they met.[15] Byrnes had sent a request to have these questions studied. Responsively the State Department had sent Byrnes (on July 13th) a memo on the "U.S. Interpretation of the Yalta Agreement and the terms which China might appropriately accept in regard to Outer Mongolia and Manchuria."

But if the President and Byrnes read it, they did not pay much heed to its suggestions. In any case, they did not take full advantage of the chance which Stalin gave them in this talk on the 17th to urge more consideration for Chinese interests and attitudes. Stalin explained in a passing fashion that among the questions still undecided was the regime for the port of Dairen. That, Truman remarked, most certainly ought to be maintained as an open port. Stalin's bland answer was that if the Soviet Union obtained control of that port it would have the status of an open port. Byrnes pointed out that under the Yalta agreement China was to retain control of Dairen. Stalin said that he planned to resume discussions with Soong as soon as he got back from Potsdam. Byrnes at least was left ". . . with the distinct impression that he [Stalin] was not

[15] *Ibid.*, Documents 203 and 204.
A Briefing Book Paper prepared in the State Department in close consultation with War and Navy Departments vigorously recommended that we seek at Potsdam a detailed understanding with the British and Soviet governments on the courses to be pursued by them in all of the many avenues of change opened by the war and the impending disintegration of the Japanese Empire. Among the main objectives named would be (1) to get the Soviet government to subscribe to an agreement on measures to encourage unity in China and the formation of a representative Chinese government and (2) the revival of the Nine Power Treaty of 1922 which pledged all to respect the sovereignty, independence, and territorial integrity of China and to refrain from seeking special privileges. *Potsdam Papers*, Document 574.
Two other Briefing Book Papers stressed the importance of securing Soviet adherence to the Cairo Declaration as a supplement to the more comprehensive understanding. *Potsdam Papers*, Documents 606 and 607. Still others contained recommendations on "Special Manchurian Problems." Document 575.

anxious to see an end to the fighting until Soviet entry into the war could help secure the concessions he expected of China."[16]

That evening, the President told Stimson that he thought he had clinched the open door in Manchuria; or so Stimson understood him.[17] But the Secretary of War remained unconvinced and continued to try to impress Byrnes with the importance of supporting the Chinese government in its resistance to Soviet claims for exclusive rights.

As far as is known, this was the only attempt of the President in the course of the conference to induce Stalin to moderate his demands upon China and give the American government adequate assurances regarding the protection of American interests in Manchuria. We are left to surmise the reasons for his abstention. Was the President merely still intent on avoiding any possible accusation that the American government was responsible for the terms and consequences of a Sino-Soviet pact? Or did he believe that Stalin's terms were on the whole unobjectionable, and that the Chinese National Government would be well advised to accept them in order to get in return Soviet neutrality in its struggle against the Chinese Communists and Soviet cooperation in the occupation of Manchuria? Or was he influenced by the thought that if he made a serious issue of this matter, the Soviet government might be provoked into postponing its entry into the war on Japan, or possibly into responding to Japanese overtures?

Or were his thoughts running underground in the opposite direction; and was he secretly hoping that no agreement would be reached, and that the Soviet government would therefore postpone its entry into the war, and the American assault, including that most powerful new weapon which had just been successfully tested, would bring the war to an end before the Soviet government got into it? The President has denied any intention of this sort and the import of the available record supports his denial. Nothing in it indicates a change in his desire or intention which he later recalled and recorded in his Memoirs, "There were many reasons for going to Potsdam, but the most urgent, to my mind, was to get from Stalin a personal reaffirmation of Russia's entry into the war against Japan, a matter which our military chiefs were most anxious to clinch."[18]

After lunch, while Churchill was escorting him to the gate of his residence, Stimson told the Prime Minister of the first message about the outcome of the New Mexico test. Churchill was "intensely interested

[16] *All in One Lifetime*, page 290.   [17] Stimson Diary, July 17.
[18] *Year of Decisions*, page 411.

and greatly cheered up." But he spoke strongly against any disclosure of information about the new weapon.[19]

That night, a second brief report from Harrison was conveyed to Stimson. "Doctor has just returned most enthusiastic and confident that the little boy is as husky as his big brother [the still untested U-235 gun type bomb]. The light in his eyes discernible from here to Highhold [Stimson's home on Long Island] and I could have heard his screams from here to my farm [in Upperville, Virginia]."

The note of pleased surprise about the demonstrated explosive force of the bomb used in the New Mexico test has only recently become understandable. For, as has been told, that bomb was of the implosion (compression) type. Unexpected scientific difficulties had been met in its development, which had only lately been solved by a change of design. However, even at the time of the test, Oppenheimer has since related, ". . . our estimates of the yield were quite uncertain, and for the most part quite low. We established a pool in the laboratory to record the guesses as to the yield of the first bomb. An overwhelming majority made estimates under a few thousand tons; figures in the hundreds of tons were popular. Two visitors, Lee DuBridge and I. I. Rabi, picked the extreme values of zero and 18,000 tons. On July 16, after the test, our first measurement of what had really happened gave 20,000 tons."[20]

On this same day Arthur Compton, a member of the Scientific Panel of the Interim Committee, forwarded to Harrison a petition signed by some sixty-odd scientists in Chicago who had been concerned with the production of the bomb and knew of the test. This group asked attention for a recommendation that an atomic bomb should not be used, particularly against any cities unless (1) the Japanese had been given the chance to surrender on terms which were to assure them the possibility of peaceful development in their homeland; (2) a convincing warning had been given them that a refusal to surrender would be followed by the use of a new weapon; and (3) that responsibility for its use against Japan was shared with our allies.[21] I do not know whether this petition, which was addressed to the President, was sent on to Potsdam for the information of Stimson and the President, but it is improbable.

---

[19] Churchill's own account of this first notice of the bomb test was brief. "In the afternoon Stimson called at my abode and laid before me a sheet of paper on which was written 'Babies satisfactorily born.' By his manner I saw something extraordinary had happened. 'It means,' he said, 'that the experiment in the New Mexican desert has come off. The atomic bomb is a reality.'" *Triumph and Tragedy*, page 637.

[20] Letter, Groves to Marshall, December 30, 1944, in Yalta Documents, pages 383-384, and letters of Oppenheimer and Groves in *Science Magazine*, December 4, 1959.

[21] *Atomic Quest*, pages 242-243.

During the day, further thought was being given to the contents and time of issuance of the Proclamation to be addressed to Japan. General Hastings L. Ismay (Chief of Staff to Churchill and a member of the Chief of Staffs Committee) informed the Prime Minister of the views that had been expressed the day before by the Combined Chiefs about the advisability of explaining the way which we intended to act when Japan made an unconditional surrender. He related that all were agreed that there would be an advantage from the military point of view in retaining the Emperor as a central authority who could command obedience, since there might not be anyone else who could effectively order the end of resistance in China and the outlying areas. The American Chiefs of Staff, Ismay reported, would be glad to have the Prime Minister raise this question with the President. That group, in fact, was at this very time preparing a memo for the President advising that nothing be done before the end of hostilities that would indicate the removal of the Emperor since his authority might be needed to end the fighting in places outside of Japan.[22]

But the Secretary of State had decided that the Declaration should not contain any promise that the Japanese would be allowed to retain the Emperor; and also that the issuance of the Declaration should be postponed.[23] When Stimson, in the course of the day asked him about these matters, Byrnes said he was opposed to a prompt and early warning and outlined the timetable in mind. Since he gathered that this schedule had been approved by the President, Stimson did not press further for its immediate issuance.

The available records do not tell what calculations determined the schedule. It is fairly safe to surmise, however, that it was related to two wishes. One was to make sure that the relatively lenient policies in the Declaration would not be denounced in the United States. The other was to take advantage of the anticipated conjuncture of events: the further effect of our continued air and naval assaults, the Soviet entry into the war, the impact of the atomic bomb.

A message which the Japanese Foreign Minister sent to Sato in Moscow that same day (Tokyo time), if it was intercepted, would have confirmed the opinion that the call to surrender would not be heeded until Japan was hurt still worse and the Japanese government was more

---

[22] Potsdam Papers, Document 1239, and Minutes of Meeting of the Joint Chiefs of Staff, July 17, 10 a.m.

[23] In a message received by Hull in Washington on the morning of the 17th. Cordell Hull, *Memoirs*, Vol. II, page 1594.

thoroughly convinced of the necessity. "Not only our High Command," this interpretative message read in part, "but also our Government firmly believes that even now our war potential is still sufficient to deal the enemy a severe blow, but against an enemy who can make repeated attacks we cannot always be completely free from anxiety. In such times, we continue to maintain our war strength; if only the United States and Great Britain would recognize Japan's honor and existence we would terminate the war and would like to save mankind from the ravages of war, but if the enemy insists on unconditional surrender to the very end, then our country and His Majesty would unanimously resolve to fight a war of resistance to the bitter end. Therefore, inviting the Soviet Union to mediate fairly does not include unconditional surrender; please understand this point in particular."[24]

No record known to me tells whether this message was intercepted by the American monitors and if so whether its substance was relayed to Potsdam. But sometime during the afternoon in Potsdam, probably just after the Plenary Session, Stalin told Churchill of the Japanese overtures for Soviet mediation, of which the American government had learned from intercepts of earlier Japanese messages.

Churchill told Stalin that he thought he should send the President a note "in order to warn him before the next session." The Marshal remarked that he did not want the President to think that the Soviet government wanted to act as an intermediary, but he would have no objection if the Prime Minister passed it on to the President. Churchill agreed to do so, while pointing out that he also did not wish the President to feel that Britain was not at one with the United States in its "aim of achieving complete victory over Japan."[25]

JULY 18

In the morning Stimson told the President of Harrison's second exultant message about the astonishing results of the bomb test. Stimson's impression was that the President was highly delighted and very greatly reinforced.[26] General Marshall gave the same information to the Combined Chiefs of Staff.

At lunch that day Truman talked over with Churchill problems connected with the use of the bomb, particularly how much and when to

[24] Potsdam Papers, Document 1224.
[25] British memo of Churchill-Stalin talk, July 17, in *Grand Strategy*, Volume VI, page 302.
[26] Stimson Diary, July 18.

tell Stalin.[27] Since no American record of this conversation has been found, we are dependent for knowledge of what was said on Churchill's account and the report which he sent to the War Cabinet within the hour:

"The President showed me telegrams about the recent experiment, and asked what I thought should be done about telling the Russians. He seemed determined to do this, but asked about the timing, and said he thought that the end of the Conference would be best. I replied that if he were resolved to tell it might well be better to hang it on the experiment, which was a new fact on which he and we had only just had knowledge. Therefore he would have a good answer to any question, 'Why did you not tell us this before?' He seemed impressed with this idea, and will consider it.

"On behalf of His Majesty's Government I did not resist his proposed disclosure of the simple fact that we have this weapon. He reiterated his resolve at all costs to refuse to divulge any particulars. . . ."[28]

The President and Prime Minister also touched on the question of whether to retain after the defeat of Japan the existing arrangements for consultation between the American and British Chiefs of Staff—the Combined Chiefs. The British Chiefs had sent a memo to their American colleagues in favor of doing so. They foresaw various situations, having important military implications, in which American and British interests would be affected in somewhat the same way; and they indicated various desirable purposes that could best be effected by preserving the organization of the Combined Chiefs, such as assuring an adequate exchange of information and arranging for a measure of uniformity in the design of weapons and training of forces. But no member of the Joint Chiefs had been enthusiastic over the prolongation of this special and intimate association. Leahy, Marshall, King, Arnold—none were convinced at this time of its advantages or necessity.

When Truman was told by Leahy of the views of the Joint Chiefs, he remarked that he also did not think that American relations with our allies were yet stable enough to warrant consideration of a permanent relationship between the military commands.[29] But when he talked

---

[27] Churchill in *Triumph and Tragedy*, pages 638-639, wrote that on the morning of the 18th ". . . a plane arrived with a full description of this tremendous event in the human story" and that the President invited him to confer forthwith, Marshall and Leahy being present. However, the courier bringing the "full description" did not get to Potsdam before July 21. All that Stimson had on the 18th were the two first brief reports from Harrison.

[28] *Ibid.*, pages 640-641. The excision is in the text printed by Churchill.

[29] Potsdam Conference, Meeting of Joint Chiefs of Staff, July 18, 10 a.m.

with the Prime Minister the President took pains not to appear to be rebuffing him.

Churchill expanded upon the difficulties faced by Britain as a result of its unrestrained expenditure for the common war cause. Truman, sympathetic, said that he would do what he could to help them out. The President, in turn, complained to the Prime Minister about the difficulties we were facing in regard to the continued American use of the air fields in British territory. Churchill said if he were retained in office he would strive to work out an arrangement in the common interest. What he had in mind was an accord not only for the joint and reciprocal use of air fields but also of naval bases and stations. "Why should we not share facilities for defense all over the world?" he asked the President.[30] When Truman answered that any such plan would have to be fitted with the policy of the United Nations, the Prime Minister said that was all right provided the accord assured ". . . under whatever form or cloak, a continuation of the existing war-time system of reciprocal facilities between Britain and the United States about bases and fuelling points."

The Prime Minister got the impression that the President was in accord with this notion if it could be presented in a way that did not make it appear crudely a military alliance between the two of them. Encouraged by this, Churchill went on to put forward his cherished idea of keeping the organization of the Combined Chiefs in being. But his hope was doomed. To foretell, the next day the U.S. Chiefs informed their British associates that they could not discuss any such arrangements during their current meetings.[31] A week later Churchill learned that he had been voted out of office.

The two Heads of Government in their mid-day conversation also discussed the proposed attempt to induce Japanese surrender by informing the Japanese people what would be in store for them. Churchill relayed what Stalin had told him the day before of the Emperor's offer to send Konoye to Moscow and the request that the Soviet Union act as mediator. The Prime Minister then went on to say that like Stalin he did not want to say anything that would make it seem that Britain was reluctant to go on with the war against Japan as long as the United States thought fit. But such action, if skillfully taken, might save many lives. He would leave it to the President to decide whether the call for unconditional surrender could not be expressed in some other way so

[30] *Triumph and Tragedy*, page 633.
[31] Potsdam Papers, Minutes of the Meeting of the Combined Chiefs of Staff and Document 1197.

that the allies got all the essentials for future peace and security, and yet by leaving the Japanese some show of saving their military honor, some assurance of their national existence after they had complied with necessary safeguards, might cause them to give up quickly. In effect, the Prime Minister thus gave the President a free hand.[32]

A few hours later Truman and Byrnes returned the call of the Soviet leaders and they had a second private talk. Stalin gave Truman a copy of the letter which the Japanese Ambassador in Moscow had presented (on the 13th), enclosing a message from the Emperor asking the Soviet government to receive a special envoy.[33] He asked whether it might be best if he made no answer at all, since the Soviet Union was going to declare war on Japan "eventually." Truman gave no sign that he already knew of this correspondence. He said that while he had no respect or regard for the good faith of the Japanese, he thought Stalin ought to decide for himself what to say. Stalin then remarked that in view of the fact that the Soviet Union was not yet at war with Japan, it might be advisable to "lull" them to sleep; and he asked, what if I just told the Japanese government that since the Emperor's message was vague and did not explain concretely the purpose of Konoye's visit, I could not give a conclusive reply. Truman said that seemed all right. Whereupon Stalin remarked that this is what he would tell the Japanese and he volunteered to show the President his answer before sending it. Truman said that although this was not necessary he would appreciate it.

Byrnes asked Molotov why he thought the Japanese had solicited Soviet mediation. Did it mean that they were nervous about Soviet intentions and hoped to avert the suspected danger? Molotov said he thought that was very likely; it would be surprising if they did not suspect anything.

At the end of the Plenary Session of the conference later that afternoon Stalin showed Truman a copy of the answer he proposed to send. The President said that it seemed to him satisfactory.

In the evening (Moscow time) after five days of silence the Soviet Deputy Commissar for Foreign Affairs, Lozovsky, gave the Japanese Ambassador a note in reply to the Japanese request that the Soviet government act as mediator for peace. This stated that the Soviet gov-

---

[32] *Grand Strategy*, Vol. VI, pages 302-303.

[33] The only available first hand record of this talk is a memorandum which Charles E. Bohlen, who served as interpreter, wrote up in March 1960 from the fragmentary notes that he had made at the time to aid him in translation. Potsdam Papers, Document 1418.

ernment regarded the Emperor's message as general, and that since it did not contain any concrete explanation, the Soviet government was not clear about the purpose of the proposed Konoye mission. "The Government of the U.S.S.R., accordingly, is unable to give any definite reply either to the message of the Emperor of Japan or to the dispatch of Prince Konoye as special envoy. . . ."[34]

This left the way clear for the American government to proceed with the intended address in which the Japanese were to be told the terms on which they could have peace. The one element in the Declaration for which the authors were still trying to find the best formula concerned the treatment of the Emperor.

Admiral Leahy, acting for the Joint Chiefs, sent Truman a memo, summing up their discussion of the day before. They thought that from the "military point of view" the current text of the proclamation to be addressed to the Japanese was "generally satisfactory." However, they believed that one sentence should be clarified—the one reading "This may include a constitutional monarchy under the present dynasty if it be shown to the complete satisfaction of the world that such a government will never again aspire to aggression." The Joint Chiefs were afraid that extreme devotees of the Emperor might construe this as obliging the United Nations to depose or execute the present Emperor and install some other member of the Imperial family on the throne, while "radical elements" might interpret it as a promise to continue the institution of the Emperor and Emperor worship. So they suggested different language, to wit: "Subject to suitable guarantees against further acts of aggression, the Japanese people will be free to choose their own form of government." In conclusion Admiral Leahy wrote that the Joint Chiefs "From a strictly military point of view consider it inadvisable to make any statement or take any action at the present time that would make it difficult or impossible to utilize the authority of the Emperor to direct a surrender of the Japanese forces in the outlying areas as well as in Japan proper."[35]

JULY 19

In the morning the U.S. Joint Chiefs discussed what the Russians were to be told about the course of the war in the Pacific; and how, and by whom. Commenting on a suggestion of the British Chiefs that the

[34] *Ibid.*, Documents 1226 and 1227.
[35] *Ibid.*, Document 1239. This advice of the Joint Chiefs was based on a recommendation of the Joint Strategic Committee which had been sent from Washington to Marshall at Potsdam.

flow of information to the Soviet Union should be controlled jointly, General John R. Deane, Head of the U.S. Military Mission in Moscow, said he thought the British had two purposes in mind. One was to secure the chance to play a part in the direction of military operations. The other was to share in any benefit that might be received from the Russians in return.

The arrangement favored by the Joint Chiefs was set out in three proposals which Marshall presented at an afternoon meeting with the British Chiefs of Staff. They were: that the Joint Chiefs should retain freedom to pass purely operational information and intelligence from American sources to the Russians; that on other matters such as technical equipment the Joint Chiefs would consult the British Chiefs before informing the Russians; and that the British Chiefs should be free to determine for themselves what information and intelligence from British sources they wished to pass on to the Russians.

Marshall explained that the American military commanders intended to pass on operational information to the Russians liberally rather than to keep it back in order to bargain for similar favors. His idea was that anything that might contribute to the efficiency of the Russian armies or help in the prosecution of the war should be given to the Russians whether or not they reciprocated. Alan Brooke said that he was of the same opinion.

At the end of the session the Combined Chiefs agreed that both the American and British Chiefs should be free to pass on to the Russians information regarding operations in the theaters in which each was responsible as either might wish, and without bargaining. They would consult with one another, however, before passing on other information and neither would convey to the Russians information derived from the other without permission.

Two officials of the State Department, John Carter Vincent and Eugene Dooman, submitted to the Secretary of State a memo concerning the interrupted Sino-Soviet negotiations. They expressed their opinion that the terms which the Soviet government was trying to impose upon the Chinese government in return for its cooperation would place the Soviet Union in a special position in Manchuria that would be harmful to the United States. They thought that Soong's offers met the requirements of the Yalta accord. Thus they concluded that a chance ought to be sought at once to talk over these matters with Stalin and Molotov, and if they were willing, to invite Soong to come to Potsdam to continue the discussions.

Presumably this recommendation was based on the thought that if the Sino-Soviet negotiations were conducted at Potsdam, American support would lead to a moderation of Stalin's demands, and to a quick closing of an accord. Perhaps it would have done so. But it might have worked out quite otherwise. The Chinese National Government might have been emboldened not to compromise and the talks might have ended in discord; or if not that, their conclusion might have been delayed until Soviet forces were in occupation of Manchuria and perhaps infringing on North China.

But the advice that Sino-Soviet negotiations be transferred to Potsdam was not heeded, and the President and Byrnes did not revert with Stalin to this area of interest until after they had departed from Potsdam.

JULY 20

A special group of American B-29 bombing planes began a series of combat flights over Japan. The purpose was to accustom the Japanese to the presence of small formations of high flying planes of this type, which was going to carry the atomic bomb.

Stimson, in Potsdam, discussed with Harriman a memo on which he was working on the importance of transforming the Soviet political system—as a necessary condition for sharing knowledge of atomic fission with the Soviet Union. Harriman discouraged his hopeful belief that the Soviet government could be led into adopting a program for the protection of individual freedoms equivalent to our Bill of Rights.

The Japanese Ambassador in Moscow conveyed to Togo in a long message his "unreserved opinion" about the situation of Japan. His review left no hope of preventing ultimate and complete defeat. One possibility to which he pointed was that the enemy could destroy the Japanese rice crop by burning up the plants when the paddies were dry.

Thus Sato pleaded for hurry in the decision to seek peace as soon as possible. To obtain it he believed that Japan should yield to most of the enemy's demands. In fact, he thought the Japanese government ought to make only one absolute condition: that the national polity be protected, the fundamental form of the Japanese government be preserved. The next to the last paragraph read "I realize that it is a great crime to dare to make such statements, knowing that they are contrary to the views of the government. The reason for doing so, however, is that I believe that the only policy for national salvation must coincide with these ideas."[36]

JULY 21

Just before noon, a courier handed Stimson the special report from the scene of the test in New Mexico, relating the results as witnessed and measured by the scientists. The Secretary of War found it to be "an immensely powerful document, clearly and well written, and with supporting documents of the highest importance"; and he thought that "It gave a pretty full and eloquent report of the tremendous success of the test and revealed far greater destructive power than we expected in S-1."

Who would not have been deeply impressed by this account of the experience and effects of this detonation? Re-read now, it seems like a try-out for judgment day. But since it is well known and longish, it need not be given space in this calendar.[37] The explosive effect of the tested bomb was estimated to be equivalent to about 20,000 tons of TNT. The searing burst of light, the tremendous blast, the mushroom cloud of illuminated dust sent up into the sky, and its wide impact upon physical objects—all were awesome, a vision of wonder and dread.

No reader of this report, nor witness of later detonations of other nuclear bombs, were more struck by the terrible marvel that had been accomplished than were the scientists who had contributed to it. As told by General Thomas F. Farrell who was in the control shelter (and whose account is included in the Groves Report), "All seemed to feel that they had been present at the birth of a new age—the Age of Atomic Energy—and felt their profound responsibility to help in guiding into the right channels the tremendous forces which had been unlocked for the first time in history."

Stimson at once sought an engagement with the President. Having talked with Marshall in the interval, he went on to the "Little White House" and asked the President to call in the Secretary of State. When Byrnes arrived, Stimson read the report aloud. The President was

[36] *Ibid.*, Document 1228. It is not known for certain whether or when this message was intercepted and relayed to Potsdam. The entry in the *Forrestal Diaries* for July 24 gives the gist of a message from Sato which resembles the one which Sato sent on July 20. Erroneously, however, Forrestal states that this was sent on the first of July.

[37] The full text of the report is given in Document 1305 of the Potsdam Papers and is reprinted in the author's recent book, *Between War and Peace: The Potsdam Conference.*

"tremendously pepped up by it . . . and said it gave him an entirely new feeling of confidence. . . ."

Stimson then hurried over to Churchill's quarters with the same stirring report in his hand. The Prime Minister could not read it through before he had to leave for the Fifth Plenary Session of the Conference. So he asked his visitor to come again the following morning.

On returning to his quarters, Stimson found a message from Harrison relating that all the military advisers concerned with selection of a target for the bomb favored "your pet city" as first choice. The "pet city" was Kyoto, earlier the lovely capital of Japan. Stimson at once dispatched a reply reaffirming his refusal to approve an attack on that city.[38] The President and General Arnold concurred.

Using the privilege of an author, I cannot refrain from inserting in the narrative a personal flash of perception of the irony and singularity of history. A few months after the war ended, I was on a tour of Japan as a member of a group accompanying Stimson's successor as Secretary of War, Robert Patterson. We had spent the day looking over the mangled ruins of the shipyards, steel plants and other industrial sections of bombed Kobe. In the dying daylight we drove along the road to Kyoto, the city that was spared. Both sides of every small country lane which we passed were crowded with Japanese; the smallest round-faced children in front, the larger ones behind them, then the women, then the men, many waving small American flags. We asked our escort, the English speaking mayor of Kyoto, the reason for this cordial acknowledgment of our presence. Turning to the Secretary of War, Patterson, whom he thought mistakenly had been in office when the decision to spare Kyoto was made, the Mayor explained, "It is gratitude. They all know that your soldiers and airmen wanted to drop the atomic bomb on Kyoto and you did not allow them to do so."

The irony was in the fact that those people of Nagasaki who substituted in death for those of Kyoto were not there to wave us on. The singularity was in the chance events which fostered Stimson's determination not to permit the bombing of Kyoto. The Secretary had not known of the distinction of Kyoto as former capital of Japan. But one evening during the early spring of 1945, a young man in uniform, son of an old friend, who was a devoted student of Oriental history, came to dinner with the Stimsons. The young man fell to talking about the past glories of Kyoto, and of the loveliness of the old imperial residences which remained. Stimson was moved to consult a history which told of the

[38] Potsdam Papers, Documents 1307 and 1308.

time when Kyoto was the capital and to look through a collection of photographs of scenes and sites in the city. Thereupon he decided that this one Japanese city should be preserved from the holocaust. To what anonymous young man may each of the rest of us owe our lives?

To revert to the narrative—still another message from Harrison arrived before Stimson went to sleep. This informed him in the same clinical code that work on the bomb to be used against Japan was progressing rapidly and it would be ready for use during the first good weather period in August.[39] It may be remarked that this was precisely the time that had been mentioned by Groves in the progress report that he had sent to Marshall in December 1944, the date at which the scientists had advised him that they believed the first specimen of the gun-type bomb would be operative.

The Japanese Foreign Minister sent his unhappy Ambassador in Moscow another evasion of the summons to face reality. "We cannot," Togo averred, "accept unconditional surrender in any situation." The Japanese government realized, however, he continued, that before entering on mediation the Soviet government would want to know Japanese conditions. "Thus, it is impossible at this time to ask the Soviet Union unconditionally for assistance in obtaining peace; at the same time, it is also impossible and to our disadvantage to indicate the concrete conditions immediately at this time on account of internal and external relations. Under such delicate circumstances, we hope to have Prince Konoye transmit to the Soviet Union our concrete intention based on the Emperor's wishes . . ."[40]

A propos the last sentence, other sources reveal that there was no approved "concrete plan" because the Supreme War Council was still harshly and widely divided on several of the leading matters that would necessarily enter any surrender terms; among them were the acceptance of the Cairo Declaration (involving loss of Formosa), a permanent ban on military activities, and the occupation of Japan.[41]

JULY 22

Right after breakfast, Stimson called on the President.[42] He got the

[39] *Ibid.*, Document 1309.
[40] *Ibid.*, Document 1230. For unknown reasons this message did not get to the Japanese Ambassador in Moscow until July 24th.
[41] Shigenori Togo, *The Cause of Japan*, page 311.
[42] Stimson's immediate reason for doing so was to find out what the President thought of the memo which he had left with him the day before, which examined the problem

impression that the President was intensely pleased by the timetable for the production of the atomic bomb of which Harrison had informed him. Then on to the residence of the Prime Minister he went, and stood by while the message from Groves was being read in full. On putting it down, Churchill, all animation, leaned forward in his chair, waved his cigar and said, "Stimson, what was gunpowder? Trivial. What was electricity? Meaningless. This atomic bomb is the Second Coming in wrath."

The Prime Minister then remarked that at the Plenary Session in the afternoon the day before, Truman was evidently much fortified for some reason and had stood up to the Russians in a most emphatic manner, telling them that they absolutely could not have certain demands and the United States was entirely against them. He said, "Now I know what happened to Truman yesterday. I couldn't understand it. When he got to the meeting after having read this report he was a changed man. He told the Russians just where they got on and off and generally bossed the whole meeting."[43]

Here it may be interjected that the even-toned minutes of the Plenary Session of July 21 do not convey any such marked change in the President's address to the Russians as Churchill perceived.

The Prime Minister then went on to say to Stimson that he felt the same way as the President. He now not only was *not* worried about giving the Russians information about the weapon but was rather inclined to use it as an argument in our favor in the negotiations.[44]

---

of our relations with the Soviet Union and its relevance to sharing knowledge of the new weapon. The text of this memo is given in the Potsdam Papers, Document 1157.

The Secretary of War concluded that "The foregoing has a vital bearing upon the control of the vast and revolutionary discovery of X (FN 2: i.e., atomic energy) which is now confronting us. Upon the successful control of that energy depends the future successful development or destruction of the modern civilized world. The Committee appointed by the War Department which has been considering that control has pointed this out in no uncertain terms and has called for an international organization for that purpose. After careful reflection I am of the belief that *no* world organization containing as one of its dominant members a nation whose people are not possessed of free speech but whose governmental action is controlled by the autocratic machinery of a secret political police, cannot [can] give effective control of this new agency with its devastating possibilities.

"I therefore believe that before we share our new discovery with Russia we should consider carefully whether we can do so safely under any system of control until Russia puts into effective action the proposed constitution which I have mentioned. If this is a necessary condition, we must go slowly in any disclosures or agreeing to any Russian participation whatsoever and constantly explore the question how our head-start in X and the Russian desire to participate can be used to bring us nearer to the removal of the basic difficulties which I have emphasized."

[43] Stimson Diary, July 22, 1945. Potsdam Papers. Minutes of Stimson-Churchill conversation, July 22.
[44] *Ibid.*

Truman conferred with his military advisers about the Groves report on the atomic bomb. Byrnes and Stimson were present, as well as the members of the Chiefs of Staff, Leahy, Marshall, Arnold, and King.[45] No official record of this discussion was found in the papers which I have read. But the succinct account given by Knebel and Bailey is evidently based on some official source. They relate that Leahy repeated his reservations, that Arnold stressed that the Air Force thought Japan could be forced to submit by "conventional bombing," but that Marshall maintained that invasion from the sea would be necessary if the atomic bomb were not used.

Then around noon the President invited Churchill's views. The Prime Minister definitely believed that the bomb should be used as soon as possible to end the war as quickly as might be, and the President so decided.

Remembrance of Churchill's impressions can be conveyed by a few extracts from his later account. "Now all this nightmare picture [of the invasion of the Japanese homeland] had vanished. In its place was the vision—fair and bright indeed it seemed—of the end of the whole war in one or two violent shocks. . . . Moreover, we should not need the Russians. The end of the Japanese war no longer depended upon the pouring in of their armies for the final and perhaps protracted slaughter. We had no need to ask favors of them."[46]

"I have no doubt," he later stated in his memoirs, "that these thoughts were present in the minds of my American friends." They were. But I think others will infer as I do from the record of the following days that knowledge of the new weapon did not affect the American inclination to have Russia enter the war as incisively as the Prime Minister remarked in the minute he sent Eden shortly after his talk with Truman, "It is quite clear that the United States do not at the present time desire Russian participation in the war against Japan."[47]

JULY 23

In the morning Byrnes asked Stimson when the atomic bomb would be ready for use against Japan. Stimson told him what he knew. Then he rushed off a message to Harrison, reminding him, "Whenever it is

[45] *No High Ground*, pages 120-121.

[46] I am assuming that this statement of his thoughts flowed primarily from the discussion at the meeting on July 22, even though he relates them to a previous talk with Truman on July 18, *Triumph and Tragedy*, pages 638-639. On this point, see Potsdam Papers, Minutes, Truman-Churchill meeting, July 22, 12:15.

[47] *Triumph and Tragedy*, page 639.

possible to give us a more definite date please immediately advise us here where information is greatly needed."[48]

Stimson let the President know that he was trying to find out just when the great new device of war could be put to the use for which it was destined. The President informed him that the draft of the warning to be addressed to Japan was on his desk, that he had accepted "our most recent change in it," and that he proposed to dispatch it as soon as he learned the date on which the bomb would be available.[49]

In the course of the evening, Stimson heard from Harrison that the bombing operation could be carried out soon after August 1, depending on the progress of essential preparatory measures and upon weather conditions; probably by August 4-5, almost certainly before August 10.[50]

Stimson asked the President whether it was true that Stalin was expanding his demands in all directions, not only seeking to extend Soviet influence over Poland, Austria, Rumania, and Bulgaria, but also striving to get bases in Turkey and one of the former Italian colonies in the Mediterranean. The President confirmed that that was so. But he said that he and the other members of the American delegation were standing firmly against all unjustified Soviet pretensions. Stimson got the impression that Truman thought that the new Russian claims were in large measure bluff, and outlined what he thought were their real ones.

In the afternoon, Stimson told Marshall that the President wanted to know whether Marshall still thought that we needed the Russians in the Pacific war or whether we could get on without them. Marshall's answer was neither direct nor conclusive. He said that the action of the Russians in amassing large forces on the Manchurian frontier was already serving one of the purposes for which we wished them to come into the war—to cause the Japanese to keep their army in Manchuria. He pointed out that even if we defeated Japan without the Russians and compelled the Japanese to accept our terms, the Russians could, if they so wished, march into Manchuria anyhow and take virtually what they wanted.

[48] Potsdam Papers, Document 1316.

[49] Since the successive drafts of the text of the Declaration that were considered at Potsdam have not been, so far as I can learn, collected and collated, I do not know to just what change Stimson refers, but it was probably of only minor importance.

[50] This is my unconfirmed interpretation of the message which was phrased in the same code as the earlier one. "Operation may be possible any time from August 1, depending on state of preparation of patient and condition of atmosphere. From point of view of patient only, some chance August 1 to 3, good chance August 4 to 5, and barring unexpected relapse almost certain before August 10." *Ibid.*, Document 1312.

Marshall informed the Secretary of War that the discussions of the Combined (U.S.-British) Chiefs about military matters of common interest to the Americans and British would end on the morrow. He suggested that it might be a good way of bringing the Russians to a decision about entering the Pacific War one way or another, if the President said to Stalin tomorrow that "In as much as the British have finished and are going home, I suppose I might as well let the American Chiefs of Staff go away also."[51] In sum, Marshall gave Stimson the impression that since we had the atomic bomb, Russian participation was no longer really needed nor much wanted; but that, if they came in, it would bring the end quicker and with smaller loss of life; and since in any event, the Soviet forces would be able, if they chose, to secure control of Manchuria (and possibly Korea and the Kuriles) it was still expedient to solicit their entry.

That night Churchill was host at a banquet for his conference associates. Stalin, without seeming to care that the waiters and orderlies were still in the room, proposed a toast "that our next meeting should be in Tokyo." Churchill took that to mean that the Russian declaration of war would come at any moment. Stalin seemed to him to have ". . . no inkling of the momentous information about the new bomb the President had given me. He spoke with enthusiasm about the Russian intervention against Japan, and seemed to expect a good many months of war, which Russia would wage on an ever increasing scale. . . ."[52]

JULY 24

Stimson saw the President in mid-morning. The Secretary of War had shown him the latest message from Harrison, indicating the probable time when all would be in order for use of the bomb against Japan. Truman was pleased, remarking that this knowledge was just what he wanted, and gave him his cue for the issuance of the declarative warning to Japan. He said that he had just asked Chiang Kai-shek to subscribe to the text, and it would be released as soon as he had done so. Stimson then went on to say that in his opinion it was important to assure the Japanese that they could continue the imperial dynasty, so important that its inclusion or exclusion might well determine whether Japan would yield. So he was sorry to hear from Byrnes that this assurance

[51] Stimson Diary, July 23.
[52] *Triumph and Tragedy*, pages 668-669.

was to be left out of the summons to surrender. He presumed it could not now be reinserted because the text had been sent to Chiang Kai-shek. But Stimson persisted. He urged that in the event that the Japanese refused to accept the proffered terms because we failed to extend this assurance it might then be conveyed orally to them. The President said he had the point in mind and would take care of it.

Truman then joined Churchill in a meeting to review the Final Report of the Combined Chiefs of Staff. This recorded the conjunction of views reached after a week of animated discussion.[53]

The British Chiefs had previously been seeking a chance to confer with their American colleagues. They had urged the U.S. Chiefs of Staff to stop off in London for three or four days, and thereafter set off together for Potsdam. But the Americans had not thought this advisable or necessary. They had suggested that if the British Chiefs had matters in mind which had to be settled with the U.S. Chiefs before the scheduled meeting of the Heads of Government, these could be discussed with the British staff mission in Washington, or if all common business was not finished at Potsdam then the Joint Chiefs would stop off in London after the conference. The President had asked Harriman to find out if Stalin would be disturbed if the U.S. Joint Chiefs were to accompany him to Potsdam, in view of the possible Japanese reaction. Stalin had answered that he would not mind. It was arranged in the outcome that the American and British Chiefs of Staff should hold their converse in Potsdam either before or while the talks with the Russian Chiefs of Staff were carried on.[54]

The report of the Combined Chiefs was comprehensive. However, in this narrative, there is need to note only a few of its main items, and these briefly.

(1) The British Chiefs had been maintaining that the British Commonwealth should henceforth be given a bigger part in the control of strategy in the Pacific, because they would be deploying in that area much larger combat forces than before. They sought cooperative parity

[53] This summary account of the decisions of the American and British Chiefs of Staff, as approved by the President and Prime Minister on July 24, is derived primarily from the collection of papers on the Potsdam Conference. This includes (1) memos recording the views and proposals of the U.S. Joint Chiefs which are printed as numbered Documents, (2) the minutes of the meetings of the Joint Chiefs and Combined Chiefs, and (3) the text of the Final Report of the Combined Chiefs to the President and Prime Minister and the minutes of the meeting of the Combined Chiefs with them on July 24, which are printed in the Potsdam Papers as Document 1381.
[54] *Ibid.*, Documents 57, 65, 85, 86, 94.

under an arrangement whereby the Combined Chiefs would exercise general jurisdiction over strategic policy and the coordination of allied efforts against the Japanese in all areas; and the Combined Chiefs would confer control over the conduct of operations in the Pacific Ocean area and China to the Joint Chiefs as their agents, and over those in the Southeastern Asia and Southwestern Pacific areas to the British Chiefs as their agents.

But the U.S. Chiefs of Staff would not accede to these proposals. They were disposed to consult with their British colleagues on all major decisions but they were not willing to share authority or powers of decision so evenly. Moreover, they were convinced that any such system of combined control would result in serious hindrances and complications. They did not want to have to argue with the British about what they might undertake to do with their much greater combat force.

In their conception there would be two clearly delineated areas of activity outside of the mainland of Asia. The Joint Chiefs were agreeable to having operations in one, the expanded Southeast Asia area, under British direction, provided they were given the chance to consider in advance prospective operations in this area in order to determine their impact on operations elsewhere and to make sure they were adjusted to the main effort. That was to be made in the other area, the Pacific Ocean area, and there the Joint Chiefs wanted to be unhindered in their conduct of the war.

On July 18th Marshall had told the British Chiefs that he was aware that in the past they had not had all the information wanted, and he assured them that this would be remedied. But, he had gone on to say, he was convinced that the operational strategy in the Pacific area must remain the undivided responsibility of the U.S. Chiefs of Staff. They could not, he had concluded, engage in a debate of pros and cons of operational strategy with their British colleagues because of the difficulties arising from the great distances over which the war extended, and the enormous land, sea, and air forces engaged.

Without disturbing the U.S. Joint Chiefs, the Final Report satisfied the British wish to be consulted about operational strategy and to have a chance to make effective any dissent they might have. It was stipulated that "The control of operational strategy in the Pacific Theatre will remain in the hands of the United States Chiefs of Staff." But they agreed to consult the British Chiefs about general strategy and to provide full and timely information about their plans and intentions. This was supplemented by a further provision that in the event that the Soviet

Union entered the war against Japan "the strategy to be pursued should be discussed between the parties concerned."

In the Southeast Asia theater, strategy was to be determined in conference between the British and American Chiefs of Staff; but, as before, the directives to the Supreme Commander of SEAC were to be sent by the British Chiefs. The scope of this command was to be extended to include a large part of the southwest Pacific which was under MacArthur's command, including Borneo, Java and Celebes. The task of reaching suitable accords about command arrangements in this vast area with Australia, New Zealand, and the Netherlands was turned over to the British.

(2) Such differences as there were between the American and British Chiefs about the over-all strategic concept had been easily resolved. Their objective was defined as being "In conjunction with other Allies to bring about at the earliest possible dates the unconditional surrender of Japan." This was to be achieved ". . . by: lowering Japanese ability and will to resist by establishing sea and air blockades, conducting intensive air bombardment, and destroying Japanese air and naval strength; invading and seizing objectives in the Japanese home islands as the main effort; conducting such operations against objectives in other than the Japanese home islands as will contribute to the main effort; establishing absolute military control of Japan; and liberating Japanese-occupied territory if required."

(3) The invasion of Japan was conceived to be "the supreme operation." All forces and combat resources needed to accomplish this "at the earliest practicable date" were to be made available. After preparing the way by air bombardment and blockade, a landing was to be effected on the southernmost main island, Kyushu, to create a tactical position favorable to "the decisive invasion of Honshu."

As defined in a separate directive for the Southeast Asia area, the order of operations there was to be: as a primary target the opening of the Straits of Malacca at the earliest possible time, and then with the forces reduced by contribution to the assault on Japan, the liberation of the Malay Peninsula; action across the frontier of Burma into Siam to seize key areas in that country; and then landings in Java and Sumatra.

(4) The Soviet Union was to be encouraged to enter the war; and such aid to its war-making capacity as might be needed and practicable was to be provided.

(5) China was to be given such help and support as might be necessary and practicable to enable it to be an effective ally against Japan. No

landings from the sea either in China or Korea were included in the vista of operations.

(6) For the assault on the Japanese home islands the British Commonwealth was to provide a long-range bomber force, a naval task force, a ground force with a small tactical air force if possible, subject to a satisfactory solution of operational problems. The size and numbers of these several contingents were, in fact, as great—or greater—than the American commanders thought they needed or could use well. The British, now that they could, were eager to prove their will to play their due part in the struggle, just as the Americans had in the war in Europe. Thereby, they hoped to improve their right for consideration of their wishes about the disposition of the situations in the Pacific and Asia after the war was won.[55]

[55] The French government had offered to provide an Army Corps of two infantry divisions, with service and supporting units at the entire disposal of the American command. One was already equipped; Lend-Lease equipment was wanted for the other. The Joint Chiefs of Staff were disposed to accept this contribution subject to various conditions. First among them was a clear understanding that the French forces would be subject to the complete command and control of the American commander in the same manner as American divisions. Truman had bluntly told this to the French Foreign Minister on May 16. As recounted by the President, "I wanted Bidault to understand clearly that if French troops were used we would have to have prior agreement from the French that they would be under our command. I added that I would insist on the condition that the French troops obey the orders of our commanding general. We are now going through an unhappy experience in the European Theatre, and I had no wish to see it repeated." *Year of Decisions*, pages 240-241. The British Chiefs of Staff suggested that any French contingents could be most advisedly used in due course in Indo-China, and the U.S. Joint Chiefs finally agreed.

On July 19 an answer approved by the Combined Chiefs had been sent from Potsdam for the French government which stated that its offer was accepted "in principle." Decision as to whether this French corps were to serve under American or British command and in what area would be determined later. In any case the corps would be moved in accord with the priority of the operation in which it was used; and "Whether used in the main effort or in the South China Sea area, it will not be possible to commit it to operations prior to the spring of 1946." (Potsdam Papers, Document 1291.)

The government of the Netherlands had offered to contribute some Dutch forces for the war in the Pacific, particularly to participate in the recapture of the Netherlands East Indies. The response approved by the Combined Chiefs and sent on the same day from Potsdam was similar to that made to the French offer.

The reserve shown in these responses to both these offers of aid was due mainly to skepticism of the U.S. Joint Chiefs as to whether the benefit would warrant the possible troubles that might arise, such as friction over command, misunderstandings due to differences of language, differences of training and equipment. Moreover, it was thought that the shipping necessary to move the French forces and their equipment from France and North Africa and the Dutch forces from Holland would not be available for months because of more urgent uses.

Both governments let it be known very quickly that they found the responses disappointing. Their Ambassadors pointed out to Acting Secretary of State Grew that the war might well be over before the spring of 1946; and they stated they were afraid that if their forces were not enabled to play a part in the liberation and occupation of their former possessions that their prestige would suffer. The Dutch government was all the

(7) The Combined Chiefs conceived that the struggle might go on almost until the end of the next year, 1946. But that the end might come much sooner was recognized in one paragraph of the Report which directed the preparation of plans for ". . . operations to effect an entry into Japan proper for occupational purposes in order to take immediate advantage of favorable circumstances such as a sudden enemy collapse or surrender."

Having examined this report paragraph by paragraph, Truman and Churchill approved these arrangements.

The Combined Chiefs, thereupon, adjourned their meeting and rode over to the Cecilienhof Palace for a conference with the Soviet military chiefs.[56] The primary purpose of the meeting was, as Truman later wrote, ". . . to co-ordinate strategy in the Far East, an important step toward bringing Russia into the war on our side."[57]

Leahy presided. The Soviet group were General Alexei E. Antonov, Chief of Staff, Red Army, his deputy General Slavin, Admiral of the Fleet Kutznetsov, and Marshal of Aviation Fallalev, Chief of the Soviet Air Staff; the same men with whom General Deane had been dealing in Moscow.

Antonov outlined Soviet intentions and plans. He said "that Soviet troops were now being concentrated in the Far East and would be ready to commence operations against Japan *in the last half of August.*[58] The actual date, however, would depend upon the result of conferences with Chinese representatives which had not yet been completed."

He defined the objectives of Soviet forces in the Far East as the destruction of the Japanese army in Manchuria and the occupation of the Liaotung Peninsula. After the defeat of Japan, he added, it was the Russian intention to withdraw their troops from Manchuria.

Antonov estimated that in Manchuria there were about 30 divisions of Japanese troops and 20 divisions of Manchurian puppet troops, that is, about 50 divisions in all on what would be the Russian front. He thought that the Japanese might try to bring into Manchuria 10 divisions from China and 7 other divisions from the Japanese home islands. He said this must be prevented and asked whether we could do so. Marshall, King, and Arnold all assured him that we could.

---

more aggrieved because the allies were refusing to make available for this purpose even the Dutch ships which were in the allied shipping pool.

[56] Potsdam Papers. Minutes of Tripartite Military meeting, July 24, 1945, 2:30 p.m.
[57] *Year of Decisions*, page 382.
[58] My italics.

Marshall then went on to tell how the actions of American submarines in the Sea of Japan, the mines laid by B-29's at the western entrance of the Inland Sea, and the blockade of the main harbors on the west coast of Honshu had almost severed communications between Japan and the mainland.[59] The ferry service between Japan and Pusan (in Korea) and shipping service in the Yellow Sea between Korea and the mainland had been almost ended. In sum, "As a result of increased naval action and mining by super-bombers there is little likelihood of any Japanese troop movements between Japan and Manchuria. By September or October we expect it to be impossible for the Japanese to move any cargo over this route."

As for possible movement of reinforcing troops from China into Manchuria, the Japanese were withdrawing from the south, leaving fortress garrisons to defend the Hong Kong-Canton area, Shanghai and Hankow. "But there was evidence . . . that . . . the continued air attacks on the single-track railroad and sabotage by Chinese guerrillas will prevent the Japanese from moving more than a trickle of troops to the north." The Japanese were, therefore, largely dependent on water transportation. However, in the course of time the Japanese could move troops from North China to Manchuria through the Peking-Kalgan route or via Tientsin.

Then, after telling of the movements of American troops from the European theater en route to the Pacific, Marshall concluded, "In the Pacific at the present time the principal difficulty is to find ground room for troops and aircraft we wish to deploy there."

General Arnold stressed the decided supremacy in the air that had been achieved over the whole region—so decided that many American bombing expeditions were meeting with no enemy air resistance. He thought that the Japanese air force was in its weakest state, having lost most of its more experienced pilots, many of its maintenance crews, and being very short of gas and oil. He reckoned that about 1,200 planes had been set aside for suicide operations, however, and that crews were being trained in such attacks against planes and ships. He foretold that from airfields established in Okinawa our B-24's would be able to operate north of Port Arthur and our B-29's would range 200 miles north of Harbin. They would be able to carry maximum bomb loads against Japanese industries and lines of communication in Manchuria.

[59] The Sea of Japan is the sea that runs between the Japanese main islands and Korea and Soviet Far Eastern shores. The Inland Sea is the narrow passage between the three main islands of Honshu, Shikoku, and Kyushu.

Discussion ensued as to several questions of coordination and division of operations as between the American and Soviet forces. Would American forces, naval or amphibious, Antonov asked, operate *against* the Kurile Islands to open a line of communications to Siberia? He thought this would be most important to assure a continued flow of supplies to the Soviet armies. Admiral King answered that the American navy did not think it possible to operate *against* the Kuriles but saw no reason why a line of communications should not be established *through* the Kuriles, since the passages between these islands were deep and wide.

Would American forces, Antonov also asked, operate against the shores of Korea in coordination with the Russian ground forces which would be on the offensive against the Korean peninsula? Marshall said that such amphibious operations against Korea had not been planned for in the near future. He explained why. Our shipping would be exposed to Japanese suicide attack, both by planes and small surface vessels. We would need all our assault shipping for the three contemplated landings at Kyushu. He realized, he added, the importance of Korea to the Russian operations but the possibility of an American attack on that country would have to be determined after the landings on Kyushu. However, he thought Korea could be controlled from air fields in Kyushu, and he pointed out again that communications between Japan and Korea were virtually cut. King added that after the Kyushu operation we would have such control of the waters of Japan and Korea that we could establish a line of communications through them to Vladivostock.

King then raised the question as to how, and by whom, control of the La Perouse Strait, between Hokkaido, the northernmost of the Japanese main islands, and Sakhalin was to be exercised. He said he understood the Russians would undertake this by capturing the southern end at Sakhalin Island. Antonov said that their first task would be to destroy the Japanese forces in Manchuria. Because of the distance to Sakhalin, additional troop movements would be needed to complete its capture in time to be of value in opening La Perouse Strait; therefore the attack on Southern Sakhalin would be only the second offensive.

Next Field Marshal Sir Alan Brooke explained prospective British operations in Southeast Asia under Admiral Mountbatten. That commander planned first to complete the destruction of the remnants of the Japanese Army in Burma, and then continue on to Siam; and as soon thereafter as possible try to recapture Malaya and Singapore and open the Straits of Malacca, and thereby shorten the line of support for British troops in the Pacific Theater. Admiral of the Fleet Andrew Cunningham in his account of British naval operations, narrated that only remnants of the Japanese fleet remained in Southeast Asian waters, and British naval forces were not restricted in their movements except in narrow parts of the Strait of Malacca. Air Marshal Sir Charles Portal reported that the British and American air forces in the Southeast Asia area were in unchallenged control.

After the discussion was over, Marshall gave Antonov a memo containing several questions. The most important ones concerned the boundaries between the prospective naval and air operations of the American and Soviet forces. The U.S. Chiefs proposed that American surface vessels operate freely in the Seas of Japan and the Sea of Okhotsk, and that American submarines operate south and east of a described line within these two seas, and Russian submarines north and west of this line.[60] A line was also suggested for air operations. As President Truman later explained, "No lines were set up for land operations since it was not anticipated by our military leaders that we would carry out operations to Korea."[61]

The record corroborates what Leahy wrote later about the session: "The entire meeting was very friendly and none of the suspicion that so often frustrated our military mission in Moscow was apparent."[62] Another meeting was arranged for the 26th, by which time Antonov promised to have answers to the American queries and proposals.

Before going on to tell of the other discussions and events of this day—July 24—it is of retrospective interest to compare the estimates of the combat strength of the Kwantung Army presented at this meeting with the Soviet Chiefs of Staff with the facts about the actual condition of that army after the war, as portrayed later by members of the Japanese High Command.[63]

---

[60] The Sea of Okhotsk is the name of the body of water between the Kurile Islands and southern Sakhalin.

[61] *Year of Decisions*, page 383.

[62] *I Was There*, page 416.

[63] This summary of the Japanese military situation in Manchuria at the time of the Potsdam Conference is derived from four monographs prepared by former members of the Japanese High Command under the auspices of the Military History Section of the Headquarters of the Far East Command of the U.S. These monographs were:

No. 45, Imperial General Headquarters Army High Command Record, Mid-1941-August 1945.

No. 138, Record of Operations Against Soviet Russia.

No. 154, Record of Operations Against Soviet Russia—Eastern Front, August 1945.

No. 155, Record of Operations Against Soviet Russia on Northern and Western Fronts of Manchuria and in Northern Korea, August 1945.

They tell that the Japanese armies in Manchuria and Korea had been greatly depleted in the attempt to counter American assaults elsewhere and to prepare for the anticipated American invasion of Japan. The best trained and equipped divisions of the Kwantung Army stationed in Manchuria had been diverted to other battlefields so that by the close of 1944 its total strength had been reduced to about half of what it had been at the maximum at the end of 1943. During the first half of 1945, Japan had tried to correct this situation by mobilizing reservists in Manchuria who had not previously been called into service, men who had been deferred as unfit and civilians. These were hastily formed into nine divisions and some brigades and deployed in areas formerly held by much stronger, better trained and better equipped troops. With these additions, the Kwantung Army itself was a force of about 24 divisions and 9 mixed brigades (about 450,000 men). However, their real combat strength as compared with well-trained and well-equipped divisions was much less, perhaps less than half. Furthermore the force had only enough ammunition to enable perhaps half of it to maintain battle for about three months. It had relatively little up-to-date armor and virtually no air protection.

The operational plans of the Japanese High Command contemplated that in the event of a Soviet invasion the Korean Army was to pass under the command of the Kwantung Army to establish a unified structure for the conduct of operations in both countries. With this group of 7 divisions from the Korean Army, the Kwantung Army would have controlled 31 divisions. It was also planned that about 6 divisions would be transferred from the China Expeditionary force to the Kwantung Army. Had all these additions been effective the Kwantung Army would have had a numerical force of about 37 divisions—far smaller than the Soviet forces which were being deployed along the frontier for the sweep through and around Manchuria, and without their armored equipment and air strength.

The Japanese High Command had a rather accurate view of their comparative weakness, and during the early summer of 1945 revised their combat plans accordingly. The concept of trying to hold almost all of Manchuria on all fronts was abandoned. Instead a plan was adopted for a defensive retreat southward, and the amassing of defensive strength in southeastern Manchuria to defend that area and Korea.

Groves notified the Chiefs of Staff of the dates on which bombs would be ready in Tinian: the first about August 1st, the second by August 6th, and the third by about August 24th, and others in September. This report provided a definite basis for the directive instructing General Carl A. Spaatz, Commanding General of the U.S. Army Strategic Air Forces, in the operational use of the new weapon against Japan. In the afternoon the historic order was written in Washington.

It read "The 509 Composite Group, 20th Air Force, will deliver its first special bomb as soon as weather will permit visual bombing after about 3 August 1945 on one of the targets: Hiroshima, Kokura, Niigata, and Nagasaki. . . .

"Additional bombs will be delivered on the above targets as soon as made ready by the project staff. Further instructions will be issued concerning targets other than those listed above. . . .

"The foregoing directive is issued to you by direction and with the approval of the Secretary of War and the Chief of Staff, USA. It is desired that you personally deliver one copy of this directive to General MacArthur and one copy to Admiral Nimitz for their information." (signed) Thos. T. Handy, General G.S.C. Acting Chief of Staff.

The draft of this directive was sent from Washington to Stimson and Marshall at Potsdam for their approval, no doubt with the knowledge that they would consult the President.

In the text of the proposed Declaration as it had finally evolved, the Japanese were to be warned that the alternative to an acceptance of the terms offered would be "prompt and utter destruction." But they were not to be told that the United States had come into possession of a much more destructive weapon than the world had ever known. Among the several reasons for not being explicit regarding the existence or nature of the atomic bomb was quite possibly the fact that the American government could not reveal these matters to the Japanese without also revealing them to the Russians. This the American government was not as yet disposed to do except in a vague and casual way.

On one central point ruling official opinion had been fixed: that we ought not to tell the Russians *how the weapon was made* until or unless an agreement was reached for international inspection and control. Stimson had meditated over the dilemma and worried about it during sleepless hours of the night, for he had taught himself to live by the maxim that the way to win trust was to give it. But his impulse in that direction was checked by his despondent view of the system of dictatorship under which the Russians lived. General Marshall was convinced that it would be unwise to pass on information that would aid the Soviet government to make this weapon until we were surer of Soviet intentions. Byrnes had been steadfastly opposed to being open with the Russians. In his mind our exclusive possession of this ultimate weapon might well be of use to him in the conduct of American diplomacy; for in the time immediately ahead it would free us of the need for Russian aid in the war against the Japanese; and in the time beyond it would make it safer for us to stand out firmly against Russian actions or demands of which we disapproved.

The President had discussed the question with Churchill several times. At first the Prime Minister had been dubious when the President told him that he intended to tell Stalin the basic fact that we had this weapon, and for the time being nothing else. But Churchill changed his mind and became inclined to let the Russians know we had it, thinking it might affect Soviet attitude toward certain of the disputed issues in the conference.

On the 24th, at lunch after the meeting with the Combined Chiefs, Truman once again talked over with Byrnes the way in which Stalin might be told just enough to invalidate any complaint that information of military importance to the Soviet Union had been kept from him, and no more. The former Secretary of State has since explained that as a result of his experience with the Russians during the first week of the Conference he had come to the conclusion that it would be regrettable if the Soviet Union entered the war, and that he was afraid that if Stalin were made fully aware of the power of the new weapon, he might order the Soviet Army to plunge forward at once.[64] However, Truman does not recall that Byrnes then, or at any time, had any such thought in mind.[65]

Whatever the reasons, it had been settled that Stalin should be told in an offhand way that we had a new and powerful weapon—that much and no more. Thus after the formal session ended and the members of the delegations were lingering in small groups waiting for their cars to come, the President sauntered over to Stalin. In order the better to seem to be casual, and to make what he was about to say seem unsensational, he did not ask Charles E. ("Chip") Bohlen to accompany him as interpreter. The only American account of what he said to Stalin and of Stalin's response is the terse one in his Memoirs. "On July 24 I casually mentioned to Stalin that we had a new weapon of unusual destructive force. The Russian Premier showed no special interest. All he said was that he was glad to hear it and hoped we would make 'good use of it against

---

[64] Interview of author with Byrnes, February 27, 1958.
[65] Interview of author with Truman.

the Japanese.' "[66] About the precise words spoken by the President, how Pavlov the Russian interpreter understood them, how he translated them to Stalin, we are left to wonder.

In any case, Stalin did not ask any questions. Truman at the time and later was sure that he did not understand the significance of what he was being told. This may be so. If, however, Stalin did grasp that he was being informed of a matter of importance, we are left to guess whether his expression of satisfaction and lack of curiosity was genuine or simulated. For we have since learned how information about the physics and chemistry of the bomb, about the engineering problems mastered, and about the structure and method of detonation of the bomb were illicitly sent to the Soviet government by its agents in the United States and elsewhere. Stalin was not ordinarily slow in grasping the significance of even the most glancing remark nor incurious about any improvement in weapons. He was quite capable of concealing any glimmer of previous knowledge and of suppressing any sign that he realized that the diplomatic or military balance between the West and the Soviet Union might be affected by the new weapon.

My own best surmise—but it is pure surmise—is that Stalin knew that the American government had been making a great effort to produce the weapon and that it was on the verge of success, but that he did not know that it had been proven in test and did not realize how great its demonstrated destructive power could be.[67]

In retrospect, the reticence—the casualness and the vagueness—that marked the communication to Stalin about the new weapon seems now to have served no purpose. It is hard to discern any advantage gained, while it is conceivable that relations with the Soviet Union were adversely affected. If the purpose of the reticence was to deter, or rather not to precipitate, Soviet entry into the war, it failed to do so, since the

---

[66] Truman, *Year of Decisions*, page 416.

[67] The impression left by careful reading of the story of Soviet Atomic Espionage recorded in the Report of that name made by the Joint Committee on Atomic Energy in 1951 is that the Soviet authorities must have been well informed about the nature of the weapon and the progress being made in its production. But this does not contain any definite report from any of the now known Soviet agents about the New Mexico test. As late as August 9, 1945, the Soviet liaison officer in Canada, Zabotin, was transmitting to "The Director" in Moscow facts given by Alek (Dr. Allan Nunn May): "The test of the atomic bomb was conducted in New Mexico, (with '49,' '94-239'). The bomb dropped on Hiroshima was made of uranium 235." Page 55.

My surmise accords with the impression which Harriman got during his first talk with Molotov after their return from Potsdam. As recalled by Harriman, Molotov in referring to Truman's statement to Stalin about "the great secret weapon (or secret device) which the American government had developed" spoke with a sneering emphasis which caused Harriman to infer that Stalin had known much if not everything about the S-1 project.

Russians entered the fray as soon as the bomb was used against Japan. If the cause for restraint was fear that candor would lead to questioning about the way in which the atomic weapon was produced, that could have been denied on grounds which could have been shown to be reasonable.

With the benefit of knowledge gained since, it is possible to delineate what would have been a wiser course. Truman and Churchill might have told candidly and adequately of the nature of the new weapon, of what had been learned about it in the New Mexico test, and of the intention to use it against the Japanese early in August. Further queries could then have been met with a statement of our willingness to share knowledge about production of the weapon, and even to enter into partnership, as soon as a satisfactory agreement was reached on joint control of its production and use. Had that been done it is just possible that the Soviet response to proposals soon to be made for the control of the weapon would have been more cooperative. Even if it had not been, the idea that secrecy preserved by the West was due to a wish to keep the weapon in reserve for possible use against the Soviet Union might not have flourished in that country as it did. But it is too easy to assert that policies conceived in the aftermath and never subjected to the proof of experience would have been better than policies conceived at the time which were defeated by experience.

JULY 25

The War Department was informed that Stimson and Marshall approved the Directive for General Spaatz, and it was given to him. In telling later of this instruction, Truman wrote: "With this order the wheels are set in motion for the first use of an atomic weapon against a military target. I had made the decision. I also instructed Stimson that the order would stand unless I notified him that the Japanese reply to our ultimatum was acceptable."[68]

Truman wrote Churchill that he would let him know as soon as Chiang Kai-shek had replied, giving his concurrence to the Declaration that was to be addressed to the Japanese government, and proposed that it be issued jointly from Potsdam, if that was satisfactory to the Prime Minister.[69] Churchill, who was about to leave for England, returned the copy which Truman had sent him the day before with a note saying, "I am willing to sign it on behalf of His Majesty's Government in its present form, and I hope you will issue it as you propose whenever you choose and as soon as possible."[70]

[68] *Year of Decisions*, page 421.
[69] Potsdam Papers, Document 1248.
[70] *Ibid.*, Document 1249.

At seven in the evening (Tokyo time) the Japanese Foreign Minister instructed the Japanese Ambassador in Moscow to take advantage of the recess in the Potsdam Conference.[71] He was told to offer to go to any place chosen by Molotov and, by emphasizing that the mission to be headed by Konoye was being sent by the Emperor's personal command, to try to get an immediate positive answer. Sato was authorized to "make it clear that we are fully prepared to recognize the wishes of the Soviet Union in the Far East." But the Japanese government still did not choose, or dare to be more definite in regard to the conditions of the peace for which it was asking the Soviet government to mediate. Sato was informed merely that (1) "As for Japan, it is impossible to accept unconditional surrender under any circumstances, but we should like to communicate to the other party through appropriate channels that we have no objection to a peace based on the Atlantic Charter. . . . Should the United States and Great Britain remain insistent on formality [of unconditional surrender], there is no solution to this situation other than for us to hold out until complete collapse because of this one point alone." And (2) "Also it is necessary to have them understand that we are trying to end hostilities by asking for very reasonable terms in order to secure and maintain our nation's existence and honor."

Sato was in fact just getting around to acting on the instructions which had been sent to him from Tokyo on the 21st, and which for unascertained reasons, had not been received by him until the 24th. He managed to see Molotov's deputy, Lozovsky, the night of the 25th (Moscow time). After Lozovsky listened to Sato's message, he asked with false ingenuousness whether he was correct in thinking that the Japanese government wanted the Soviet government to mediate. Sato said he was correct. Lozovsky then asked whether the concrete proposals which Konoye would bring would have to do with Russo-Japanese relations or the termination of the war. Sato said that they would deal with both. The Ambassador took this questioning to mean that Lozovsky was giving earnest heed to the Japanese proposal, especially since the Soviet official asked him to give him a written text and promised him an answer.[72]

[71] *Ibid.*, Document 1233.

[72] Late that night, July 25 (Moscow time), the Ambassador sent two reports of this talk with Lozovsky to the Japanese Foreign Office which are printed in the Potsdam Papers, Documents 1234 and 1235. Even if this exchange of messages was intercepted, it is improbable that their contents were known by the Americans and British at Potsdam before the Declaration was issued on the next day, July 26. But the written statement made by Sato was presumably the one read by the Soviet interpreter at the Tenth Plenary Session on July 28.

JULY 26

In the morning the cruiser *Indianapolis* arrived at the small island of Tinian with the fissionable material for the first atomic bomb that was to be used against Japan.

In the afternoon the American Chiefs of Staff met alone with the Soviet Chiefs of Staff. They were then given the answers to the five questions which Marshall had given Antonov on the 24th. These dealt with elements in the plans for coordinated operations.[73]

The main items were few and quickly settled; and since these arrangements did not really become effective because of the quick ending of the war, identification without detail will suffice, I think, to indicate the outlook of the American and Soviet Chiefs of Staff.

They agreed on dividing lines for their respective naval operations in the seas around Japan, and air operations over Manchuria, Korea, and the islands and waters near Japan.

General Antonov, for the Soviet Chiefs, urged the Americans to open a line of communications from Kyushu through the Straits of Tsushima to Vladivostock. General Marshall, for the U.S. Chiefs, expressed willingness to do so, but explained that because of the fight which the Japanese would put up against the forces we expected to land in Kyushu, and the danger from mines and suicide planes, it might not be possible to open this southern route through the Straits of Tsushima ". . . until the middle of December or about six weeks after the first landing on Kyushu."

They agreed that with the beginning of Soviet operations against Japan, Soviet liaison groups be attached to General MacArthur and Admiral Nimitz, as well as a Soviet mission in Washington; and that American liaison groups be located at the headquarters of the Soviet High Commander in the Far East, Marshal Vasilevski, and of the Commander of the Soviet Pacific Fleet, Admiral Yemashev.

At the end of the conference Marshall expressed the appreciation of the U.S. Chiefs of Staff for the chance to discuss these important matters with the Soviet Chiefs; and Antonov expressed his pleasure and satisfaction over the results of the conference.

[73] The minutes of this meeting are given in the Defense Department publication, "The Entry of the Soviet Union into War Against Japan: Military Plans 1941-1945," 1945. Pages 92-104.

Late in the afternoon the message from Chiang Kai-shek approving the text of the Declaration was received. Copies were given to representatives of the press and radio in Potsdam at 7:00 p.m. for dispatch at 9:20 p.m.

The pronouncement was phrased as a joint statement by Truman, Churchill, and Chiang Kai-shek. Stalin had been told by Truman a day or two before that a combined (American-British-Chinese) Declaration was going to be addressed to the Japanese. But he had not been consulted about its contents or asked to subscribe to it. As soon as it was released Byrnes sent a copy to Molotov's residence. Sometime in the course of the evening Molotov's interpreter telephoned a request that its issuance be postponed for several days. No reasons were given.

Contents of this Declaration corresponded so closely to that of the earlier draft versions which have been reviewed that attention need be directed to only two points.[74]

The question of the future status of the Emperor was left ambiguous. The Japanese were informed that their country would be occupied until the purposes named in the Declaration had been accomplished and ". . . there has been established in accordance with the freely expressed will of the Japanese people a peacefully inclined and responsible government." These statements could be construed as leaving open the disposition of the Imperial institution. For while they did not explicitly acknowledge the authority of the Emperor by calling on him to announce the surrender, they did not state that he might not continue in office. Byrnes thought they would indicate that the Emperor might be kept, without reviving controversy within the delegation.

The final paragraph read: "We call upon the government of Japan to proclaim now the unconditional surrender of all Japanese armed forces, and to provide proper and adequate assurances of their good faith in such action. The alternative for Japan is prompt and utter destruction."

The Japanese were not told that the allies had acquired a wholly novel weapon which gave intense import to this terse description of the consequences of refusal.

In my judgment the Declaration was a generous offer to a willful aggressor except in one respect. The confirmation of the decision which had been announced publicly by Roosevelt and Churchill after their meeting with Chiang Kai-shek at Cairo in December 1943: to deprive Japan of all its territories except the home islands was a harsh penalty and shortsighted. There was conclusive justification for requiring Japan

[74] The text was printed at once in the State Department Bulletin for July 29, 1945.

to give up the territory that it had cruelly conquered in China (including Manchuria) and Korea. But it would have been wiser, I believe, to have allowed it to retain control of Formosa, the Kuriles, and the Ryukyus.

That same evening news of the results of the election in Britain was received. Churchill and Eden were out of office. Clement Attlee was to be Britain's new Prime Minister, and Ernest Bevin the new Foreign Secretary. The formal sessions of the conference were suspended until they arrived.

JULY 27

The text of the Potsdam Declaration was picked up by the Japanese radio monitoring stations at 6:00 A.M. Tokyo time. All day long the Japanese officials, civilian and military, discussed what heed, if any, should be taken of it.

The rapid analysis made by experts in the Foreign Office focused on three points: (1) That although the Soviet government was almost certainly consulted at Potsdam, it was not party to it, thereby still preserving its legal neutrality; (2) that the issuing power for the first time gave rather precise indications of the effective intent behind their menacing demand for unconditional surrender; and (3) that the term "unconditional surrender" appeared only once in the document, and was then only in reference to the Japanese armed forces.

But the Foreign Minister, Togo, was upset by several of its main features—by the territorial provisions, the extent of occupation of Japan and the ambiguity of the statement about the eventual form of the Japanese government.[75] Despite the firm statement in the Declaration that the allies would not deviate from the announced terms, he believed it might be possible for Japan to get them through Soviet mediation. So he advised the Prime Minister that until the still-awaited Soviet answer about the proposed Konoye mission was received, the Japanese government should neither accept nor reject the allied ultimatum.

In the course of the day Prime Minister Suzuki gave the Cabinet to understand that he agreed with Togo's advice, and that while waiting for the Soviet reply he was going to refrain from official comment on the Declaration, that he would "kill it with silence."[76] He said he would publish a censored version to keep up the nation's will and instruct the press to play down its importance. But all the senior military officials,

[75] *The Cause of Japan*, pages 311-312.
[76] Robert C. J. Butow, *Japan's Decision to Surrender*, page 145.

except the Minister of the Navy, Yonai, were urging him to reject the proffered terms explicitly at once, since in their view they provided no basis for negotiation and hesitation might weaken the national morale. It may be assumed that all construed the threat of "prompt and utter destruction" to mean merely a continuation of the assault from the air and from the sea, as prelude to the invasion which they hoped to repel and thereby to win better terms. None conceived of a new weapon that would give an astounding new meaning to this threat.

During the day many thousands of leaflets were dropped from American planes over eleven Japanese cities, warning of enormous air bombardment to which they would be subjected if Japan did not surrender at once on allied terms.

Talking privately with Molotov in the evening, Byrnes explained that he had learned only that morning of Molotov's request for delay in the issuance of the Declaration; by then the statement had been widely distributed. When Molotov pointed out that he had made his request as soon as he had received Byrnes' letter giving him a copy of the Declaration, Byrnes remarked that even if the message had been conveyed to him at once it would have been too late, since the Declaration had been given out to the press at 7:00 p.m. on the 26th. The Secretary of State went on to explain that the Soviet government had not been consulted about the substance of the Declaration or the choice of the time of issuance because it was not at war with Japan and the American and British governments had not wished to embarrass it.

It is interesting to speculate what might have happened if Stalin had been asked to subscribe publicly to the Potsdam Declaration. Had he agreed to do so, it is possible that the immediate response by the Japanese government might have been quite different—and indicative of a willingness to surrender on the proffered terms if given assurances about the future of the Imperial Institution. In that case there would have been no need or occasion to use the bomb. However, the best guess is that Stalin would not have agreed to subscribe to the Declaration unless its issuance was delayed until after Soviet entry into the Pacific war.

JULY 28

The U.S. Senate ratified the Charter of the United Nations by a vote of 89 to 22.

The morning papers in Japan, guided by government, published the Declaration in abridged form. They refrained from editorial comment.[77] In the news columns they reported briefly, and without attribution, that the government was not paying any attention to the Declaration which appeared to be an attempt to separate the military from the people.[78]

Military leaders (particularly the War Minister, General Korechika Anami, the Army Chief of Staff, General Voshijiro Umezu, and the Navy Chief of Staff, Admiral Soemu Toyoda) were dissatisfied with the frail understanding reached by the Cabinet the day before—that the government should refrain from official comment until it had heard from the Soviet government. They had pressed the tired Prime Minister to speak out openly against the Declaration. Suzuki agreed to do so at a press conference that afternoon. The Foreign Minister, Togo, was absent from the Palace and did not know of this change of intention.

At 3:00 p.m. (in Tokyo) Suzuki was asked by reporters for his views about the Declaration. His answer was, "I believe the Joint Proclamation by the three countries is nothing but a rehash of the Cairo Declaration. As for the Government, it does not find any important value in it, and there is no other recourse but to ignore it entirely and resolutely fight for the successful conclusion of this war."[79] Asked about the great attacks on the Japanese mainland by allied sea and air forces,

[77] Among the passages omitted were the ones which stated (a) that the allies did not intend to enslave the Japanese as a race or destroy them as a nation, (b) that Japanese troops after being disarmed should be allowed to return to their homes with the chance to lead peaceful and productive lives.

[78] For example, Asahi Shimbun on July 28 reported that the viewpoint of the government was that "Since the joint declaration of America, Britain and Chungking is of no great value it will only serve to re-enhance the government's resolve to carry the war forward unfalteringly to a successful conclusion."

[79] Potsdam Papers, Document 1258. In a footnote to this document it is explained that the text given is a translation of portions of a Domei transmission in *romanji* carried by Radio Tokyo's Greater East Asia Service at 3:00 a.m. Eastern War Time, July 29, and monitored by the Foreign Broadcast Intelligence Service of the U.S. Federal Communications Commission.

The Japanese word therein translated as "ignore" was "mokusatsu." There has been a subsequent attempt to question whether by using it Suzuki intended to reject the Proclamation. Toshikazu Kase, who was then a member of the Japanese Foreign Office, in his book, *Journey to the Missouri*, page 211, comments, "True, the Cabinet decided to 'ignore' the proclamation, but to ignore it should have meant simply that we refrained from commenting on it. To state expressly that we would ignore the proclamation was entirely contrary to the purpose of the decision. . . ." However, it is notable that Foreign Minister Togo in his later account, while telling that he was surprised by the Prime Minister's statement, since it was at variance with the decisions of the Supreme Council and the Cabinet, and deploring it, does not question its meaning as understood by the American authorities. *The Cause of Japan*, pages 313-314. For a considered discussion of this point, see Butow's *Japan's Decision to Surrender*, pages 143-149. He gives alternative translations of the verb "mokusatsu": "take no notice of it," or "treat it with silent contempt," or "ignore it."

he said "I leave this with absolute confidence in the hands of our strategists."[80] The Japanese press gave a leading place to this statement and it was broadcast to the United States.

Stimson has tersely recorded the grim conclusion that was drawn. "In the face of this rejection we could only proceed to demonstrate that the ultimatum had meant exactly what it said when it stated that if the Japanese continued the war, the full application of our military power, backed by our resolve, will mean the inevitable and complete destruction of the Japanese armed forces and just as inevitably the utter devastation of the Japanese homeland."[81]

No document or memoir or diary tells whether news of the Prime Minister's comment on the Declaration reached Potsdam before the Heads of Government met in brief Plenary Session at 10:30 that evening, the first session at which Attlee and Bevin were present.

In any case, Stalin said to Truman and Attlee that although the Soviet government had not been informed when the Declaration to Japan was drawn up, he wished to advise them of the latest Japanese overture. An interpreter thereupon read in English Sato's renewed application for reception of the Konoye Mission. Stalin then remarked that it was merely a repetition of the earlier request, but since it was more definite, the answer would also be more definite. It would be "no."[82] The President knew of these Japanese messages which had been intercepted.[83] He just cursorily thanked Stalin, as did Attlee.

JULY 29

Molotov told Truman that Stalin would find it helpful if the American and British governments would address a formal request to Russia to enter the war against Japan. He suggested this might be based on the refusal of the Japanese government to accept the Potsdam Declaration, and the wish to shorten the war and save lives. He added that the Soviet government was assuming it would have signed an agreement with the Chinese before entering the war.

[80] *New York Times*, July 30, 1960.
[81] *On Active Service in Peace and War*, page 625.
[82] Sometime during the day, Forrestal had told Byrnes in detail of the intercepted messages. Byrnes, *All in One Lifetime*, page 297. Truman told Department of State historians that he was familiar with the contents of this instruction sent to Sato (Editor's note in Potsdam Papers Vol. I, page 873 and Document 1234).
[83] Minutes of the Tenth Plenary Meeting, July 28, 10:30 p.m.

The President was surprised. He told Molotov he would have to consider the suggestion carefully. Leahy advised him not to make such a request of the Soviet government since it would place us under a permanent obligation. The President also talked with Attlee about it later in the day.

Byrnes, who had been present at the talk between Truman and Molotov, was also displeased with the request; the Soviet government would be violating the terms of its Neutrality Pact with Japan and he did not want to have the American government share the responsibility for this measure, and anyhow he did not want to urge the Russians to enter the war.[84] But, nevertheless, he and the legal adviser, Benjamin V. Cohen, devoted themselves to finding some way of avoiding a positive refusal without committing the American government. They recalled that in the Moscow Declaration (of October 1943) the Soviet government and the Western Allies had agreed ". . . to consult with each other . . . with a view to joint action on behalf of the community of nations" and that in Article 103 of the United Nations Charter it was provided that if there was a conflict between obligations of member states under the Charter and previous international understandings the Charter should prevail. Thereupon they wrote out a draft of a communication which Truman might send to Stalin. This concluded, "It seems to me under the terms of the Moscow Declaration and the Provisions of the Charter, above referred to, it would be proper for the Soviet Union to indicate its willingness to consult and cooperate with other great powers now at war with Japan with a view to joint action on behalf of the community of nations to maintain peace and security."[85]

All the citations around which this sophistical statement was woven were taken out of context, it may be said bluntly. Yet the President approved it, and Attlee concurred in it.

JULY 30

The headline of the story in the *New York Times* telling of the response of the Japanese Government to the Potsdam Declaration read: JAPAN OFFICIALLY TURNS DOWN ALLIED SURRENDER ULTIMATUM.

---

[84] *All in One Lifetime*, pages 297-298. The day before, Byrnes had told Forrestal that "he was most anxious to get the Japanese affair over with before the Russians got in, with particular reference to Dairen and Port Arthur." *The Forrestal Diaries*, entry for July 28, 1945.

[85] Byrnes, *op.cit.*

And the story itself began "Premier Kantaro Suzuki of Japan has put the official Japanese stamp of rejection on the surrender ultimatum issued to Japan by the United States, Great Britain and China. . . ."

Stimson was back in Washington. In conference with Groves and Harrison, he went over the text in hand for the announcement which the President would make after the first atomic bomb was dropped on Japan. Then he sent a message to the President at Potsdam telling him that he was sending on the draft revised in the light of the Potsdam Declaration, the dramatic results of the test, and certain minor suggestions made by the British. He advised the President that the time schedule for the use of the bomb was progressing so rapidly that he thought it essential that an approved text of the statement be available for release no later than Wednesday, August 1.[86]

Groves informed Marshall of the inferences being drawn from the New Mexico test about the probable results of the first atomic bomb to be dropped upon Japan. The blast effect, it was reckoned, would be equivalent to between 14,000 and 17,000 tons of TNT; it would be lethal in a radius of at least 1,000 feet from the point of fall, and extremely serious within a range between 2,500 and 3,500 feet; the generated heat and flame would be fatal in a radius of from 1,500 to 2,000 feet. However, no damaging effects on the ground from radioactive materials were anticipated; those experienced in New Mexico resulted from the low altitude at which the bomb had been detonated. All structures within an area of one to two miles would be demolished, and those within an area of six to seven miles would be badly damaged.

The Japanese Ambassador in Moscow that night made two reports to his government.

In the first, after reviewing the circumstances under which the Joint Declaration had been issued at Potsdam and speculating about Soviet intentions, he concluded, "Therefore I believe that Stalin feels that there is absolutely no necessity for making a voluntary agreement with Japan. On this point I see a serious discrepancy between your view and the actual state of affairs."[87]

In the second he recounted the course of a talk he had had with Lozovsky late in the afternoon. The Deputy Commissar had explained the continued delay in responding to the Japanese petition by the fact

[86] Potsdam Papers, Document 1313.
[87] Ibid., Document 1260.

that Stalin and Molotov were still in Berlin. Sato had said that he understood. "However," he continued, "the three countries—Great Britain, the United States and China—issued a joint declaration against Japan. Unconditional surrender is, after all, out of the question for the Japanese Government. Our view remains the same as was stated on the 13th, at our meeting before the last. If it is possible to avoid such a formula, however, Japan desires to end the war, with an extremely conciliatory attitude, so long as Japan is guaranteed the nation's honor and existence. For this purpose we asked the Soviet Government for assistance."

Ambassador Sato earnestly requested Lozovsky to inform Molotov that the Japanese government was still eager to send Prince Konoye, and that he would have the authority to discuss a wide range of subjects with the Soviet government, and that he hoped that the Potsdam Declaration would not deter the Soviet government from aiding the Japanese government as mediator.[88]

In Tokyo various groups were urging the Lord Keeper of the Privy Seal Kido to arrange for the acceptance of the Declaration without further demur. But the military members of the Supreme Council remained opposed and threatening. Thus the decision to continue to wait for a reply from the Soviet government was reaffirmed, permitting the division to prolong itself without reaching a climax. Despite the warnings from Sato and lack of any evidence of Soviet interest, the hope lingered that the answer from Moscow, when it came, might bring a solution for this ruinous internal crisis. The Emperor, having taken one weak initiative, was quiescent during this crucial flight of hours and days.

JULY 31

Truman informed Stalin of the text of the letter which he was willing to send to him, suggesting reasons which the Soviet government could give for entering the war against Japan, although the Soviet-Japanese Neutrality Pact was still in effect.

In a covering note, Truman wrote that he proposed to send the actual letter after Stalin notified him that the Soviet and Chinese governments had come to an accord. "If you decide to use it, it will be all right. However, if you decide to issue a statement basing your action on other ground or for any other reason prefer not to use this letter, it will be satisfactory to me. I leave it to your good judgment."[89]

[88] *Ibid.*, Document 1261.
[89] *Year of Decisions*, pages 403-404.

Stimson and his advisers devoted the morning to study of the statement that he himself was planning to issue when the atom bomb was dropped. He thought it much better than the original draft.

In the late afternoon Grew told Stimson that General Arnold was planning in a speech of celebration of Air Force Day to include what Stimson thought was "virtually a new ultimatum" to Japan. Grew and Stimson agreed the speech ought not to be cleared since it would confuse or obscure the whole situation. Stimson so advised Marshall and Arnold, and the speech was changed.

That same afternoon, General Thomas F. Farrell, who had consulted with General Curtis E. Le May at Guam and then hurried on to Tinian, informed Groves that it would be possible to arrange to cast the bomb on the very next day, everything being in readiness, and said that they interpreted the directive [of July 25] to mean that this action could be taken then if atmospheric conditions favored. Groves did not correct this interpretation. Thus the bomb might have been dropped some days earlier than it was, had not a typhoon struck that very day.[90]

AUGUST 1

In Potsdam, Attlee acknowledged with warm thanks a letter from Truman ". . . about the new weapon to be used on Japan." He said that if it was convenient he would come to see the President for a few minutes after the Plenary Session that afternoon. Regrettably no copy of Truman's letter, written in longhand, is available, and no record of this private talk between Truman and Attlee has been made known.[91]

Stimson discussed with Bundy, Harrison, and Groves the report that had been written by scientists connected with the Manhattan Project about the history of the effort and the nature of the result.[92] Because of the length of this narrative, about two hundred pages, they went over only an outline of it. The Secretary confided in his diary that the aim of the study was to offset any possible reckless statements by independent

[90] *No High Ground*, page 126. Confirmed by General Groves.

[91] Potsdam Papers, Document 1314. Attlee subsequently wrote, "Agreement for the dropping of the bomb by the United States had already been given by Sir Winston Churchill on behalf of Britain. I was, therefore, not called upon to make a decision, but if I had been I should have agreed with President Truman. . . . His was the decision and courageously he took it." Article by Lord Attlee, "The Hiroshima Choice," in the *Observer* (London) September 6, 1959.

[92] Subsequently published in book form under the name of its chief author, Henry De Wolf Smyth, *Atomic Energy for Military Purposes*, 1945.

scientists after the bomb was used, and observed that if he and his colleagues could be sure that no such statements would be made they would prefer not to give it out. But Groves had reached the conclusion that the best course would be for the government to issue a carefully prepared report, one which, while not revealing any vital information, would "take the stage away" from the accounts and comments that might be made by others.

AUGUST 2

The Conference at Potsdam ended. Beneath the usual assurances of the three leaders that their talks had resulted in progress toward a just state of peace, a tone of weariness and disappointment could be detected.

The joint press release was silent about the war in the Pacific. Its professional readers were left to make what they could out of the one brief paragraph headed "Military Talks," which read, "During the conference there were meetings between the Chiefs of Staff of the three governments on military matters of common interest."

The President then flew from Potsdam to England, lunched with King George VI on the battleship H.M.S. *Renown*, and departed from Plymouth on the U.S.S. *Augusta* for the voyage home. Byrnes and Leahy accompanied him.

Stimson, in Washington, met with Harrison, Bundy, Groves, Conant, and Sir James Chadwick, Roger Makins (of the British Embassy), and Dr. Richard Tolman, one of the technical advisers to Groves, to discuss the historical report of the scientists for issuance after the statements that he and the President would give out. He recorded in his diary that he still felt very doubtful about it, as did some of the others, including the British. But on the other hand, he was impressed by the fact that not only Groves, who was very careful, but also Conant and the scientists were very strongly in favor of having such a statement made, and assured him that it contained no information that would be of use to our national rivals.

Togo once again pressed Sato to get a helpful answer from the Russians. His message was rambling, almost excusing. "The battle situation has become acute. There are only a few days left in which to make arrangements to end the war. . . ." When the Soviet government agreed to receive the special envoy who was being sent to ask her mediation, ". . . efforts will be made to gather opinions from the various quarters regarding definite terms. (For this, it is our intention to make the Potsdam Three-Power Declaration the basis of the study regarding these terms). . . ."[93]

I do not know whether this message was intercepted; and if it was whether a copy was sent to Truman and Byrnes. In any event, it could have made no difference, since all that the Japanese who wanted peace dared offer at the time—judging by this distressed message—would not have affected either American or Soviet plans. As Ehrman has observed, "It was indeed as reasonable to deduce from the latest developments that an atomic bomb might now enable the peace party to force surrender on its opponents as it was to deduce that the two parties would together accept defeat without it. Togo and the Emperor were desperate; but they still could not prevail. The situation seemed to have reached the point where the bomb—and perhaps the bomb alone—would have the required effect."[94]

In his message to Sato, Togo had also said, "It is requested that further efforts be exerted to somehow make the Soviet Union enthusiastic over the special envoy. . . . Since the loss of one day relative to this present matter may result in a thousand years of regret, it is requested that you immediately have a talk with Molotov." Poor Sato! Stalin and Molotov were just starting back from Potsdam, and they traveled by train and did not reach Moscow until the plane carrying the bomb had left Tinian.

[93] *Grand Strategy*, Vol. VI, page 308.
[94] *Ibid.*, pages 308-309.

PART THREE
Japan Is Forced to Surrender

Time is a child moving counters in a game; the royal power is a child's.

—HERACLITUS

7. Japan's Plight and Stubborn Folly; The Resort to Ultimate Measures

By EARLY August little was left standing in the three urban areas that supported Japan's war effort—Tokyo-Kawasaki-Yokohama, Nagoya, and Osaka-Kobe. Most of the essential industrial plants in the smaller towns had been damaged or destroyed. The harbors and channels along the Japan Sea and the Inland Sea were closed by mines. Transit of men and goods in and out of Japan and even between the ports of Japan had diminished to little, to what could be carried on small coastal vessels. The system of protection against American air and naval bombing assaults had collapsed and the organization to control fires after incendiary raids was exhausted. The few remaining large air bases were being smashed and cratered. Over eight million people were homeless and dispersed. After a large air raid the absenteeism from work was between seventy and eighty per cent. American airplanes launched from land bases and from naval carriers were able to fly freely over any part of Japan, and shells from our battleships safely cruising within gunfire range of the home islands were compounding the destruction.

Production of weapons and ammunition was falling fast. Vital raw materials were scarce. The small remaining stocks of oil, only about seven per cent of what they had been at the start of the war, were being reserved for use in the battle against the invaders.

The Japanese soldiers and airmen were still being more or less adequately fed; but stocks of rice for civilians were forty per cent less than in 1941, and because of the dwindling supply of rice and other basic foods, the ration was less than 1,500 calories. Before the next harvest and winter there was the worrisome prospect of the end of all imports, the burning of crops in the fields, near famine or famine.

Some elements of combat strength remained to serve the will of those who were still arguing that Japan must continue to stand, fight on, and die. There were over a million and a half men in the Japanese Home Army. Of these, a ground force of about seventeen able and determined divisions were being assembled in Kyushu, but with barely enough oil and ammunition for one great battle. Aircraft production had been sustained better than any other branch of war industry. Thousands of planes, mostly of a sort that could be used only for suicide attacks, were being hoarded—as a special assault armada that was to be launched from hundreds of secret small airstrips in the interior.

[119]

The men around the Imperial Throne would not give in to despair, and continued to look for a chance to retrieve the situation. Some, mainly civilians, clung to the hope that the Soviet government would, if properly rewarded, stay out of the war and act as mediator. Others, the heads of the Japanese military organization that was doomed to extinction, still avowed that they would be able to repel the invasion of Kyushu with great losses to the attacking ships and men, and that when this happened the President and the American military commanders would lose face, and the will of the enemy to accept great losses would break, and thus the American government would be receptive to the idea of a compromise peace.

The governing American officials knew how damaging their air and naval assaults on Japan were, and how awful the plight of the Japanese people was becoming. But rather than await the gradual descent into helplessness which would lead to unconditional submission, they were in a hurry to bring this about as soon as possible. Impatience to end the strain of war blended with a zest for victory. They longed to be done with smashing, burning, killing, dying—and were angry at the defiant, crazed, useless prolongation of the ordeal. The Japanese government had rejected reasonable conditions of peace. This sustained the impression that no matter what the odds the Japanese might fight on in their homeland until death. There was the problem posed by the presence of large Japanese armies on the mainland of Asia and in various islands in the Central and South Pacific; these might continue to resist after the homeland was occupied. And there was the conjunctive desire of the British to regain control of their territories in South-East Asia.

These considerations were thought to add up to the conclusion that the use of any means that would bring the war to a quick end was justified—to save lives of Americans and their allies and to save the Japanese from their pitiable folly. Two measures, long in preparation, were about to be taken: dropping the atomic bomb and the entry into the war of a great new antagonist, the Soviet Union. By this time in fact the impetus of both was so great, and the plans for their execution were so complete, that only a most resolute and courageous act of will—of a kind rarely recorded in history—could have stayed them.

8. The Bomb Is Dropped on Hiroshima

BENEATH the relaxed formalities on board the U.S.S. *Augusta* there was the vibrant secret that an air group at Tinian was under orders to drop an atomic bomb on Japan on the first day in August that the weather permitted visual bombing. This event was awaited with subdued impatience.

The group at Tinian who were in readiness to drop the bomb had been compelled to wait out unfavorable weather over all of Japan during the first days of August. But reconnaissance planes which flew over the target area on the night of the 5th reported back that the prospect for the next day was better. The order was given to the planes to set forth on the historic mission.

At 2:45 on the morning of the 6th by the watches of the crew of the plane, the *Enola Gay*, which was carrying the bomb, started on the long flight from Tinian. It was followed closely by two observation planes which carried cameras, scientific instruments, and trained witnesses. The take-off was dangerous because the bomb load was heavy, and it took skillful piloting to gain the necessary upward lift even from the lengthened runways. Three other B-29's of other air groups had crashed in practice not long before.

The trip to Japan was smooth. Dawn over Japan was sultry but somewhat clear. About 7:00 o'clock (Hiroshima time) the Japanese early-warning radar net detected a small number of air craft headed toward southern Japan, and a preliminary alert was sounded throughout the Hiroshima area. Soon afterwards an American weather plane circled over the city, but withdrew without bombing. So an "all clear" signal was sounded. The people began their daily activities thinking that the danger was passed.

At 8:00 Japanese watchers spotted two B-29's heading toward Hiroshima. The radio stations broadcast a warning advising the people to take shelter if these appeared over the city, adding, however, that the mission seemed to be one of reconnaissance rather than bombing. Most factory and office workers were already at their places of employment and those who were enroute continued on their way. Many school children and some industrial workers were engaged in building fire-breaks and evacuating valuables to the country. The two planes were seen in the skies over the urban area at high altitude. But since many of those below who watched their flight thought the intruders had come merely to reconnoiter, they did not heed the advice to seek protective shelter.

Aboard the *Enola Gay*, the assembly of the bomb had been completed, making it a "final bomb." Colonel Paul W. Tibbets, the pilot, received word from the weather plane near Hiroshima indicating that the chance of placing the bomb on the target was good. "This," to quote the Air Force official history, "sealed the city's doom."[1] The *Enola Gay* swung into its purposeful run-in at 8:11. The bombardier, navigator, and radar operator took charge; the altitude was over 31,600 feet. The bomb was released. It was of the type different from that tested in New Mexico. It was known by its makers and attendants as the Lean Boy or Thin Boy. It contained uranium 235 as its fissionable material enclosed at the opposite ends of a gun barrel. The two sections of material were brought together in the critical mass and exploded by a proximity fuse when a gun mechanism at one end of the barrel shot the smaller of the two parts into the other.[2]

The detonation had been timed to go off before the bomb hit the ground to increase the radius of the blast. There was a terrible explosion over the central section of the city. A white flash of blinding intensity was all that many saw before they were blown to bits or struck down by flying fragments, or burned by the wave of searing heat that flashed out from the explosion. A heavy cloud of smoke and dust spread, cloaking the city in a pall of darkness. Hundreds of fires breaking out everywhere soon transformed it into a blazing inferno and, as the fires kept on, into a waste of ashes and smoldering ruins. Those who had escaped with their lives, many of them burned, in agony and confusion sought refuge elsewhere.

The members of the crew of the *Enola Gay*, on their return to Tinian, had a far-away look in their eyes at the memory of what they had seen and when they tried to talk about it the words fell over one another.[3]

On board the *Augusta*, while the President was at lunch with the crew in the mess hall, a rushed message was handed to him. "Big bomb dropped on Hiroshima August 5 at 7:15 p.m. Washington time. First reports indicate complete success which was even more conspicuous than earlier test." A few minutes later a corroborating report with more details came

---

[1] *The Army Air Forces in World War II, Volume Five. The Pacific: Matterhorn to Nagasaki, June 1944 to August 1945*, page 716. Many of the details about this flight and the bomb drop are derived from the account given on pages 716-717 of this volume.

[2] Groves' letter, *Science Magazine*, December 4, 1959. Article by William L. Laurence in *New York Times*, August 7, 1960.

[3] Interview with Admiral William R. Purnell, Navy representative on the Committee on the Military Uses of the Atomic Bomb, quoted in the *New York Times* of August 20, 1945.

in. After reading these messages to Byrnes, he signaled to the men that he wanted them to listen to news he had just received. Leaving them clapping and cheering, he went to the wardroom to tell the naval officers of the great exploit. "I could not," he has recalled, "keep back my expectation that the Pacific War might now be brought to a speedy end."[4]

In Washington, August 6th was rainy. As soon as Marshall got word the bomb had gone off, he telephoned Stimson who was at his home on Long Island. The President and the Secretary of War authorized the issuance to the press of the prepared statements. The tenor of these had been made more ominous after receipt of the reports of the New Mexico test. Presumably the involved British officials, possibly Churchill himself, were consulted about the final changes, since during the whole process of composition they had been given ample opportunity to comment and propose amendments.

The one over Truman's name made known that an atomic bomb had been dropped on the city of Hiroshima, an important Army base; and that it had more explosive power than twenty thousand tons of TNT. "It is an atomic bomb. It is a harnessing of the basic power of the universe. The force from which the sun draws its power has been loosed against those who brought war to the Far East."

Astounded and awed, the world read on to the closing lines: "It was to spare the Japanese people from utter destruction that the ultimatum of July 26 was issued at Potsdam. Their leaders promptly rejected that ultimatum. If they do not now accept our terms, they may expect a rain of ruin from the air, the like of which has never been seen on this earth. Behind this air attack will follow sea and land forces in such numbers and power as they have not yet seen, and with the fighting skill of which they are already well aware."

The President also used this most dramatic circumstance to tell the world how the American government proposed to deal with the new force which had been broken out of the atom, saying in part:

"It has never been the habit of the scientists of this country or the policy of this Government to withhold from the world scientific knowledge. Normally, therefore, everything about the work with atomic energy would be made public.

"But under present circumstances it is not intended to divulge the terminal processes of production or all the military applications, pending

[4] *Year of Decisions*, pages 421-422, and *Speaking Frankly*, page 264.

further examination of possible methods of protecting us and the rest of the world from the danger of sudden destruction.

"I shall recommend that the Congress of the United States consider promptly the establishment of an appropriate commission to control the production and use of atomic power within the United States. I shall give further consideration and make further recommendations to the Congress as to how atomic power can become a powerful and forceful influence toward the maintenance of world peace."[5]

Stimson, revealing the vast undertaking which had been conducted with such guarded care, reviewed the effort on the part of science, industry, and government that had culminated in the production of the bomb. The new military weapon, he solemnly stressed, had an explosive force which staggered the imagination. Improvements in sight, he predicted, would increase its effectiveness several fold. "But more important for the long range implications of this new weapon is the possibility that another scale of magnitude will be evolved after considerable research and development."[6]

[5] The text of the statement issued by the White House on August 6 is in Potsdam Papers, Document 1315.
[6] Statement by the Secretary of War (Stimson) August 6, 1945.

9. The Calendar of Days before the Surrender

A U G U S T 7 - 8

ON THE afternoon of August 7th the Foreign Minister, Togo, informed the Cabinet of the statements which Truman and Stimson had issued about the bomb, and the War and Home Ministers presented preliminary reports on the destruction at Hiroshima.

All that the morning papers on the 8th (Tokyo time) told the Japanese people was that Hiroshima had been "considerably" damaged by "a new-type bomb." But later that day Togo, with Suzuki's approval, advised the Emperor that the atomic bomb would revolutionize warfare and that more would be dropped on Japanese cities unless the Potsdam offer was accepted. The Emperor agreed that no time should be lost in seeking an end to the war. However, when the Prime Minister tried to convoke an immediate meeting of the Supreme Council, some of the military members said they could not be present. While the Japanese authorities were thus wasting their last slim chance to ward them off, the next blows against them were set in motion.

The U.S.S. *Augusta*, completing a record run, put into Chesapeake Bay on the afternoon of the 7th (Washington time) and the President was back in the White House by 11 p.m., the Potsdam journey over. Truman in his *Memoirs*, after telling of the reception of his statement about the drop on Hiroshima which had been given out in Washington, wrote, "Still no surrender offer came. An order was issued to General Spaatz to continue operations as planned unless otherwise instructed."[1] If such an order was sent, it was intended as a confirmation of authority to drop a *second* bomb. But the President in a letter to the authors of the official history of the Army Air Force, reproduced by them, stated that the order to drop the first bomb was given by him only after Japan rejected the Potsdam Declaration; and he repeated this avowal later; and Admiral Samuel Eliot Morison gave it professional diffusion in his naval history.[2] But almost certainly Truman's memory tricked him.[2a]

---

[1] *Year of Decisions*, page 423.

[2] Morison wrote, "Not until after the [Potsdam] Conference had broken up with no further word from Tokyo, when President Truman was at sea on board the *U.S.S. Augusta*, did he give the final order to drop the bomb on two Japanese cities." *History of U.S. Naval Operations in the Pacific*, Vol. XIV, page 352.

[2a] Any such order was unnecessary because of the terms of the order to Spaatz on July 25th. (See page 91 of this book.) And no copy of this order has been found in the files of the War Department or of the Manhattan Project, or of messages sent from the *Augusta*. See Morison's review of *Japan Subdued* in *American Historical Review*, October 1961, and my letter in the *American Historical Review*, October 1962.

In the forenoon of the 8th (Washington time), presumably with the knowledge that the other bomb was about to be thrown into the balance of battle, Stimson showed the President a report from headquarters of the Strategic Air Force on Guam on the extent of the damage wrought by the first atomic bomb, and also reports from Tokyo and Air Force photographs showing the area and thoroughness of the destruction. Truman had somberly remarked that such destruction placed a terrible responsibility upon himself and the War Department. Stimson, oppressed by the need to cause the Japanese to suffer more in order to compel them to accept their fate, urged that we ought to make it as easy as possible for the Japanese to accept our terms for surrender. He also advocated a measure of leniency in dealing with the Japanese after they had submitted. The American government, he told the President, ought to recognize the difference between the Japanese and Germans and treat them differently. He thought it important to show tact in dealing with the Japanese, since they were naturally a smiling people and if you wanted to get on good terms with them it was best to show kindness. When the Secretary repeated this observation to General Marshall, the Chief of Staff told him that General MacArthur was inclined to follow this policy.

Even as they were talking the crews of the B-29's on Tinian that were to carry the second atomic bomb were completing their last minute preparations for their mission.

The Soviet government was poised to throw its forces against the Japanese armies in Manchuria and Korea. Stalin and Soong were still at odds over some elements in the Sino-Soviet accord about which they had resumed talks. But the Soviet government did not wait, as Stalin and Molotov had repeatedly said it would, for Chinese concurrence in the Yalta accord, before plunging into the war. The Red Armies were hurried to be in at the kill. At 5:00 in the afternoon of the 8th (Moscow time), Molotov summoned the Japanese Ambassador. Sato hopefully thought he was going to get at long last a response to the Japanese petition to receive the special envoy from the Emperor, Konoye. But Molotov, with wooden face and abrupt manner, gave him a statement which ended in the affirmation that "In view of the foregoing the Soviet government declares that as of tomorrow, that is of 9 August, the Soviet Union will consider it is in a state of war with Japan."

The explanation of this action was so phrased as to make it appear that it was being taken in response to an allied request after Japan had rejected the Potsdam Declaration, and in accord with the obligation of the Soviet government to its allies and to the United Nations. This was a false and deceptive explanation.

An hour or two later, Molotov asked the American and British Ambassadors, Harriman and Clark Kerr, to call. After reading to them the statement given Sato, he tried to make sure that the timing of the entry should be regarded as a simple matter of good faith. He called attention to the fact that the Soviet troops would go into action against the Japanese almost precisely three months after the surrender of Germany. At one time, he added, he thought this step could not be taken until the middle of August, but now the Soviet government was living strictly up to its original promise.

That night after dinner Harriman and Kennan saw Stalin. The Generalissimo told them that the first Soviet units had already crossed the frontiers of Manchuria from west and east, that they had already gone forward ten or twelve kilometers in some sections, and that the main armies were entering Manchuria as they talked. Jovially he remarked how much better the course of the war in the Pacific was going than he had anticipated; he had not known what successes the American Navy would have in the Pacific. "Who would have thought," he asked, "that things would have progressed so far by this time?"

Harriman, not ingenuously, asked Stalin what effect he thought the news of the atomic bomb would have on the Japanese. Stalin answered that he believed that they were looking for a pretext to get rid of their government and to replace it with one that would be qualified to arrange a surrender; the bomb might give them that pretext. Harriman remarked that it was a good thing that their side had invented this weapon and not the Germans; that no one had dared think that it would be a success; and that the President had learned that it would work successfully only a few days before he told Stalin about it. Stalin was—or pretended to be—impressed; the Soviet scientists, he remarked, had told him that it was a very hard problem to work out. Harriman said that if the allies could keep it and apply it for peaceful purposes, it would be a good thing. Stalin assented, saying that it would mean the end of war and aggressors—but the secret would have to be well kept. He then went on to tell the Ambassador that the Red Army had found one laboratory in Germany where the Germans had been working on the same problem and without result. If they had found out how to make the weapon Hitler would never have surrendered. Even England, Stalin continued, although it had excellent physicists, had gotten nowhere with its research in this field. Harriman explained that the British had pooled their knowledge with us since 1941, but that it had required enormous installations to conduct the experiments and to achieve the results—and an expenditure of over two billions of dollars.[8]

The first message from Harriman informing the President of the hastened Soviet action arrived in the early afternoon. Truman, in one of the shortest appearances of the sort on record, told the representatives of press and radio, "I have only a simple announcement to make. I can't hold a regular press conference today, but this announcement is so important I thought I would like to call you in. Russia has declared war on Japan. That is all."

Senator Alexander Wiley of Wisconsin was reported to have said, when told of the news, "Apparently the atomic bomb which hit Hiroshima also blew 'Joey' off the fence."[4]

AUGUST 9-10-11

At about eleven o'clock on the morning of the 9th (Tokyo time) an atomic bomb fell upon Nagasaki, on the west coast of the southern island of Kyushu.[5]

The same preliminary measures were taken for the second bomb launching as for the first. But it did not go so smoothly. Kokura had been selected as the best target. The plane with the bomb traversed the skies over that city three times without getting a glimpse of it through the clouds. So, with fuel running low, the pilot flew on to the next on the list, Nagasaki, some eighty miles to the southwest. Just as he was ending his first run over the city, the clouds broke and Nagasaki stood

[8] Memo, Stalin-Harriman talk, August 8th. The historian cannot be sure whether the impression derived from this memo that both Stalin and Harriman were taking polite refuge from their innermost thoughts in the harbor of what could be safely expressed, is in accord with the actual character of the conversation or due to the somewhat stilted and condensed record contained in the memo. Would the Soviet government please oblige by publishing its version?

[4] *New York Times*, August 9, 1945.

[5] William L. Laurence, the correspondent of the *New York Times*, who was in Tinian, wrote in his book *Dawn Over Zero*, that General Farrell, who was General Groves' deputy in Tinian for the atomic bomb operation, told him on the evening of the 6th, just before the planes set off for Hiroshima, that the second atomic bombing mission was scheduled for August 11; and that because of forecasts of bad weather on that date the mission was advanced by two days. Laurence dryly comments that "It is quite possible, though I have no direct knowledge of it, that the forecasts of bad weather came all the way from Potsdam." Spaatz and Groves knew that all their colleagues, military and civil, were eager to strike the second blow as quickly as possible to get the most impressive effect and hasten the surrender. Groves was in constant contact with his deputy in Tinian, General Farrell. Subsequently Farrell told Groves that he discerned in Groves' messages an urgent wish to have the second bomb dropped as soon after the first one as possible; and so he, Farrell, decided to rush and risk the attack on the 9th rather than wait out the forecasted worse weather.

out clearly in the daylight. The bomb was dropped. It was the implosion, plutonium-using type that had been tested in New Mexico, not that which had fallen on Hiroshima. It fell four miles away from the heart of the city, exploding, as it happened, on an industrial center beyond the target area, but only an easy walk around the bay to the harbor hillside where the house and garden of Madame Butterfly still stands.

Stimson had determined that this second atomic strike was necessary to enable the Emperor and those of his advisers who wanted to surrender to overcome the opposition. Thus behind the grim satisfaction with which he read the rushed report of the results of the drop on Nagasaki was the hope that his mission was "accomplished," and that there would be no need to use the third bomb which was about to be shipped to Tinian.[6] He urged Byrnes to treat the Japanese sympathetically if they showed any disposition to surrender, and to make it as easy as possible for them.

The Secretary of War went over to the White House along with Groves, Bush, and Conant, scientific members of the Interim Committee, in order that the President might hear the arguments for and against the publication of the long report by scientists telling of the development of the bomb.[6a] These three had been strongly in favor of issuing

[6] General Spaatz had asked for permission to make an atomic attack on Tokyo when another bomb was available. Craven and Cate, *op.cit.*, page 730.

[6a] In a memo which General Groves sent to General Marshall on August 6th to keep him informed of the various statements that were to be released after the fall of the bomb on Japan, he said: "Within forty-eight hours thereafter we expect to issue a scientific release. This was prepared under my direction by a competent scientist. This release . . . might shorten, by at most one to two months, the time it would take to duplicate our work, which time I estimate at no less than five years and probably well over ten. This release has been formally assented to by the British but the Secretary desires that its issuance be cleared in advance by the President. In my opinion, it is essential that this release be made promptly if we are to have any hope of success in our efforts to retain the maximum amount of secrecy in our work."

Their reserve about the publication of the Smyth Report may have had some validity. Professor Heinz Barwich, a German physicist who voluntarily went to Russia in 1945 and worked for ten years in one of the Soviet laboratories, then became the Director of the Institute for Nuclear Research in Rossendorf, East Germany, and who defected to the United States in 1964, so attested.

He said that his particular task was to separate the uranium isotopes and to devise a method for producing U-235 on a large scale. He was asked whether they tried a different method from the one used in America (the Barrier method) for separating U-235, and answered, "We had to try every idea which we had. The Barrier method was the only one established to be possible. . . . Other methods were . . . not yet clear. Until the Smyth Report, nothing was clear, and after the Smyth Report everything was clear. . . . For instance, after the Smyth Report we heard about failure in thermal diffusions, in liquid UF. This was reported in the Smyth Report. . . ."

Mr. Sourwine: "You found the Smyth Report valuable, did you?"

Mr. Barwich: "I think it was very valuable for Russia."

Nuclear Scientist Defects to the United States. Hearing before the Sub-Committee to investigate the administration of the Internal Security Act of the Committee on the Judiciary, U.S. Senate, December 15, 1964, page 11.

it at once; but the British scientific member of the Combined Policy Committee, Chadwick, had been dubious; and Stimson had wavered. In talk with the President a day before, Stimson had assured him that all care had been taken not to give away any secret which would really help a rival to build on our originating work. He explained that he was swayed by Groves' opinion, but since the bomb had been used he had the impression that the public attitude had changed and he no longer felt it essential to give out the report at once. Stimson and Byrnes, who was present, allowed their experienced scientific associates in the atomic bomb project to have the lead. They explained why they thought that the publication of the controlled study would prevent harm that might result from reckless and excited versions which were sure to circulate if the subject was shrouded in deep secrecy. The President said he was convinced, and approved immediate issuance of the report.

The President, in the course of a radio report that night on the results of the Potsdam Conference, said, "I realize the tragic significance of the atomic bomb"; and then later on, "Having found the bomb we have used it. We have used it against those who attacked us without warning at Pearl Harbor, against those who have starved and beaten and executed American prisoners of war, against those who have abandoned all pretense of obeying international laws of warfare. We have used it in order to shorten the agony of young Americans. We shall continue to use it until we completely destroy Japan's power to make war. Only a Japanese surrender will stop us."[7]

In this determination all but a very few Americans were with him, certainly all of the men in uniform and their families.

When the Supreme War Direction Council gathered at the Imperial Palace late that same morning of the 9th—as it was in Tokyo—the members had the grave knowledge that the Soviet Union had declared war, a Tass broadcast having been intercepted. Then soon after their talks began, they learned that another atomic bomb had been dropped on Nagasaki.

There was no respite or refuge left anywhere in Japan. The stricken cities of Hiroshima and Nagasaki were still under heavy clouds of dust. The three-prong advance of the Red Army through Manchuria, sluggish at first, was revealing its superiority over the weakened Kwantung Army. Relentlessly, huge daytime flights of fighters and bombers were flying

[7] This address was probably prepared before the news had been received of the bombing of Nagasaki. Its text is in Department of State *Bulletin*, August 12, 1945.

at chimney-top level over Kyushu, and over Japan's "Little Ruhr" area around Yawata, smashing what was left of the iron and steel and chemical industries. Planes from the carriers of the Third Fleet were assailing all settlements on Northern Honshu, and American naval vessels, having moved in close, were sending salvo after salvo along the northeast coast of that main island. Millions of leaflets were being dropped to convince the Japanese that their cause was hopeless. Every allied radio facility broadcast over and over the "quit or die" message.

But the Japanese government was unable to act until the Emperor imposed his will upon the military leaders. For them surrender meant at least humiliation and loss of career, at most disgrace and condign punishment—death.

At this tense and disputatious meeting of the Supreme Council, Suzuki proposed that the allies be informed at once that Japan accepted the Potsdam Declaration, provided it was assured that it would not endanger the national polity or mean the suppression of the Imperial Family. The Minister of War and Chief of the Army General Staff said they would not yield so abjectly, and insisted that the Japanese government must attach three other conditions to its acceptance: that the Japanese military forces should be allowed to disarm and demobilize themselves; that there be no allied occupation of Japan; and that all war criminals were to be prosecuted by the Japanese government itself. In the face of the pleas of the Prime Minister, the Foreign Minister, and the Navy Minister, they maintained that the real test of Japan's power to resist was still ahead, and that when the enemy invasion force suffered severe casualties the war could be ended on better terms.[8]

The grim and protracted debate, first in the Supreme Council and then in the Cabinet, went on until almost midnight, and then was resumed at a meeting of the Council with the Emperor in an air raid shelter deep inside the Imperial Palace. Once more in the Imperial presence the War Minister argued that all four conditions were essential since unqualified acceptance of the Potsdam terms would result in national ruin. The Chiefs of the Army and Navy Staff stood by him, once more expressing the belief that Japan could get better terms, and warning that if the government surrendered on the basis of the Potsdam Declaration, chaos would follow. The hours of argument had only accentuated the difference. The Prime Minister at 2:00 o'clock in the morning

[8] Their faction was supported at a Cabinet Meeting later that day by the Home Minister, Genki Abe, and the Minister of Justice, Hiromasa Matsuzaka.

stepped forward, and in an act unprecedented in modern Japanese history asked the Emperor to decide.[9]

The issuance of an absolute command by the Emperor was known among the Japanese as the Voice of the Sacred Crane. This was a reference to an old saying that even when the crane was hidden from sight its voice was heard from the skies. At last the Voice of the Sacred Crane was heard. Remaining seated and speaking softly, the Emperor said that he was in complete accord with the views of the Foreign Minister: to end the war upon the terms of the Declaration on one sole condition— on the understanding that the allied demand would not prejudice the prerogatives of the Emperor as a sovereign ruler. To continue to fight, he averred, would be suicidal; to end the war this way was the only way to save the nation from destruction. Turning to the military men, he remarked that their performance had been far short of their promises. He was deeply aware of the feelings of the sorrowing families of those who had died in the war, and of the very great sacrifices made by all those who had fought and served in the war—but there was now no choice for him or the nation.

All members of the Council bowed to the imperial will. The Cabinet unanimously approved the decision before its weary members separated at 4:00 o'clock in the morning (of the 10th, Tokyo time) for their short rest. At 7:00 the Foreign Office transmitted the message of submission to the American, British, and Soviet governments through the Swiss and Swedish governments. "The Japanese government," it stated, "are ready to accept the terms enumerated in the Joint Declaration which was issued at Potsdam on July 26th . . . with the understanding that the said declaration does not comprise any demand which prejudices the prerogatives of His Majesty as a Sovereign Ruler."

The Cabinet was afraid of a revolt in the armed forces. So it was decided that no announcement of the negotiations would be made until an Imperial Rescript proclaiming Japan's acceptance was issued. The interval was to be used to direct the nation toward peace obliquely and gradually.

Early on the morning of the 10th in Washington American radio monitors picked up the message which had been sent from Tokyo to the Japanese Ministers at Berne and Stockholm.

[9] The Prime Minister, Suzuki, and the Lord Privy Seal, Marquis Kido, had been assured by the Emperor before the conference that he was ready to issue an imperial order as soon as the government wished him to do so. See the account by Mamoru Shigemitsu, former Foreign Minister, *Showa: Years of Upheaval*, page 360.

The President summoned Stimson, Forrestal, Byrnes, and Leahy to the White House before nine o'clock. He asked each whether he thought this message ought to be treated as an acceptance of the Potsdam Declaration, an unconditional surrender of the type we had sought. Stimson spoke up vigorously in favor of a reply which would make clear that the Japanese could retain the Emperor. Byrnes remained hesitant, recalling the public statements that had been made by both Roosevelt and Churchill which had so definitely specified that surrender would have to be unconditional. The Secretary of State thought another reason why we could not immediately assent to the Japanese proposal was that since the British and Chinese governments had concurred in the Potsdam Declaration we could not depart from it without consulting them. The discussion was adjourned until the official version of the message was received.

Stimson went back to the War Department and Byrnes returned to the State Department. Stimson talked with Marshall and his civilian aides and they started to draft terms of surrender to be included in the answer to the Japanese government. McCloy thought that this would be a fine chance to introduce the elements of a democratic government into Japan. But Stimson did not favor the idea. He believed that our response should be simple and aimed to bring about the surrender just as soon as possible, and so not allow Soviet claims for a share in the occupation and control of Japan to gain validity with the advance of the Red Army.

Concurrently a reply was written in the State Department. It was responsive to the Japanese request for assurances about the Emperor. Grew had urged Byrnes also to spare the Emperor the necessity of having to sign the surrender terms personally; Byrnes rejected the suggestion; but he adopted it when the British government put it forward.[9a] Various important indications of what would be required of the Japanese government after acceptance of the Potsdam Declaration were introduced into the reply. By indirection it was the determination of the American government to entrust the execution of the surrender terms to one supreme commander—and one only. The Supreme Commander was signified.

When Byrnes read its text to Stimson, the Secretary of War thought it wise and careful and more likely to secure acceptance than the one written in the War Department. Forrestal agreed. Thereupon, with the whole

---

[9a] The reply was based on a draft by Cohen. Byrnes did not solicit Grew's advice or assistance, but the latter mastered his pride and twice opened the door between his offices and Byrnes' to say he thought he and some other members of the Department could be helpful. Byrnes allowed him to bring Dooman and Ballantine to join the discussion.

Cabinet in accord, the President approved it. The proposed answer, addressed to the Swiss Chargé d'Affaires, read:

"With regard to the Japanese Government's message accepting the terms of the Potsdam proclamation but containing the statement 'with the understanding that the said declaration does not comprise any demand which prejudices the prerogatives of His Majesty as a sovereign ruler,' our position is as follows:

"From the moment of surrender the authority of the Emperor and the Japanese Government to rule the state shall be subject to the Supreme Commander of the Allied Powers who will take such steps as he deems proper to effectuate the surrender terms.

"The Emperor and the Japanese High Command will be required to sign the surrender terms necessary to carry out the provisions of the Potsdam Declaration, to issue orders to all the armed forces of Japan to cease hostilities and to surrender their arms, and to issue such other orders as the Supreme Commander may require to give effect to the surrender terms.

"Immediately upon the surrender the Japanese Government shall transport prisoners of war and civilian internees to places of safety, as directed, where they can quickly be placed aboard Allied transports.

"The ultimate form of government of Japan shall, in accordance with the Potsdam Declaration, be established by the freely expressed will of the Japanese people.

"The armed forces of the Allied Powers will remain in Japan until the purposes set forth in the Potsdam Declaration are achieved."

Messages were hurried out at once to our Embassies in London, Moscow, and Chunking, instructing them to secure quick approval of this reply.

The British government hastened to say that it thought our proposed reply was satisfactory except in one respect. Attlee and Bevin were of the opinion that it was not advisable to ask the Emperor personally to sign the surrender terms. They proposed that this passage be amended as follows:

"The Emperor shall authorize and ensure the signature by the Government of Japan and the Japanese General Headquarters of the surrender terms necessary to carry out the provisions of the Potsdam Declaration, and shall issue his commands to all the Japanese, military, naval and air authorities and to all the forces under their control wherever located to cease active operations and to surrender their arms, and to issue such other orders as the Supreme Commander may require to give effect to the surrender terms."

Churchill also liked the proposed reply, with this one change. The American officials and the President at once adopted the suggestion.

No one was sure how the Soviet government would respond. If it delayed or objected, the President was disposed to go ahead anyway and send our answer to Tokyo and act upon it.[10]

The Soviet government, it turned out, did not miss any element of significance in the text to which it, the newcomer in the war, was being asked to subscribe. Around midnight of the 10th (Moscow time) Harriman and Clark Kerr, the British Ambassador in Moscow, were seeing Molotov at his request.[11] The Secretary of State for Foreign Affairs had called them in to inform them that because of a delay in transmission, the Soviet Ambassador in Tokyo had not been able to deliver the Soviet declaration of war to the Japanese government until the morning of the 10th; that when he did so, the Japanese Minister of War [the Foreign Minister?] had given him a statement similar to that transmitted to the governments of the United States, England, and China.[12] Molotov remarked that the Soviet attitude toward the Japanese response to the Potsdam Declaration was "skeptical," since by making conditions in regard to the Emperor it was neither unconditional nor concrete. He said that the Soviet government intended in turn to give its answer by continuing to advance in Manchuria, the Red Army having already moved forward about 170 kilometers. To Harriman it seemed that Molotov was giving every indication that the Soviet government was willing to have the war continue.

The talk was at this turn when Kennan appeared, having hurried over from the Embassy with a copy of the answer which the American government wanted to send to Tokyo and a message expressing the hope that the Soviet government would associate itself with it. Harriman explained the reason why we were replying in this sense was that the American government thought that only the Emperor could issue effective orders that would cause the Japanese troops everywhere to stop fighting at once. Molotov appeared to agree with this observation. But

[10] *Forrestal Diaries,* August 10, 1945.

[11] Memo, conversation Harriman and Clark Kerr with Molotov, August 10-11. Subject: Japanese Surrender Negotiations. Truman in *Year of Decisions,* pages 430-431, has recorded Harriman's report of this conversation virtually in full.

[12] Togo in his book of memoirs, *The Cause of Japan,* page 322, explains the cause of the delay differently, relating that when Ambassador Malik requested an interview on the 9th he, Togo, had been unable to receive him because of his preoccupation with important conferences.

when Harriman went on to emphasize the wish of the American government to transmit this answer to Japan as quickly as possible in order to end the war and save lives, Molotov's first response was temporizing. He said he would let Harriman know the opinion of the Soviet government the following day. But Harriman, guided by the tone of the message from Washington, insisted that the American government would have to have an answer that same night (or rather before daylight came). Molotov said he would see if he could get one.

At 2:00 a.m. on the 11th (Moscow time) he asked Harriman and Clark Kerr to call again. He then read them a statement signed by himself.

"The Soviet Government considers that the above mentioned reply should be presented in the name of the principal powers waging war with Japan.

"The Soviet Government also considers that, in case of an affirmative reply from the Japanese Government, the Allied powers *should* (or *must*) reach an agreement on the candidacy or candidacies for representation of the Allied High Command to which the Japanese Emperor and the Japanese Government are to be subordinated."[13]

Harriman asked what this meant. Molotov answered that since there was not a combined command in the Far East, it would be necessary to reach an agreement as to which allied representative or representatives would deal with the Japanese. He proposed that the American government should make some suggestion and the allies could subsequently agree as to who the Supreme Commander was to be. Harriman said this would give the Soviet government a chance to veto the choice of the Commander; that was utterly out of the question, and he knew the American government would not agree to it. He proceeded to ask Molotov whether the Soviet government would be willing to have MacArthur as Supreme Commander. Molotov said he thought so but he would have to consult his colleagues. Harriman remarked that an agreement whereby the United States would undertake to consult its allies regarding the choice of the Commander was one thing, but as the Soviet answer read, it seemed to mean that the Soviet government was asking for a right to veto the selection. Thus it was only a qualified approval, which he was sure would not be acceptable to the American government. Molotov remarked it was conceivable that there might be

---

[13] The Russian translator (Pavlov) in reading the English version translated this to read: "the Allied Powers *must* reach an agreement." (my italics) The Russian word may have either meaning.

two Supreme Commanders: MacArthur and Vasilevski. Harriman said that was "absolutely inadmissible."

Molotov turned brusque. He asked Harriman to send the Soviet answer to Washington whether he liked it or not. Harriman said that he would do so, but pointed out that the United States had carried the main burden of the Pacific war for four years, keeping Japan off the back of the Soviet Union, while the Soviet Union had only been in the war for about two days. So it was only just that the Soviet government should let the American government choose the Supreme Commander, and it was unthinkable that he could be other than American. Molotov asked Harriman again and more sternly to send on the Soviet answer to Washington, no matter what he thought.

Harriman returned to his office at the Embassy with the intention of doing so. But before his message was written and coded the interpreter, Pavlov, telephoned him. He said that Molotov had talked with Stalin— and there had been a misunderstanding; the Soviet government had intended to suggest only that there should be "consultation" before the selection of a Supreme Commander, not a requirement for "reaching an agreement." Therefore the Soviet government was willing to have an appropriate change in the wording of its answer to the American government. Harriman expressed satisfaction, but he said he also thought the phrase in the Soviet answer "or candidacies" would also be found objectionable in Washington and he asked Pavlov to tell this to Molotov. A few minutes later Pavlov telephoned Harriman again and said that this phrase might also be struck out of the Soviet answer.

Whereupon Harriman hurried the Soviet answer to Washington. The final paragraph read, "The Soviet Government also considers that, in the case of an affirmative reply from the Japanese Government, the Allied Powers should consult on the candidacy for representation of the Allied High Command to which the Japanese Emperor and the Japanese Government are to be subordinated."

Truman at the end of his subsequent account of these talks with Molotov succinctly wrote: "Harriman was, of course, expressing our set policy. The State, War and Navy Co-ordinating Committee had some time ago formulated our position on the post-war control of Japan, and I had approved it. We wanted Japan controlled by an American Commander, acting on behalf of the Allies. . . . I was determined that the Japanese occupation should not follow in the footsteps of the German experience. I did not want divided control or separate zones."[14]

[14] *Year of Decisions*, pages 431-432.

The Chinese government made known its concurrence with enthusiastic comment.

Thus the American government was in a position by the morning of the 11th to send along its response to the Japanese government and did so. Truman was not persuaded by Stimson and Forrestal simultaneously to suspend air and naval action against Japan, as a humane act and one that would appeal to the Japanese people. The President said that he thought it best to keep up the war in all its intensity so as to allow no letup which might cause the Japanese to attempt to bargain further. But he did agree that we should not use any other atomic weapon in the interval.[15]

The *New York Times* on the next morning captioned its report on the jubilant reaction of the American fighting men in the Pacific to the news: "GI's in Pacific Go Wild With Joy; 'Let 'Em Keep Emperor,' They Say."

But the Japanese people were not yet aware of the step taken by their government to seek peace.

The morning papers in Japan (August 11 in Tokyo) carried an appeal over the name of the President of the Board of Information. The last veiled sentences read, "In truth we cannot but recognize that we are now beset with the worst possible situation. Just as the government is exerting its utmost effort to defend the homeland, safeguard the polity, and preserve the honor of the nation, so too must the people rise to the occasion and overcome all manner of difficulties in order to protect the polity of their Empire."

Its vagueness and sponsorship reflected fear of revolt by military elements or of assassination. So deceptive was this language that most readers took it as another call to fight to the death. How could they not when in the adjoining column of the same newspapers there was a statement in the name of the War Minister which was directly contrary to the spirit and intent of the decision that had been made by the Cabinet at dawn of the day before.

Here is its text:

"Instructions to all officers and men of the Army:

"The Soviet Union has finally taken up arms against this Empire. Try as she may to disguise the facts by rhetoric, her aspirations to conquer and dominate Greater East Asia are obvious. In the face of this

---

[15] *Forrestal Diaries*, August 10, 1945.

reality we shall waste no words. The only thing for us to do is to fight doggedly to the end in this holy war for the defense of our divine land.

"It is our firm belief that though it may mean chewing grass, eating dirt, and sleeping in the field, a resolute fight will surely reveal a way out of a desperate situation. . . ."

"Minister of War."

The Americans waited with strained excitement to learn whether our indication that the Emperor was to be spared would enable the end-of-the-war elements in the Japanese government to prevail over the more fanatical. "Never," Secretary Byrnes recalled, "have I known time to pass so slowly!"[16] The hours were spent in completing the orders and statements that would be issued when and as soon as Japan surrendered.

AUGUST 12

Very early in the morning the Japanese Foreign Office intercepted an American short-wave broadcast from San Francisco which revealed the allied reply to the Japanese offer to surrender.

The dispute among the Japanese officials and senior advisers around the Throne was renewed in full intensity. The chiefs of the Army and Navy General Staffs, General Umezu and Admiral Toyoda, went over to the Imperial Palace together and pleaded with the Emperor to reject the allied terms. They argued that Japan would be reduced to vassalage and the Emperor to a subordinate position; they predicted that acceptance would invite internal disorder and result ultimately in the removal of the Imperial Family. The Foreign Minister and his staff construed our response more favorably. After getting the Emperor's support for acceptance of Byrnes' reply, Togo went on to persuade Suzuki that it meant that the allies intended to respect the Emperor and allow him to remain as supreme head of the Japanese polity and nation.

Undeterred by the pleas of the High Command, the Emperor called together at the Palace in the afternoon the imperial princes and the families of the princes to solicit their support for his determination to make peace. While they convened the Cabinet was having another of its anguished sessions. Togo bore the brunt of the opposition, standing fast on his judgment that although the allied terms were harsh, even odious, it would be dangerous to delay acceptance by asking for clarification; the allies could interpret this act as a sign of Japan's intention to break off negotiations; or it might cause those elements in the allied

---

[16] *All in One Lifetime*, page 306.

government who were opposed to the retention of the Imperial system to prevail. The same Ministers, led on by the Secretary of War, who had previously wanted to attach various conditions to Japan's acceptance, denied Togo's interpretation. Disconcertingly the Prime Minister, Suzuki, vacillated—going so far as to avow that there was no alternative to continuing the war.

Using as reason the fact that the formal allied reply had not yet been received, Togo managed to have the Cabinet meeting adjourned. During the night hours the beset Prime Minister had been prevailed upon to fall in with Togo's views of the allied terms and to go ahead and accept them. Meanwhile, the official text of the allied response which had arrived in Tokyo just as the Cabinet meeting was ending, was held in secrecy at the personal order of the Vice-Minister of Foreign Affairs, Shumichi Matsumato, in order to allow tempers to cool off and give the Foreign Office time to develop new arguments why it should be accepted. The delay in the announcement of receipt of our reply by the Japanese official agencies puzzled Grew.

In the United States, this Sunday was another day of anxious waiting. Press and radio reporters swarmed through the Executive offices and large crowds drifted by the gates of the White House.

All branches of the American government worked late into the night to get ready for the expected and glad event. The President instructed Harriman to inform Stalin of the arrangements for the acceptance of the surrender of Japan which Washington was determining. Harriman did so by way of a letter to Molotov which explained those features of our plans of most direct concern to the Soviet government. They were:

That General MacArthur be designated as Supreme Commander for the Allied Powers to accept, coordinate, and carry into effect the general surrender of the Japanese Armed Forces.

That if Stalin would designate the officer whom he wanted to represent the Soviet Union the President would instruct MacArthur to make arrangements necessary for him at the time and place of surrender.

That it was contemplated that MacArthur would direct the Japanese Imperial General Headquarters to have the Japanese forces "in your [the Soviet] area of operations" surrender unconditionally to the Soviet High Commander in the Far East. There was not, it may be remarked in passing, any explicit understanding about the limits of the Soviet area of operations on land.

"I am assuming," the President added, "that you [Stalin] are in general accord with the above procedure and am issuing preliminary instructions to General MacArthur to this effect." Truman correctly surmised that whether he liked it or not, Stalin would have to assent. He did so at once, and named General Derevyanko as representative of the Soviet High Command.

AUGUST 13

Three full days had gone by since the Japanese government, under the shock of the atomic bomb and the Soviet entry into the war, had stated that it would surrender under the terms of the Potsdam Declaration if the authority and dignity of the Emperor were not impaired. Though the Japanese people on each of these days were subjected to great suffering, and the fact that they would not be able to sustain effective resistance was displayed by every burning or smashed town, those who thought it imperative to bring the ordeal to an end were still being checked, and the agony of decision in Japan continued.

In the sessions of the Supreme War Council and the Cabinet which followed each other on the 13th (Tokyo time) the Minister of War and the Chiefs of Staff of the Army and Navy were even more obdurate in their contention that the allies must be told that the Emperor could not be subjected to their orders, and that Japan should not be compelled to submit the form of its government to the will of the people. The group supporting the Foreign Minister answered as before with the statement that the Emperor's prerogatives would be affected only in those matters that came within the surrender terms, and that in any event the loyal Japanese people could not be coerced into renouncing the Imperial institution.

Late in the evening the Chiefs of the Operations Sections of the Army and Navy General Staff and the Chief of the Military Affairs Section of the War Ministry agreed that one of their senior admirals (Onishi) should appeal to Prince Takamatsu to urge Navy Minister Yonai and Admiral of the Fleet Nagano not to yield. He went off on that errand at midnight. Prince Takamatsu refused, since neither the Army or Navy had a definite or realistic plan to strike the enemy a telling blow.

Truman and Byrnes let it be known to their associates that their patience was running out. But they remained confident that the incessant discussion that was going on in Tokyo, of which fragmentary indications were learned from the Japanese radio, would end in submission.

Truman went ahead and sent the first important directive to Mac-Arthur, as Supreme Commander for the Allied Powers.

He was told to require the Emperor to issue a proclamation, the text of which had been written in Washington, authorizing his representatives to sign an instrument of surrender.

He was informed that:

"From the moment of surrender, the authority of the Emperor and the Japanese Government to rule the state will be subject to you and you will take such steps as you deem proper to effectuate the surrender terms.

"You will exercise supreme command over all land, sea and air forces which may be allocated for enforcement in Japan of the surrender terms by the Allied Powers concerned."

He was advised that the British, Chinese, and Soviet governments were being asked to designate representatives to be present at the time and place of surrender.

AUGUST 14

Early in the morning (Tokyo time) American planes dropped over Tokyo leaflets containing a Japanese language version of the offer of the Japanese government to accept the Potsdam terms and the allied reply. It was no longer possible to conceal what was going on from the people.

Kido took one of the leaflets to the Emperor. He warned the Emperor that if he did not act at once, disclosure of the secret negotiations would give the extremists a chance to defy even his wish. The Emperor agreed to take the initiative in convoking an imperial conference since none of the military representatives could evade or refuse his call. Before it assembled, he took the precaution of calling Fleet Admiral Nagano and Field Marshals Sugiyama and Hata, the senior military commanders in Japan at the time, to the Palace and asked them to secure the obedience of the armed forces to his decision.

At 11:00 o'clock there assembled before the Emperor in the air raid shelter in the Palace the whole Supreme Council for the Direction of the War and the President of the Privy Council. They were so hastily summoned that they had no time to change to court clothing; some, being in warm weather garb, had to borrow neckties from their secretaries. After hearing once again the reasons given for continuing the war, the Emperor waited, before breaking the grim silence. Foreign Minister Togo in his memoirs quotes him as saying in part "As to . . .

the [Potsdam] declaration, I agree with the Foreign Minister that it is not intended to subvert the national polity of Japan; but, unless the war be brought to an end at this moment, I fear that the national polity will be destroyed, and the nation annihilated. It is therefore my wish that we bear the unbearable and accept the Allied reply, thus to preserve the state as a state and spare my subjects further suffering. I wish you all to act in that intention."[17]

The Emperor went on with choked voice to speak of the plight of the war sufferers and the families of the war dead and said he would do everything he could to console them. Admitting that the decision would be a shock to the armed forces, he said he was ready to appeal directly to the troops if necessary. He offered to broadcast his decision to the people and asked the leaders to draw up an imperial rescript which would announce the end of the war. All those about him wept aloud. This imperial conference was concluded in grave silence at noon.

That night the Swiss government was asked to relay to the allied governments the notice of surrender. It stated:

"1. His Majesty the Emperor has issued an Imperial rescript regarding Japan's acceptance of the provisions of the Potsdam declaration.

"2. His Majesty the Emperor is prepared to authorize and ensure the signature by his Government and the Imperial General Headquarters of the necessary terms for carrying out the provisions of the Potsdam declaration. His Majesty is also prepared to issue his commands to all the military, naval, and air authorities of Japan and all the forces under their control wherever located to cease active operations, to surrender arms and to issue such other orders as may be required by the Supreme Commander of the Allied Forces for the execution of the above-mentioned terms."[18]

The struggle was over. The Japanese people, overcrowded in their home islands, had chosen war rather than frustration of their effort to make themselves dominant in all of East Asia. The land in which they lived, the territory they commanded, was to be reduced to what it was when Commodore Perry in 1853 came as intruder from the Western world.

At the end of the afternoon (Washington time) the news was telephoned from our Embassy at Berne to the Secretary of State. He hurried across to the President's office to let him know, and almost at once a

[17] *The Cause of Japan*, page 334.
[18] *Department of State Bulletin*, Vol. 13, No. 321, page 255.

message was sent out addressed to the Foreign Ministers of Great Britain, China, and the Soviet Union advising them that the American government regarded this Japanese message as a full acceptance of the Potsdam Declaration and wished to release it to the public at once.

The Japanese government was notified accordingly. It was ordered to command all Japanese forces everywhere to stop fighting at once, and to send envoys to the Supreme Commander, General of the Army Douglas MacArthur, to discuss arrangements for the formal surrender. Truman made this known in the statement which he gave out that evening.

All the people of the West rejoiced. Among the soldiers, sailors, and airmen in the far-off Pacific there was exultation as they let their fancies run free over the prospect of soon seeing their country and their homes again. In the military quarters which MacArthur had at Manila a sense of triumph was blended with pride in the new responsibilities and with worried thoughts of what troubles might be met when the Americans set foot in Japan.

The British people, too, gave voice to their gratefulness. Prime Minister Attlee in his radio address to the nation reviewed the long ordeal. In celebrations throughout the British Commonwealth and Empire Churchill was not forgotten.

But the Soviet government was not to be so abruptly arrested in its assault against the Japanese in Manchuria. It allowed the campaign in Manchuria to develop a little longer.

Meanwhile at midnight on the 14th (Moscow time) Stalin and Soong finally completed their negotiations and signed a series of accords which, it was conceived, would regulate Sino-Soviet relations after the war. Since the story of these negotiations, and of the American part in them, and of the substance of the agreements reached has been amply told elsewhere, it would be irksome to retell it here.[19]

The resultant accords at the time gave satisfaction as an augury of peace on the continent of Asia and healing unity in China. They were hailed not only by the Soviet and Chinese governments but by the American government also, although a few informed members of the State Department and the American Embassy in Moscow were worried and displeased by the acquisition by the Soviet Union of a special, maybe dominant, position in Manchuria.

---

[19] *The China Tangle*, Chapter 30.

During these same crucial days of which we have been telling, the Russians had a distinguished visitor from the United States, General Eisenhower, formerly Supreme Allied Commander, now Commander of U.S. forces in Western Europe and American member of the Control Council for Germany.

He had been invited to come just after the surrender of Germany while the sense of comradeship in arms was most alive. But the War Department had at that time asked him to defer the trip, and then an unexpectedly prolonged visit to the United States and his duties in Germany had compelled him to put off the day. On August 2nd, just before leaving Potsdam, Truman had told Stalin he would be pleased if Marshal Gregory Zhukov (Soviet member of the Control Council for Germany) visited the United States. Thereupon Stalin had renewed the invitation to Eisenhower to visit Moscow. The date of August 10th was set. Unrecorded, but possibly among the reasons for Stalin's selection of this date, was the thought that Eisenhower's presence would coincide with Soviet entry into the Pacific war.

Soon after his arrival Eisenhower was engaged in talk with Marshal Zhukov and General Antonov. They related for him the progress of the Soviet offensive on the three fronts in Manchuria and told him of their plans to isolate Manchuria from North China and gain entry into Korea. On the next day not only he but Ambassador Harriman and General Deane were invited by Stalin to stand alongside him on Lenin's tomb to review an enormous Physical Culture Parade. This was the first time any foreigners were stationed on this lofty spot. The spectators applauded Eisenhower; Stalin and his colleagues were most cordial to him. Eisenhower might have wished he had been less singularly honored, since the whole official group remained standing throughout the entire five hours of the spectacle.

The Red Star, in its issue of August 12th, printed an item entitled "Statement of General Eisenhower to Red Star Correspondents" which in part read, "That was a very magnificent spectacle, and I think that people of other countries would have been very astonished if they could see what is being done in this country for the physical training of the younger generation. I personally was amazed at the preciseness with which the exercises were performed, and I was especially deeply impressed by the happy expression which I saw on the faces of the participants in the parade. They looked full of strength and happiness."

Before the General left on the 15th there were dinners, and tours of Moscow and Leningrad and other talks with Soviet military men. Marshal Zhukov left on the same plane with him for Berlin. Eisenhower issued a cordial statement of appreciation for the city and people of Moscow, whom he was leaving as friends. On returning to his headquarters he sent messages of thanks to Stalin and Antonov for their warm reception and superb hospitality. Stalin sent back a framed portrait of himself with the inscription: "To the famous strategist General of Armies D. Eisenhower with very best wishes—I. Stalin." In the course of a talk with Harriman a few days later the Generalissimo remarked that he thought Eisenhower a great man, not only because of his military accomplishments but because of his human, friendly, kind, and frank nature. He was not a "grubyi" (rude, coarse, brusque) man like most military men.

10. The End of the Fighting

DURING the night of the 14-15th there were some disorders in Tokyo. A section of the Imperial Guards Division rebelled and tried to seize and suppress the phonograph record of the rescript before it could be broadcast, but they were foiled. The homes of the Prime Minister and Marquis Kido were attacked. From Atsugi airfield (twenty-five miles southwest of Tokyo) one of the "Divine Wind Squadrons" flew ominously low over Tokyo, and dropped leaflets proclaiming that this was the final day of reckoning (Gyokusai). There were alarming street scenes in front of the palace.

At noon on the 15th the imperial rescript proclaiming surrender was broadcast. As remembered by a sensitive member of the Japanese audience, "First came a squawk and a sputter, then a band playing the national anthem, then the hoarse, strained voice of aged Prime Minister Kantaro Suzuki in a few words of introduction. In a moment followed the voice of the Emperor. It was a surprisingly musical voice; somewhat high-pitched but gentle, liquid and mellow, a little tired and pathetic, not very clear and sincere. The measured cadences of the classically phrased rescript which the Emperor read were not easy to follow, but there was no doubt about their general import. It meant surrender; the call was not to arms but to restraint and fortitude in enduring the pangs of defeat."[1]

Thereafter the people quietly bowed to its somber lament and command. In their hearts they welcomed peace. They worried over the fate of the husbands and sons scattered in China and a hundred islands of the Pacific, of those still in the battle line in Manchuria and of the non-combatant women and children stranded in many of these places. They turned to the tasks of securing food and shelter while they waited for their conquerors to arrive.

The Cabinet resigned. Uniquely it was decided that a member of the Imperial Family could best undertake the task of forming a new one. Prince Higashi-Kuni (the Emperor's uncle-in-law and a general on the active list) was chosen at once as Prime Minister. Prince Konoye agreed to serve as his Deputy; but he was to find memories too tragic, and rather than submit to trial as a war criminal, that victim of his own indecision committed suicide.

MacArthur assumed his post as Supreme Commander in charge of

---

[1] Kazuo Kawai, *Japan's American Interlude*, page 80.

[effectuation] *(margin annotation)*

the effectuation of the surrender and the control of Japan. On the 15th he sent from Manila an urgent message to the Japanese Emperor, the Japanese government, and the Japanese Imperial Headquarters, directing them, pursuant to the terms of surrender, to order all Japanese forces everywhere to stop fighting at once. It asked that he be notified of the effective time of such cessation, whereupon allied forces would also be ordered to cease hostilities.

This command was carried out by Imperial General Headquarters with the authority of the Emperor on the next day, the 16th (Tokyo time). Because communications had broken down, it was reckoned by the Japanese government that this order would not become known to all military units in Japan for two days, to those in Manchuria, China and the South Seas for six days, and to those in New Guinea and the Philippines for twelve. The allies were so advised. Members of the Imperial Family were sent to visit Japanese military headquarters in Japan, China, and elsewhere to impress the Imperial wishes and see that they were carried out.

American and British commanders in the Pacific were ordered to suspend offensive operations against Japanese forces insofar as consistent with the safety of allied forces in their areas. They began with eager will to plan for the rescue and reception of the woebegone soldiers who had been prisoners of war, survivors of an ordeal in Japanese camps which had caused the deaths of many.

In Manchuria, however, the war went on for some days longer. MacArthur on the 15th (Manila time) sent a message through General Deane, the head of the American military mission in Moscow, to Antonov, which the Soviet Chief of Staff understood to be an implied order that he instruct Soviet ground, sea, and air forces in the Far East to end offensive action against the Japanese. Touchy as ever, Antonov answered on the next day that he believed this request was submitted under a misunderstanding, since only the Supreme Commander of the armed forces of the Soviet Union could make that decision. The Red Army columns continued on their way forward. By this time one was deep in Chahar province, only one hundred and fifty miles northwest of Peiping.

At about 4:00 o'clock on the afternoon of the 16th (Moscow time), the Soviet government learned from a broadcast in English from Tokyo that the Emperor had ordered all Japanese forces to stop fighting at once; the same information came to them almost simultaneously from MacArthur. At 6:00 o'clock on the 17th, Marshal Vasilevski, Commander in Chief of the Soviet troops in the Far East, broadcast a radio call to the Commander of the Kwantung Army to end all action against Soviet troops along the entire front, to lay down their arms and surrender at noon on the 20th. As soon as this was done, he added, Soviet troops would cease their operations. Deane was informed that the designated interval had been accorded in order to give the Commander of the Kwantung Army time to inform all his forces, but that the Soviet Command did not want to continue the offensive until the 20th, and would accept the surrender of any Japanese units at any time. The Japanese divisions in Manchuria grounded their arms and announced their surrender.

When the Soviet armies stopped marching, they were over all sections of the "Three Eastern Provinces" known as Manchuria, and well within the adjoining Chinese provinces of Jehol and Chahar and in control of junction towns which would be important in the contest that was flaring up between the Chinese National Government and the Chinese Communists. Soviet units had pushed down to a part in Northern Hopei province and to towns along the Great Wall. A few days later, after the advance had stopped, Stalin told Harriman that Chiang Kai-shek had feared the Red Army would keep on until it reached Kalgan (in the province of Chahar) and Peiping and unite with the Chinese Communists in those areas, but he had assured Chiang Kai-shek that they would not.

The Russian press and radio had given much attention to the explosion of the first atomic bomb over Hiroshima. Thereafter they had been silent about its effect, not even reporting the drop of the second bomb on Nagasaki. The talents of their writers were devoted to elevating the feats and advances of the Soviet forces. As the fighting came to an end, the people of the Soviet Union were told that it had been the irresistible thrust of their soldiers that had brought the war against Japan to its climax, that this had been the finishing blow. Praise of the valor of the Soviet forces in the Far East and of their part in bringing the war to an end were the conventional front for the Russian intention to expand its realm of control over nearby sections of the Asian mainland and the islands and waters of the northern Pacific. This extension of Soviet influence was being facilitated even then in two ways: by the accord that had been signed with the Chinese National Government, and by the provisions for acceptance of the surrender of the Japanese forces.

11. The Plans for Acceptance of the Surrender of the Japanese Forces

GENERAL MACARTHUR had been given dual assignments. As Supreme Commander of the Allied Forces he was authorized to effectuate the surrender of Japanese armed forces everywhere and to direct the occupation and control of Japan. As Commander in Chief of the U.S. Army Forces in the Pacific, he was charged, along with Admiral Nimitz and General Albert C. Wedemeyer, with the acceptance of the Japanese surrender in a designated area.

The planners in the War and State Departments, in close touch with British associates, during that crowded second week of August, had composed instructions for him in both spheres. Having been approved by the Joint Chiefs of Staff and the President, these were hurried out to him.

MacArthur, as Supreme Commander of the Allied Forces, was to direct the Emperor to issue an order (known as General Order No. 1) setting forth the arrangements to govern the act of surrender of the widely scattered Japanese armies.

This was a comprehensive plan designating the particular allied authority to whom the Japanese forces in each area were to surrender, in order to avert confusion and misunderstanding. It was foreseen that Japanese commanders might seek to cause dissension among the members of the coalition by proffering surrender to one and refusing it to another. Or the allied commanders in the various theaters of war might quarrel about jurisdiction, or penetrate each other's field of command, or compete for shipping and naval support.

Such an inclusive program could only be formulated by the American government, but it recognized that the assignment of the right to accept surrender would have to conform to the division of areas of military operations and command among the four main allies. In deciding zones of surrender military circumstances in general were allowed to rule.

But heed was paid, tacitly at least, to political accords and consequences. In drawing up the plan delineated in General Order No. 1, several agreements regarding political and territorial situations were borne in mind. Among these, two in particular were relevant: the Cairo Declaration and the Yalta accord about the territorial rights to be granted to the Soviet Union. It also conformed roughly to certain other suppositions about prospective territorial dispositions. There was no discussion about the Pacific Islands to the south that Japan had governed, but they were or would be in the control of the Americans; and one of the suppositions was that the United States would retain them or hand some over to others, particularly Australia, as it might decide. Another supposition of greater range was that the European allies (Great Britain and the Commonwealth, the Netherlands, France) were entitled to regain their colonies and possessions in the Pacific and on the mainland of Asia, if they could do so by their own men and efforts.

Specifically, General Order No. 1 directed that:

(a) The Japanese Commanders and all ground, sea, air, and auxiliary forces within China (excluding Manchuria), Formosa, and French Indo-China north of 16 degrees north latitude surrender to Generalissimo Chiang Kai-shek.

(b) The Japanese Commanders and all ground, sea, air, and auxiliary forces within Manchuria, Korea north of 38 degrees north latitude, and Karafuto [southern section of Sakhalin] surrender to the Commander in Chief of the Soviet Forces in the Far East.[1]

(c) The Japanese Commanders and all ground, sea, air, and auxiliary forces within the Andamans, Nicobars, Burma, Thailand, French Indo-China south of 16 degrees north latitude, Malaya, Borneo, Netherlands Indies, New Guinea, Bismarcks, and the Solomons, surrender to the Supreme Allied Commander, South East Asia Command or the Commanding General, Australian Forces, as arranged between them.[2]

(d) The Japanese Commanders and all ground, sea, air, and auxiliary forces in the Japanese mandated islands, Ryukyus, Bonins, and other Pacific Islands surrender to the Commander in Chief, U.S. Pacific Fleet.

(e) The Imperial General Headquarters, its Senior Commanders, and all ground, sea, air, and auxiliary forces in the main islands of Japan, minor islands adjacent thereto, Korea south of 38 degrees north latitude, and the Philippines surrender to the Commander in Chief, U.S. Army Forces in the Pacific.

This program was on the whole well received by our allies, but several remonstrances and requests for revision were sent to the Ameri-

---

[1] The 38th parallel in Korea was selected because the State Department wanted American forces to go as far north as possible but the Joint Chiefs did not want a line that would be beyond anticipated American capabilities in relation to Russian forces in Manchuria. It was decided that it was desirable to have the capital of Korea in our zone of surrender although some of the military representatives thought this was over-reaching.

[2] The British and American Chiefs of Staff subsequently agreed that the Japanese forces on the island of Nauru should surrender to the Commander-in-Chief of the Australian forces, and those on Ocean Island to the same military authority, acting on behalf of the United Kingdom.

can government. They originated in Moscow, Chungking, Paris, London, and Melbourne.

Stalin asked for two supplements to the Soviet sphere. One was that the Japanese armed forces in the northern half of the island of Hokkaido (the northernmost of the four Japanese main islands) be directed to surrender to the Commander in Chief of the Soviet Forces in the Far East instead of to the Commander in Chief of the U.S. Army Forces in the Pacific. In that connection, he explained, "this last point is of special importance to Russian public opinion. As is known, in 1919-21 the Japanese occupied the whole of the Soviet Far East. Russian public opinion would be gravely offended if the Russian troops had no occupation area in any part of the territory of Japan proper." The other was that the Japanese armed forces in all the Kurile Islands, which under the Yalta accord were to pass into possession of the Soviet Union, should be similarly reassigned. Stalin concluded this message to Truman (of August 16) in which he proposed these amendments by saying, "I am most anxious that the modest suggestions set forth above should not meet with any objections."

The first of these proposals was read with indignation by the President and the Chiefs of Staff and rejected with firmness, for it would have meant divided occupation and control of Japan.

In regard to the Kuriles it had been the American intention to have Admiral Nimitz receive the surrender of Japanese forces on those of the Kurile Islands that lay south of the dividing line for naval operations which had been agreed on at Potsdam, while the Russians might receive the surrender of the Japanese forces on the islands of Paramushiro and Shumushu to the north of that demarcation line. But, at the same time that he refused to allow the Russians to gain entry into Hokkaido, Truman informed Stalin that he was willing to include all the Kurile Islands in the area wherein the Japanese were to surrender to the Soviet Commander in Chief. However, he added, he would be obliged if in return Stalin would accord ". . . air base rights for land and sea aircraft on some of the Kurile Islands, preferably in the central group, for [American] military purposes and for commercial use." In making this request the President was acting on advice of the Joint Chiefs of Staff, who thought it would be useful to have a suitable airfield for movement from the Aleutians to Japan and the Philippines, including rights of transit and refueling for military aircraft.

Stalin attuned his response to make it sound regretful rather than angry. He and his colleagues had not expected a refusal of their request to occupy the northern half of Hokkaido. And they were surprised and hurt by our request for air base rights in the Kuriles; this had not been visualized either at Yalta or Potsdam, and seemed to imply that the Soviet Union was either a vanquished country or unable to defend all of its territory. As he later expressed his views to Harriman, he was "astounded" at what he regarded as an American attempt to get a permanent military base in the Soviet defense zone.

Truman hastened to explain that the only reasons for asking for base rights on one of the Kuriles was that the weather was usually bad in the Aleutian-Kurile area, and so the American government wanted to have another connecting air route [via the Aleutian Islands] for emergency use during the period of occupation of Japan. Why, he asked, should this request be regarded as offensive? The Kurile Islands were not yet part of Soviet territory; Roosevelt had promised only to support their transfer to the Soviet Union at the peace conference and he, Truman, had confirmed that promise, so he felt our reasonable wish in that connection deserved consideration. Stalin said he was glad that the misunderstanding had been dispelled, and he approved the request for emergency landing rights for military craft during the period of occupation and for a reciprocal arrangement for commercial aircraft use of the Kuriles and the Aleutians. The contemplated arrangement was forgotten, it may be foretold, after the Russians took control of the Kuriles and the Soviet and American governments began to turn into antagonists for power in the Northern Pacific.

The complaint of the British government was that General Order No. 1 was ambiguous in regard to Hong Kong. The American authors had not tried to decide whether Japanese forces in that Crown Colony should be required to surrender to Chiang Kai-shek as being "within China," as the Generalissimo was averring. The British government, to foretell, did not submit the question to American adjudication. It hurriedly sent a naval force to relieve Hong Kong from Japanese occupation. The Generalissimo was aroused. He argued with the British government and pleaded with the American government. Truman, although inclined as Roosevelt had been to encourage the termination of British sovereignty over this port and outpost, was not willing to become an active agent of a compelled change. So the American government notified the British and Chinese governments that the Supreme Commander would arrange for the surrender of Hong Kong to the British military representatives, but that this action should not be construed as indicating our views about the future disposition of the territory.

Truman in his answer to Chiang Kai-shek took refuge in the idea that this problem of Japanese surrender in Hong Kong was ". . . primarily a military matter of an operational character." Thus he urged Chiang Kai-shek to coordinate his military action with the British. Unwillingly—and because he had no way of getting his own forces to Hong Kong unless the Americans were willing to move them in by air—Chiang Kai-shek had thereupon notified the British that he would delegate his authority as Supreme Commander in the China Theater to a British Commander to accept the surrender at Hong Kong, with the participation of a Chinese and an American officer. But the British government, with polite regret, rejected this proposal. Hong Kong was British territory, and they would receive the surrender in the name of the King of Great Britain. Chinese and American representatives would be welcome as guests. Being distracted by the difficulties of arranging for the quick movement of his forces even within China, although provided with transport and supplies by the United States, the Generalissimo had to desist in his attempt to wrest Hong Kong from Britain. Years later, it was to become a refuge for many of his followers.

The French government protested the instructions in regard to the surrender of the Japanese forces in Indo-China (in the northern part to Chiang Kai-shek, and in the southern to Mountbatten). It wished to have the duty assigned to its representative. But France did not have an adequate and organized military force in or near Indo-China at the time of the surrender, and no way of getting them there quickly. The dissatisfied French authorities had to reconcile themselves to an indirect admission of their tenure over Indo-China; it was arranged that a representative of France on Mountbatten's staff should be associated with the local surrender, and that a representative of the French government should be in attendance later when the formal surrender of Japan was made to MacArthur.

General Order No. 1, as revised, was given on August 20th by General MacArthur to the Japanese emissaries who went to Manila to receive his instructions about the effectuation of the surrender.

12. The Orders Issued to the American Commanders

UNDER General Order No. 1 Japanese commanders of forces in the Pacific Islands south of Japan were to surrender to the Commander in Chief of the U.S. Pacific Fleet (Nimitz), and those in command of forces in Japan proper, the southern section of Korea and the Philippines were to surrender to the Commander in Chief, U.S. Army Forces in the Pacific (MacArthur).

On August 15th the Joint Chiefs sent amplifying directives to these two American commanders and to General Wedemeyer, Commander of the U.S. Forces in China. They were informed that:

(1) Key areas of Japan proper, Korea, and the China coast were to be occupied.

(2) The swift occupation of Japan proper was to be regarded as "the supreme operation" and to have first call on available resources. The early occupation of Keijo (Seoul) in Korea and acceptance of the surrender of Japanese forces in that area were to have the second call. The operations to be undertaken on the coast of China and on Formosa were to be subject to these priorities.

(3) The immediate purpose of occupation operations on the China Coast was, by gaining control of key ports and communication points, to extend such assistance to the forces in the China theater as was practicable without involvement in a major land campaign.

Here we may glance briefly at the situation in China as it was affected by the American directives regarding the sending of troops into China and the instructions which defined and limited their assignments after they landed.

The surrender in haste of Japan caught both the Chinese Nationalist Government and the American Command in China by surprise and off balance. The few well-trained and equipped troops among the three hundred divisions in the Chinese Army were, in the south and in the interior, about to start an advance toward the Canton area on the coast. There were no arrangements or reserved means for quick transport of troops to other parts of the country. The promised equipment for other Chinese forces (up to 39 divisions) was still on its way from the United States to China. The railway and road systems were wholly inadequate. Plans for taking over the civil administration of those great sections of

China which were under control of the Japanese were in a confused and fragmentary state.[1]

Chiang Kai-shek would have been well advised to have bothered less about securing control of Hong Kong and to have been more thoroughly prepared to take over the vast areas of China from which the Japanese were to be expelled. Without extensive American aid by air and sea the Chinese Nationalist Government could not move its forces to the big cities along the coast from the interior and the south where they were concentrated. In the northern provinces its qualification, as well as its right to accept surrender of the Japanese, was being boldly challenged by the Chinese Communists. Entry into Manchuria depended on Soviet good will.

General Order No. 1 had instructed the Japanese forces in China to surrender *only* to Chiang Kai-shek or officers designated by him. This provision was intended to make it harder for the Communists to install themselves in localities held by the Japanese armies and to prevent them from obtaining large stores of arms and ammunition. But even before the Japanese announced their acceptance of the Potsdam terms, Chu Teh, the Commanding General of the Chinese Communist forces, had ordered his troops to advance against Japanese forces at all points, accept their surrender, and take control of any areas where the Japanese were found. Mao Tse Tung broadcast an announcement that the Chungking High Command did not represent the Chinese people and a demand that the Japanese troops surrender to the Communist military authorities. News of the accords which Soong signed with Stalin in Moscow, whereby the Soviet government promised to aid and support only the National Government, did not cause these Chinese Communist leaders to retract.[2] Chu Teh sent notes to the American, British, and Soviet governments in which he appealed for acceptance of Communist claims to represent the people and of the right to share in the surrender and control of Japan.

MacArthur, as instructed, notified the Japanese authorities that the promise to return Japanese armed forces to their peaceful occupations applied only to those who obeyed General Order No. 1. The American government answered Chu Teh's appeal by expressing the hope that the Communists would cooperate with Chiang Kai-shek. It sought to

[1] As described in a message from General Wedemeyer to General Marshall on August 1, ". . . if peace comes suddenly, it is reasonable to expect widespread confusion and disorder. The Chinese have no plan for rehabilitation, prevention of epidemics, restoration of utilities, restoration of balanced economy and redisposition of millions of refugees."

[2] As stated in the First Paragraph of the Note signed by Molotov relating to the Treaty of Friendship and Alliance of August 14, 1945.

secure the concurrence of the Soviet, British, and Chinese governments in a public statement which would confirm their joint resolution to see that the surrender in all of China should be carried out in such a way as to unify the country under Chiang Kai-shek. But when Bevin proposed to reduce the force of the statement and Molotov was noncommittal, Byrnes gave up the idea.

These were the circumstances in which Wedemeyer informed MacArthur that "the problem of orderly surrender of the bulk of the Japanese troops in the China theater with the preservation of law and order in presently occupied areas resolves itself to one of rapidly deploying Central Government troops into strategic areas." During the second week in August in several warning essays he tried to persuade Marshall and his colleagues of the need to take vigorous action in China if they did not wish failure of our hopes, since the Central Government was unready and would be unable to re-establish its authority without extensive aid and support. Chiang Kai-shek was appealing for the dispatch of five American divisions to China. Wedemeyer gave point to this appeal by observing that the American government might not appreciate the explosive and portentous possibilities in China when Japan surrenders—inability to disarm the Japanese, civil war, chaos in China.

Wedemeyer was directed by the War Department to arrange for the movement of Chinese troops on American transport planes and ships into all areas in China and Formosa held by the Japanese, to facilitate the surrender and repatriation of the Japanese. Furthermore, plans were approved for sending in American marines and soldiers to secure control of key ports and communication points to help the Chinese Nationalist forces when MacArthur decided they were not needed for his assignment in Japan and Korea. But Wedemeyer was advised in messages of August 7th and 14th to expect only two divisions when shipping became available and when MacArthur should conclude that the forces and the shipping were not required for his prior assignments in Japan and Korea. All provisions of his instructions, it was also stipulated, were to apply only insofar as action taken did not prejudice the basic principle that the American government would not support the Central Government of China in "fratricidal" war.[3] The quarrel with the Communists, it was then still the American official belief, could be settled by peaceful means, and must be settled in no other way.

[3] An instructive though somewhat scanty account of the messages exchanged during this period between Wedemeyer and the War Department is given in *The United States Army in World War II China-Burma-India Theater. Time Runs Out in CBI*, by Charles F. Romanus and Riley Sunderland (1959), pages 393-395.

When representatives of the three main American commands met at Manila on August 18th, Wedemeyer was told that he must not expect any American forces to land in China until ten divisions had been placed in Japan and two divisions had been placed in Korea; they might appear in China by the end of September if these operations went smoothly. MacArthur was, it turned out, greatly overestimating the number of men and of transport vessels that would be needed to assure safe entry and establish control of Japan.[4]

It was soon to become sadly clear that even with our energetic help the National Government did not have the systematic ability, the trained administration, the equipment, or the generalship rapidly to secure control of the whole of their great country, to defeat their Communist antagonists in North China and Manchuria, or to bring able and honest administration to Formosa. The American government had striven to have China accepted as an equal of the great powers; and it had conceived that China would become the stabilizing, peaceful and democratic—even dominant—influence in the Pacific. But before the first autumn after the collapse of Japan was over, China was losing strength and unity, and the National Government was needing more and more help to sustain itself.

[4] On July 27 MacArthur had advised Marshall that he thought the minimum forces necessary for the occupation of Japan and participation in the occupation of Korea would be 23 reinforced divisions and 20 air groups—in all about 800,000 men. The same anticipation disposed him to favor the inclusion of contingents of foreign troops, including Russian troops, in the occupation forces of Japan, but only on the understanding that these would be subject to his command in the same way as American troops. Soon after entering Japan the Supreme Commander reduced these estimates by half, and later he reduced them more.

13. The American Plans and Program for Japan

ON APPOINTING MacArthur Supreme Commander, the American government had advised him that from the moment of surrender the authority of the Japanese Emperor and Japanese government to rule the state would be subject to his will, and that he was to take steps as he deemed proper to effectuate the surrender terms. The breadth and depth of his authority was tersely stated in one sentence, "You will exercise supreme command over all land, sea, and air forces which may be allocated for enforcement in Japan of the surrender terms by the Allied Powers concerned."

A few days later, irritated by a message from the Japanese government which seemed to construe the Potsdam Declaration as a voluntary accord, the American government made clear that it was not to be so regarded.[1] For, as Truman later recorded, the American government did not want to ". . . begin the occupation by bargaining over its terms. We were the victors. The Japanese were the losers. They had to know that 'unconditional surrender' was not a matter for negotiations."[2]

As bluntly affirmed in a later exposition of his authority, sent by the Joint Chiefs of Staff to MacArthur on September 6th, just after he had landed in Japan:

"1. The authority of the Emperor and the Japanese Government to rule the state is subordinate to you as Supreme Commander for the Allied Powers. You will exercise your authority as you deem proper to carry out your mission. Our relations with Japan do not rest on a contractual basis, but on an unconditional surrender. Since your authority is supreme, you will not entertain any question on the part of the Japanese as to its scope."[3]

It was contemplated that the Supreme Commander should effectuate allied policies through the Japanese government to the extent that such an arrangement produced satisfactory results.[4] They would act upon

---

[1] MacArthur was greatly upset by this message. It conveyed the "conditions" which the Japanese army leaders had put forward, expressed as "desires." Perhaps Togo, knowing it would be disregarded, sent it as a gesture which might reconcile the military men. But that night (August 15th) Anami, the War Minister, committed suicide.

[2] *Year of Decisions*, page 456.

[3] State Department Publication No. 2671, *Occupation of Japan: Policy and Progress.* Appendix 16. *Authority of General MacArthur as Supreme Commander for the Allied Powers.*

[4] As stated in Paragraph 2 of the exposition of his authority sent him on September 6th, "Control of Japan shall be exercised through the Japanese Government to the extent that such an arrangement produces satisfactory results. This does not prejudice your right to act directly if required. You may enforce the orders issued by you by the employment of such measures as you deem necessary, including the use of force."

his advice or orders and under his supervision. There was to be no foreign military government of the civilian population, no prisoner of war camps, no foreign police.

It is scarcely to be wondered at that years later, having exercised this delegation of authority to rule over the eighty million Japanese people, having had his every summons heeded, and after daily obeisance of the Japanese when he emerged each day from his office with a brisk stride to his waiting limousine, MacArthur came to regard himself as having enough prestige to challenge the President of the United States, the Chief of Staff, and the Secretary of State.

Much thought had been given to the nature and basic elements of the system of allied occupation and control that was to be operative in Japan. On August 18th the President had approved a memorandum agreed on by the State, War, and Navy Departments and endorsed by the Joint Chiefs of Staff.[5] In brief summary this stated that (1) the American government recognized that it was obligated to consult with those of its allies who were at war with Japan, and also to act in concert with them in effecting the surrender and disarmament of Japan; (2) while these allies had the right and responsibility to share in the occupation and control of Japan, and in the formulation of policies for Japan, the American government must be in charge of the carrying out of these policies; (3) while the United States would provide most of the army of occupation, we wished our allies to share in this task and effort.[6] But (4) all national contingents composing the army of occupation should be combined into a unified force under a commander designated by the American government; (5) the whole of Japan was to be controlled

[5] This memorandum had been developed by a State-War-Navy Committee, known as SWNCC, completed by it August 11th, approved by the Joint Chiefs of Staff, submitted by Byrnes to the President on August 16th, and approved by him subsequently. It was called *National Composition of Forces to Occupy Japan Proper in the Post-War Period*.

[6] The reasons why the American government welcomed participation of troops of other countries in the army of occupation are explained in a memo sent by General Marshall to President Truman early in August, "It is certain that there will be no other forces other than U.S. troops to move immediately into the Japanese islands and Formosa . . . in the initial period of occupation. There are three million members of the Japanese armed forces outside of the main islands plus an unknown number of Japanese civilians. These must be collected and disarmed and according to U.S. policy returned to Japan. This will require a considerable period of time and a great deal of effort. The British, the Chinese and the Russians, if it is in accordance with U.S. policy should be asked to share this effort. It does not seem proper that the U.S. people should be made to feel they are alone sharing the cost of straightening out the Far East following Japanese capitulation. Also the Japanese people should not be allowed to focus on the U.S. alone the blame for the occupation of their country and the mass shifting of their people."

as a unit; there would not be separate zones of occupation as in Germany; and (6) the occupation authority was to provide a centralized administration for all of Japan.

As soon as the British and Soviet governments grasped these American ideas they protestingly made known that they were not pleased with their subordination, and proposed other arrangements whereby they would be assured of a chance to share more effectively in the conduct of the occupation. The differences of desire were unsolved when MacArthur landed in Japan, and troops marching behind the American flag entered Tokyo. They remained in suspense while the Supreme Commander issued his first orders to the Japanese. The Foreign Office in London thought it was being disregarded and was impatient for a start of genuine consultation. The Soviet government, Harriman warned on August 23rd, would again assert their wish for a zone of occupation with an independent command, and if rebuffed would try to interfere with the American program.[7]

After many months of arguments that were far from languid, the State, War, and Navy Departments had agreed on a statement of policies to be pursued in Japan during the initial period after surrender. The Joint Chiefs of Staff had adopted it, and on September 6th the President approved it. Thereupon it was distributed to MacArthur and to appropriate U.S. departments and agencies "for their guidance."[8]

This was to be followed, and was followed by more detailed instructions on the way in which its multiple points and sections were to be construed and applied. In the consultation over the air-waves between

---

[7] The arrangements ultimately adopted were (1) to have a Far Eastern Commission in Washington of eleven (later thirteen) allied nations which was given the assignment of formulating general policies for the conduct of the occupation. It was to function by majority vote, provided that included the votes of the United States, the United Kingdom, the Union of Soviet Socialist Republics, and China, which gave each veto power. However, it was stipulated that pending action by the FEC the American government could issue in case of need urgent interim directives to MacArthur. Mainly because of Soviet dissent this became the ruling practice. (2) An Allied Council for Japan in Tokyo composed of representatives of the United States, the British Commonwealth, the Soviet Union, and China. It was advisory in character. In practice neither MacArthur nor the American government felt constrained to heed its advice.

[8] It is printed as Appendix 13 in State Department Publication No. 2671 already cited, under the title *United States Initial Post-Surrender Policy for Japan*. The substance was sent to MacArthur by radio on August 29th, and after consideration of his comment and approval by the President, was sent to him by messenger on September 6th. It was amended during the following weeks, but only one of the changes, that concerned with reparations, is significant. The text printed in Appendix 13 is the amended one, but still bears the date of August 29th, without mention of the changes that had subsequently been made in the original text. Copies were sent to our allies and it was published.

MacArthur and the War Department during the period of composition of these instructions, the Supreme Commander was distressed over the prospect that he would be hampered in the exercise of his judgment in the light of circumstances faced. He thought some of the proposed provisions "unwise, rigid, too detailed and unnecessary." Marshall patiently explained to him the reasons for formulating detailed and comprehensive instructions: that on many matters the State Department was the primary sponsor; that not only American but foreign governments and peoples (presumably the prospective Far Eastern Commission was in mind) were attentively interested in the course pursued and actions taken; and that definiteness would enable the several government departments in the United States and the military command better to integrate their actions. Moreover, it was understood that MacArthur would be free to recommend changes and to exercise reasonable latitude in the execution of his instructions, pending any required consultations in Washington.

The chief features of the many crammed sections of the statement of our initial policies are well remembered both in Japan and the United States. Together they formed a program which would enable the Japanese people to remake their lives out of the ruin of war and the humiliation of defeat, to devote their inborn energies to peaceful progress, and eventually to live as free individuals under authority which they themselves controlled.

The designated objectives were two: to insure that Japan could not become a menace to peace and security; and to bring about a peaceable, responsible and democratic government. The Japanese within the four home islands were to be encouraged to develop a desire for individual liberties and a respect for fundamental human rights; and they were to be induced to adopt a democratic system of government, responsive to popular will.

No military organizations, forms, or careers were to be allowed. All persons who had been active exponents of militarism and militant nationalism were to be removed and excluded from public office and from any other position of public or substantial private responsibility (which became known as "the purge").

In contrast to the corresponding sections about economic affairs in the Potsdam accord about Germany, those in this outline of policy for Japan were lucid and coherent. Industries or branches of production whose chief value was in preparing for war or making weapons of war were to be eliminated, and the size and character of Japan's heavy industries were limited to its peaceful needs. The economic structure was to be reorganized so as to favor a wide distribution of income and of ownership of the means of production and trade.

During the austere time of occupation the Japanese authorities were to be directed to develop programs which would avert acute distress, assure just distribution of available supplies, restore the productive capacity of the country for peacetime needs, and meet reparations dues. These were to be paid partly through the transfer of Japanese property outside Japan, partly through the transfer of such goods or existing capital equipment as was not needed for approved purposes. No reparations were to be exacted in a form which would be counter to the aim of demilitarizing Japan. The amounts and the division among recipients were left for future determination and negotiation when it would be clearer what Japan could pay, and how it could do so.

The British government was on the whole in accord with this creed and program, but the Soviet government was displeased by the basic leniency and the favoring attitude toward private forms of economic life and democratic forms of government. Stalin allowed his displeasure to show in a talk which he had on September 14th with a group of American Congressmen and Senators. Striking the table with his clenched fist he said that the allies must keep a close grip not only on Germany but on Japan. He recalled with sarcasm how Germany had been allowed to revive after the first World War and to become strong enough to start and almost win the second one; now, he continued, the United States was making the same mistake about Japan; it ought to be dealt with as Germany was being treated now, not as it was treated after the first war.

The American government was very soon forced to recognize the necessity of giving substantial aid to the Japanese people in order to prevent the whole program from being distorted by distress or disturbed by disorder. While we ruled we nourished; while we reproved we tried to act as friends.

Time was to bring regret about several elements of the terms imposed on Japan. The sphere of Japanese rule was reduced too greatly, by depriving it of *all* of its territory outside of the four home islands. The ban on rearmament, written into the Constitution under MacArthur's direction, was too rigid.

Perhaps before long it may appear that a third major error in foresight will have to be acknowledged. Under the Constitution, which the

Japanese were urged to adopt, the authority of the Emperor was reduced to a mere symbol of the state, and the Executive branch of the government was made directly responsible to the elective Diet, which was denominated as the highest organ of state power. Whether the Japanese will be able to operate this type of government well in face of contemporary assaults on such democratic forms is being put to the test, a test made harder by the fact that in the Constitution provision for respect of individual rights was absolute and unqualified, not to be restricted or infringed on by any human authority under any circumstance.[9]

These features of our policies were owing to errors of foresight about the course of events in the Pacific, particularly to an imprudent measure of belief that China after the war would be a firm friend of the United States, and that Communist and other revolutionary groups in Japan would not threaten our relations with that country.

Concurrently, thought was being given to the policies to be pursued toward and in Korea. In the declaration issued at Cairo in November 1943, the American, British, and Chinese governments had stated "the aforesaid three great powers, mindful of the enslavement of the people of Korea, are determined that in due course Korea shall become free and independent." It had been conceived that the Koreans would have to be trained for self-government and would be willing to live under supervision until judged qualified. Thus at Yalta in February 1945, President Roosevelt in a private talk with Stalin had said that he had in mind a trusteeship to run perhaps twenty or thirty years. His idea was that this might be administered by representatives of the United States, the Soviet Union, and China, for he did not think it necessary to invite Britain to participate. Stalin had said that he thought the shorter the period the better, and that in his opinion Britain should be invited to take part in it. They had agreed that no foreign troops should be stationed in Korea during the period of trusteeship. Stalin reaffirmed his approval of a four-power trusteeship when he talked with Hopkins at the end of May.

On June 15th President Truman had informed Chiang Kai-shek that

[9] A thoughtful and lucid examination of the transformation of the Japanese political system under American tutelage has been written by Kazuo Kawai in *Japan's American Interlude*.

Chapter I of the new Japanese Constitution provided that: Article 1. "The Emperor shall be the symbol of the State and of the unity of the people, deriving his position from the will of the people with whom resides sovereign power." Article 3. "The advice and approval of the Cabinet shall be required for all acts of the Emperor in matters of state, and the Cabinet shall be responsible therefor."

the American, British, and Soviet governments were all in favor of this course. In Briefing Book Papers taken to Potsdam the same recommendations were advanced, with the explanation that arrangements should be adopted to develop in Korea a strong democratic and independent state. Judgment was left open as to whether or not this international supervisory administration or trusteeship should be under the authority of the United Nations. It was contemplated that it would function after military government in Korea was brought to an end and until such time as the Koreans were deemed able to govern themselves as a free and independent sovereign state.[10]

In the memo which Stimson, at Potsdam, sent Truman on July 16th, after referring to the Stalin-Roosevelt informal agreement for a trusteeship, he called attention to the fact that the Soviet Union was training one or two divisions of Koreans who probably would accompany the Red Army in their advance into Korea. He expressed anxiety that if an international trusteeship was not set up in Korea, or perhaps even if it were, these Korean divisions would probably gain control and influence the formation of a Soviet-dominated local government. "This is," he wrote, "the Polish question transplanted to the Far East." Therefore he advised Truman to maintain at least a token force of American soldiers or marines in Korea during the period of trusteeship.[11] But as far as the open record tells, Truman did not talk to Stalin about the future of Korea.

The agreement between the American and Soviet Chiefs of Staff on a line of separation for their respective operations in the air and on the sea cut across Korea. The Soviet Chiefs had made it known that they planned to fight their way into Korea from the north, and the American Chiefs had indicated that they had no intention of attempting a landing in Korea before the invasion of Kyushu but might do so if it was found necessary.

As told, General Order No. 1 provided that a representative of the Soviet High Command was to accept the surrender of Japanese forces north of the 38th parallel; and a representative of the Commander in Chief of the U.S. Army Forces in the Pacific would accept the surrender of the Japanese forces south of that line, a division which allowed the American commander to control the capital of the country, Seoul, and the Tsushima Straits.[12]

---

[10] Potsdam Papers, Documents 251, 252, 253.

[11] Ibid., Document 732.

[12] The article by Arthur L. Grey in Foreign Affairs of April 1951, "The Thirty-Eighth Parallel," is a reliable account of how the division of the country into two separate administrations came about and developed.

By the time (September 8th) that American troops, rerouted from Manila in haste, landed in Korea, the Soviet forces were south of the demarcation line, but they quickly withdrew to it.

While it was conceived that the temporary occupation of Korea should be a joint operation under an over-all allied command, no plan seems to have been worked out for a combined U.S.-Soviet military government.[13] The reasons remain a matter of conjecture. The governing one may have been the expectation that the two separate administrations would soon be superseded by the four-power trusteeship. Or it may have been because of a wish to wait and see what condition the several parts of the country were in when the time came to assume charge.

In any event both the Americans and Russians soon learned that the Korean people did not want to live under a trusteeship; they wished to govern themselves at once and thought that a promise had been given to that effect. Thus the harassed Commander of the American forces in liberated Korea soon found himself not only quarreling with the Russian allies but also beset by complaints of the Koreans. He was not going to find it as easy to pursue the policies formulated in the Directive sent him by the Joint Chiefs as was his colleague in conquered Japan.

The Russians in actuality knew much more definitely what they wanted to do in their sector of occupation than did the Americans in the area under their control.[14] However, the tale of developments in Korea after its liberation from Japan, and the abandonment of the plan of trusteeship, has been adequately told in other narratives.[15]

[13] Undated Briefing Book Paper in Potsdam Papers, Document 605. Testimony General Helmick, House Committee on Foreign Affairs, June 9, 1949, Korean Aid, Hearings on H. R. 5330, U.S. House Committee on Foreign Affairs, 81st Congress, 1st Session.
[14] The American Embassy in Moscow reported that the Soviet press indicated that the Soviets were following a policy in Korea similar to that in Manchuria; that Peoples Committees were functioning in Seishin where a Korean Workers Union was organizing the local Koreans to assist Soviet naval forces in the occupation of Gensam. A farsighted description and analysis of the situation in the two areas was sent to Washington on September 15th by H. M. Benninghoff, a Foreign Service Officer attached to the American Military Headquarters in Seoul.
[15] Among them, E. Grant Meade, *American Military Government in Korea*, and Leland M. Goodrich, *Korea: A Study of U.S. Policy in the United Nations*.

14. The Formal Surrender

THE formal surrender was to be impressive and dramatic. President Truman and the Joint Chiefs of Staff agreed that it would be wise to arrange to have it occur close to the capital of Japan so that all the Japanese people would realize how thorough was their submission. But fear lest there might be demonstrations or assaults by fanatics favored a place off the coast in Tokyo Bay, and on the gallery deck of our most powerful ship of war the U.S.S. *Missouri* (named after the home state of the President and christened by his daughter).[1]

On the morning of September 2nd (Tokyo time) the Japanese envoys (Foreign Minister Shigemitsu and General Umezu, Chief of the Imperial General Staff), stood before General MacArthur, stern of expression and severe in tone, and wrote their names on the marked lines in the Instrument of Surrender. Representatives of the British, Soviet, Chinese, Australian, Canadian, New Zealand, Dutch, and French people—who had all suffered from Japan's tragic attempt to extend its supremacy from its four small and poor islands to the whole of the Western Pacific and Asia—also signed with a gleam of satisfaction beneath their gravity.

The second paragraph of the Instrument of Surrender read "We hereby proclaim the unconditional surrender to the Allied Powers of the Japanese Imperial General Headquarters and of all Japanese armed forces and all armed forces under Japanese control wherever situated." Other paragraphs pledged the Japanese authorities in the name of the Emperor to carry out the provisions of the Potsdam Declaration in good faith and to issue and obey whatever orders the Supreme Commander might require to give effect to its provisions.

The President broadcast the event to the world. His V-J Day speech took memorial notice of those who had suffered and died to achieve the victory they won. In the references to our allies there was no hint of separation, no shadow of disappointment. Elation over triumph was not clouded by any sobering reflections upon the meaning of atomic fission. The last two sentences were an attempt to wrest comfort and certainty from history and destiny.

[1] American apprehensions of such trouble on this occasion were mild compared with Stalin's. On August 27th he told Harriman he thought the risks were substantial because the Japanese were treacherous and there were many "crazy cutthroats" still among them. He suggested that various Japanese statesmen and military chieftains should be taken as hostages. His judgment was that it would be better advised to have ordered the Japanese to send all their ships and planes to Manila, and have them come there to sign the surrender.

"From this day we move forward. We move toward a new era of security at home. With the other United Nations we move toward a new and better world of peace and international good will and co-operation.

"God's help has brought us to this day of victory. With His help we will attain that peace and prosperity for ourselves and all the world in the years ahead."

In Moscow Stalin announced the signing of the act of unconditional surrender. "This means," he said, "that the second world war has come to an end." Then he went on to review the "aggressions" of Japan toward Russia as far back as 1904. "The surrender means," he emphasized, "that Southern Sakhalin and the Kurile Islands will pass to the Soviet Union, and from now on will not serve as a means for isolating the Soviet Union from the ocean and as a base for Japanese attacks on our Far East."

Concurrently the heads of the American Navy were recommending a similar extension of American sovereignty in the Pacific. They were advocating the retention of a string of bases stretching from the Aleutians to the Admiralties (the island of Manus) on the score that American control would enable the United States to keep any aggressor far away from American shores.

In crowded cities and small towns and isolated farms, in ships at sea and in camps on a hundred foreign fields and islands and atolls, Americans listened and rejoiced and enjoyed the vision of a peaceful life at home and a world from which the evil and cruelty and terror of war would have gone for the rest of their lives.

The American memory of how the war started was being refreshed by the public release of reports of official investigations of the catastrophe at Pearl Harbor. Americans' attitude toward the Japanese people, as they read the first descriptions of the conditions in Japan, was hardened by the horrifying first account of the cruelties suffered by prisoners in the Japanese prisoner of war camps; they learned that many had died because of beating, insufficient food and clothes, bad sanitation, and denial of medical aid.

On September 2nd American soldiers entered Tokyo and the stars and stripes was raised over MacArthur's headquarters in the American Embassy. It was the same flag that had flown over the capitol in

Washington on December 7, 1941. The Supreme Commander had words ready for the occasion. "Have our country's flag unfurled and in Tokyo's sun let it wave in its full glory as a symbol of hope for the oppressed and as a harbinger of victory for the right."

The Japanese people had been soothed by assurances that the allies would not land as "combat units," and would not seize their food, or commandeer their houses, or confiscate their savings. Despite the fact that it had been made plain in the Potsdam Declaration, many were shocked when they grasped that the allies were going to occupy the whole of their country.

But the official authorities at once proved their intent to honor their obligations. The people and the soldiers heeded the pleas of the Emperor of the need to bow before defeat and to show fortitude and self-control. They sadly responded to the counsel given by the Emperor in the last paragraph of his imperial rescript of August 14th: ". . . We are always with ye, Our good and loyal subjects, relying on your sincerity and integrity. Beware most strictly any outbursts of emotion which may engender needless complications, or any fraternal contention and strife which may create confusion, lead ye astray or cause ye to lose the confidence of the world. Let the entire nation continue as one family from generation to generation. . . . Unite your total strength to be devoted to the construction for the future. Cultivate the ways of rectitude; foster nobility of spirit; and work with resolution so as ye may enhance the innate glory of the Imperial State and keep pace with the progress of the world."

This patient, misled, and stunned people were beginning to carry away on their backs the rubble and to clear the ground where their houses once stood. Separated members of families were planning to meet again; the Japanese soldiers on the mainland and dispersed over a hundred islands and bases in the Pacific munched their rice as they chattered and gestured. It had been promised that they would be returned home and allowed to resume, as best they could among the ruins, their peacetime ways of living. Empire was gone; glory had passed; reckless and brave men had passed on. The future was hard, sober, dreary, but not hopeless nor remorseful.

15. The Heritage: An Imperiled Eternity

THE Americans who had conducted the war were relieved by the indications that they were not going to face trouble in Japan, for even at this season of American supremacy, the more informed and thoughtful realized that the ends for which the war had been fought were in hazard. The prospect of a peaceful order in the Far East, resting on friendship between the four members of the war coalition, was fading; the working alliance between the Western allies and the Soviet Union was dissolving; and quarrels over policies for Japan and China were starting.

The atomic bomb had enabled us to bring the war to a swift end. As long as we alone had this weapon we could prevail in any quarrel over a situation engaging American vital interests, such as the control of Japan. But its possession did not assure a satisfactory settlement of other current issues. Neither the American government nor the American people were inclined to impose their will upon those who differed with them by threat or by war; we regarded ourselves as leading advocates of the principle that all disputes between nations must be settled by peaceful means, and peaceful means only.

Moreover, it was foreseen that such advantage as we might gain from having atomic weapons was only temporary, that it would last only until other countries were able to produce them. Unless a reliable agreement had been reached by then to ban or control their production and use, nations were almost sure to engage in a desperate effort to arm themselves similarly. Then, having the power to destroy each other, they would be likely to live in mutual fear and mistrust. Was the victory won by brave men and women who believed they were fighting for peace and justice going to become instead the prelude to an era of awful terror? The more percipient American officials, beset by such thoughts during the first weeks of peace, strove to formulate measures for imprisoning the force of the atom that had been released.

In the interval Truman issued an order for the purpose of safeguarding the secret as long as possible. On August 15th he directed the Secretaries of State, War, and Navy, the Joint Chiefs of Staff, and the Director of the Office of Scientific Research and Development ". . . to take such steps as are necessary to prevent the release of any information in regard to the development, design or production of the atomic bomb; or in regard to its employment in military or naval warfare, except with the specific approval of the President in each instance." Time has taught that this vigilance did not seriously hinder the Soviet efforts to develop atomic weapons.

On September 4th the *New Times* published the first detailed expression of official views about the atomic bomb to appear in the Soviet Union. The article emphasized the opinion that the American achievement did not solve any political problems and it attacked those elements in the American press (Hearst, Patterson, and McCormick) who were advocating the use of the threat of the bomb to enforce American will in international affairs. It avowed that "many other countries have scientists who studied the problem of splitting the atom and who would work with redoubled energy to invent weapons as good or better." It advocated that the control of atomic energy be entrusted to an international body "since the fundamental principles are well-known and henceforth it is simply a question of time before any country will be able to produce atomic bombs."[1]

Stimson had reached similar conclusions. After his return from Potsdam he had again consulted with both the civilian and military persons associated with him on the S-1 project.

On August 17th Oppenheimer sent him a further statement of the opinions of the Scientific Panel on various points that had arisen in previous discussions of the Interim Committee about contemplated legislation. In the course of doing so once again Oppenheimer related that the Panel did not think there was any satisfactory defense against atomic weapons; that it doubted whether our national security could be assured by the maintenance or superiority of such weapons; that even though we tried to keep our knowledge of how to produce them secret, competitive production by other nations would not be prevented. Therefore, the Panel concluded that the American government should start at once to seek an international agreement to end the production of such weapons and to control atomic energy.

When Secretary of State Byrnes learned of these recommendations he told Harrison to advise Oppenheimer that it was not feasible to reach an agreement of the sort which the Scientific Panel had in mind, either quickly or in a hurry, and therefore to ask the scientists at Los Alamos

[1] United Press dispatch from Moscow of September 3, 1945, summarizing and extracting an article in the Soviet magazine *New Times*, printed in the *New York Times*, September 4, 1945.

and elsewhere to continue to carry on vigorously their effort to produce and improve such weapons.

On September 4th Stimson discussed the nature of and prospects for an international agreement with Byrnes, who was about to leave for the first meeting of the Council of Foreign Ministers in London. Byrnes was strongly opposed to any immediate initiative towards a cooperative agreement with Russia which might provide for the control of atomic energy. Despite the opinion of the scientists he seemed to continue to believe that the American government could secure an important advantage by guarding the knowledge of how to produce these weapons; and that as long as we could retain exclusive ability to make them he would be assisted in the achievements of his diplomatic aims. By this time Byrnes had become mistrustful of Soviet good faith, believing that at Potsdam Stalin and Molotov had shown themselves to be perfidious. He had reached the conclusion that neither the United States nor the United Nations could rely on Soviet promises.

The Secretary of War told the President of this talk with the Secretary of State and explained the differences in their views. He said that while he realized that both his program and the one favored by Byrnes involved dangers, he thought those attaching to his were the lesser, and that his would get the United States on the right path toward bringing about world order and peace, while Byrnes' plan would set the world on the wrong path and cause the nations to revert to a race in armaments and power politics.

In the days that followed, Stimson completed a statement of his views and proposals, encouraged by the agreement of the group with whom he had been consulting. On September 12th he took it over to the White House and presented it to the President with a covering letter. Truman waved him into a seat at the side of his desk and then read the memo aloud, paragraph by paragraph.

Both the memorandum and the covering letter have been printed and are familiar to students of this crucial question.[2] But since no official recommendation records as clearly the prevailing wish to get along with the Soviet Union in good faith and by just accord, a few of its main features ought to be recalled:

"In many quarters it [the atomic bomb] has been interpreted as a substantial offset to the growth of Russian influence on the continent. We can be certain that the Soviet Government has sensed this tendency and the temptation will be strong for the Soviet political and military

[2] Stimson and Bundy, *On Active Service in Peace and War*, pages 642-646.

leaders to acquire this weapon in the shortest possible time. . . . Such a condition will almost certainly stimulate feverish activity on the part of the Soviet toward the development of this bomb in what will in effect be a secret armament race of a rather desperate character. There is evidence to indicate that such activity may have already commenced. . . ."[3]

"Whether Russia gets control of the necessary secrets of production in a minimum of say four years or a maximum of twenty years is not nearly as important to the world and civilization as to make sure that when they do get it they are willing and co-operative partners among the peace-loving nations of the world. It is true if we approach them now, as I would propose, we may be gambling on their good faith and risk their getting into production of bombs a little sooner than they would otherwise. . . ."

"*[American-Soviet] relations may be perhaps irretrievably embittered by the way in which we approach the solution of the bomb with Russia. For if we fail to approach them now and merely continue to negotiate with them, having this weapon rather ostentatiously on our hip, their suspicions and their distrust of our purposes and motives will increase. . . .*"[4]

"My idea of an approach to the Soviets would be a direct proposal after discussion with the British that we would be prepared in effect to enter into an arrangement with the Russians, the general purpose of which would be to control and limit the use of the atomic bomb as an instrument of war. . . . Such an approach might more specifically lead to the proposal that we would stop work on the further improvement in, or manufacture of, the bomb as a military weapon, provided the Russians and the British would agree to do likewise. It might also provide that we would be willing to impound what bombs we now have in the United States provided the Russians and the British would agree with us that in no event will they or we use a bomb as an instrument of war unless all three Governments agree to that use. . . .

[3] One bit of evidence was a report received by the War Department about this time in the middle of September that the Soviet authorities were compelling the commanders of the Czechoslovak Army to give orders that all German plans, parts, models, and formulas regarding the use of atomic energy, rocket weapons, and radar be turned over to them. Russian infantry and technical troops occupied Jachimov (Achimuv) and St. Joachimstal, the town and the factory—the only place in central Europe where at this time uranium was being produced—even though there was no stipulation in the agreement between Czechoslovakian and Soviet governments for Soviet occupation of this area.

[4] In the narrative Stimson later wrote about his official life, *On Active Service in Peace and War*, these sentences are italicized because, as explained in a footnote, these were two of the sentences that he considered to be the heart of the memorandum.

"I would make such an approach just as soon as our immediate political considerations make it appropriate."

As the President read each section he said he agreed with it. Thus Stimson left the White House with the impression that he was in accord with its general tenor. But the measures proposed by the Secretary of War would have called for great daring on the part of even an assured and experienced executive under favorable circumstances, for it would have been an act of singular faith and trust that could have resulted disastrously. On the one hand the American government would be renouncing voluntarily the singular weapon of which it was sole master; and on the other hand it would be making it easier for foreign countries to develop the same or a similar one.

What a baleful balance of dangers: those which Stimson foresaw if the American government did not make this great gesture—dangers which have largely proven real—and those which would have been incurred had it adopted the bolder policy. Perhaps the President would have tried to ascertain the response of the American people to a far-sighted course of the sort advised by Stimson if experience with the Soviet rulers at the time had been such as to inspire trust. There are no cardiograms to inform us of the syncope of his decision. But it may be surmised that the inflowing reports of Soviet policy in Germany, Poland, and the satellite states, and of the discord at the meeting of the Foreign Ministers at London, discouraged any impulse toward a risky initiative.

Moreover, it may be surmised that the President might have been more inclined to try it had all those around him shared Stimson's judgment. But they did not. At a Cabinet meeting on the afternoon of the 21st, the last day of Stimson's service in office, he made an urgent plea for the policy advocated in the memorandum. The strenuous discussion aroused made this the longest session of the Truman Cabinet. His proposal was supported by Acting Secretary of State Dean Acheson and vigorously sponsored by Henry Wallace, Secretary of Commerce. But it was opposed by Fred M. Vinson, the Secretary of the Treasury, and by Forrestal, the Secretary of the Navy, who advised further study before action was taken.[5]

The President deferred decision and sought the advice of Vannevar Bush, Director of the Office of Research and Development, and of the Joint Chiefs of Staff. This group recommended that the American government retain all existing secrets in respect to the atomic weapon,

[5] A detailed recital of the views expressed by all the members of the Cabinet at this momentous meeting is in *Year of Decisions*, pages 526-527.

pending agreement on fundamental political problems and for international control of atomic weapons. Truman paused and waited for the
expected chance to talk over the whole field of policy with the heads
of the two other governments who were our partners in the original
effort, the Prime Ministers of Great Britain and Canada.

They met in the middle of November in Washington. The procedure
they proposed in the joint declaration resulting from their consultations
was more cautious and less clear than that which Stimson had formulated,
but it was still a memorable and sincere effort to begin negotiation of
an agreement for the control of atomic weapons. It could have averted
the subsequent competitive accumulation by the West and the Soviet
Union. But I must leave to others the task of telling of the long and
confused negotiations between the former allies about the control of
atomic energy, which were about to begin.

In their statement Truman, Attlee, and King expressed realization
that the only complete protection for the civilized world from the
destructive menace was in the prevention of war, and stated that "Faced
with the terrible realities of the application of science to destruction,
every nation will realize more urgently than before the overwhelming
need to maintain the rule of law among nations and to banish the scourge
of war from the earth." *Beginning of actual Global gov. thought?*

At the end of this narrative of the great war and the terminal efforts
at peace-making, the historian must conclude that the nations have not
come to this realization. The threat of destruction has grown enormously
in the years that have since passed, grown without restraint. No one
knows the number of atomic weapons ready for use in the hands of
possible opponents, but all know that both the United States and the
Soviet Union now possess bombs the most powerful of which contain
an explosive force of a million and more tons of TNT. In contrast,
the resolve to find the ways of ending the quarrels that are dividing the
world seems to have become tired, weighed down by mutual mistrust.

Fifteen years afterwards nothing that might be written could add
to the simple and conclusive comment which General Arnold, who had
commanded the expanding and heroic American air force during the
war, included in his report to the Secretary of War. "Even before the ...
atomic bomb ... mass air raids were obliterating the great centers of
mankind. ... The Twentieth Air Force was destroying Japanese cities

at ... [a] cost to Japan ... fifty times the cost to us. . . . Atomic bombing is [even] more economical. . . . Destruction is too cheap, too easy. . . . No effort spent on international cooperation will be too great if it assures the prevention of this destruction."[6]

The war against the Axis was fought by the Western allies to protect their freedom and place in the world. The ordeal was sustained not only by courage and pride and anger, but by the aspiring belief that once the aggressive enemy was defeated, the world might live in tranquil, unclouded peace. We have, instead, a precarious truce resting on mutual terror. History at this point leaves all eternity in peril.

[6] Report to the Secretary of War, November 12, 1945, Washington, 1945.

PART FOUR

Queries and Reflections in Aftertime

Prophet

Behold!
As if the stars had fallen from their places
Into the firmament below,
The streets, the gardens, and the vacant spaces
With light are all aglow;
And hark!
As we draw near,
What sound is it I hear
Ascending through the dark?

Angel

The tumultuous noise of the nations,
Their rejoicings and lamentations,
The pleadings of their prayer,
The groans of their despair,
The cry of their imprecations,
Their wrath, their love, their hate!

—HENRY WADSWORTH LONGFELLOW,
Christus, A Mystery

16. Was a Real Chance Missed to End the War Earlier?

In his memoirs former Acting Secretary of State Grew quotes from a letter he wrote to Stimson in 1947 raising the question whether, if the President had not waited until the Conference at Potsdam (July 17th-August 2nd, 1945) to tell the Japanese of our intentions, the surrender of Japan could have been hastened; in particular if the President had made "a public categorical statement that surrender would not mean the elimination of the present dynasty if the Japanese people desired its retention. . . ."

Grew recognized how groping this, like all other efforts to learn the secrets of unacted history, must be. But he wrote, "I myself and others felt and still feel that if such a categorical statement about the dynasty had been issued in May, 1945, the surrender-minded elements in the Government might well have been afforded . . . a valid reason and the necessary strength to come to an early clear-cut decision."

Do the Japanese records that have since become available provide an answer to his question?[1] I believe they do; and I find that they indicate that the Japanese government would not have surrendered before July, either in response to such statement of policies in explanation of our call for unconditional surrender as the State Department urged the President to make, or such a statement about the dynasty as Grew had in mind.

In early April the Koiso Cabinet, which had taken over from General Tojo, had also been compelled to resign by the stress of adversity. Admiral Baron Kantaro Suzuki (retired) was chosen to be Prime Minister in this last war cabinet. Seventy-seven years old, he had been Grand Chamberlain to the Emperor and more recently President of the Privy Council. The Emperor liked and trusted him. Known as a person of integrity and moderation, he was not regarded as so convinced an advocate of the necessity of fighting on as to alienate the seekers of peace,

---

[1] The main records available in English are: (1) The unpublished history of the war written by SCAP under General MacArthur's direction, (2) records of the International Military Tribunal For the Far East, (3) Butow's perceptive account in *Japan's Decision to Surrender*, (4) Kase's *Journey to the Missouri*, a reliable and informative study by a former member of the Japanese Foreign Office, edited by Professor David N. Rowe of Yale University, (5) Shigemitsu's *Japan and Her Destiny* (Shigemitsu was Foreign Minister under Tojo, and later as Foreign Minister, one of the signatories of surrender), and (6) Togo's *The Cause of Japan*.

nor so bold an advocate of peace as to cause the more militant elements to oppose him.

When conferring the imperial mandate, the Emperor had voiced deep concern over the trend of war but had refrained from any explicit request or order that Suzuki arrange for an early peace. The new Prime Minister had agreed to have General Korechika Anami as Minister of War, though he was of the same temper as Tojo and as opposed to any initiative toward peace. Moreover, in order to get the Army to cooperate in the formation of his Cabinet, Suzuki had assented to its conditions: that he would prosecute the war to the finish; that he would form a Cabinet that would favor unification of the Army and the Navy; that the Cabinet would promptly take the measures desired by the Army to assure victory in the decisive battle of the homeland. How could Suzuki keep these promises and probe for peace?

But several of the other chief positions in the Cabinet were assigned to men who discreetly were advocating peace. Yonai had been retained as Navy Minister. Togo, who had been Foreign Minister under Tojo in 1941, was induced to serve again in that office; during the crucial months before Pearl Harbor he had been wavering and weak, but the officials near the Throne who persuaded him to take on the responsibility again in this darker time were sure that he was in favor of ending the war as soon as possible. It is not unlikely that Suzuki gave him assurances of a trend quite different from those which he gave the Army. The diffusion of conflicting promises was usual; because of the agonizing divisions within the circle around the Throne, Cabinets were able to survive and operate only by supple and constant deception of some of their members.

When it took office the Suzuki Cabinet, like the German government before it, believed that there was a fair chance of dividing the coalition, and so securing an easier peace. This it sought to do by soliciting Soviet friendship; the reliance on the good-will of the Soviet Union up to the end was one of the crucial causes of the ultimate Japanese tragedy. Foreign Minister Togo suspected that the Soviet government had entered into a secret accord with the American and British governments to enter the war, but he had no proof of it. The other members of the Supreme Council (the Prime Minister, Foreign Minister, War and Navy Ministers, and Chiefs of the Army and Navy General Staffs) thought it unlikely. The Soviet government had on April 5th given notice of its wish to terminate the Neutrality Pact with Japan which it had signed in 1941; the Japanese government was lulled by the fact that by its terms the pact was to remain in force for one year after such notice of termination.

Togo had instructed Sato, the Japanese Ambassador in Moscow, to secure assurances that the Soviet Union would continue to be neutral, but his advances had been evaded by Molotov. Suzuki and Togo had waited before seeking a more definite pledge, hoping for a more helpful response if the battle for Okinawa went well. However, it had gone worse. Then Germany had collapsed, and the allied attacks on the homeland were becoming disastrous. So Togo had decided that an effort to make peace with the Western allies should be started at once, before the Japanese power to resist was wholly exhausted. In that event he foresaw that it would be even more difficult to get any relaxation of the demand for unconditional surrender. The Emperor, Togo believed, had reached the same conclusion.

The Supreme Council considered the plight of Japan in conferences that dragged on for four days in the middle of May. Togo, for the first time, in contradiction to the military view, disclosed his own opinion that an effort to win the Soviet Union over to the Japanese side would be futile. Hence he advocated that active consideration ought to be given to measures to end the war itself. His colleagues were not convinced.

What price was the Japanese government willing to pay at this time to keep the Soviet Union neutral or cause it to be benevolently friendly? It was provisionally agreed that Togo might promise the recession to Russia of the territorial rights and privileges granted by the Treaty of Portsmouth and the neutralization of South Manchuria, but Korea was not to be discussed.[2]

And suppose the Soviet government would also agree to act as mediator between Japan and the Western allies? What terms short of unconditional surrender would be acceptable? War Minister Anami maintained that the terms ought to reflect the fact that Japan was not yet down on its knees; did it not, he argued, hold more of the territory of its enemies than they did of Japanese territory? The spokesmen for the Navy knew that the far-off areas which had been captured early in the war could no longer be defended or even supplied, but not wishing

---

[2] As so often, in Japanese decisions of the war period, the actual details of the tentative agreement reached by the members of the Supreme Council were not precise. Togo, in his memoirs describes them as ". . . abrogation of the Treaty of Portsmouth and the Russo-Japanese Basic Treaty, and the restoration in general of the status prior to the Russo-Japanese war; provided, that autonomy for Korea should not be included—that question being reserved to Japan's arbitrament—and that South Manchuria should be neutralized." *The Cause of Japan*, page 287.

to appear less courageous or to hurt fighting unity, they had not taken issue with the War Minister. Only the Foreign Minister dared try to dwell on the reality that unless they accepted terms which corresponded to the obvious trend of the war, any effort to secure peace by mediation would fail.

Unable to agree on this essential matter, the conferring group decided to defer any request to ask the Soviet government to act as mediator. Togo was constrained merely to try again to bargain for Soviet neutrality or friendship. He had asked Hirota, a senior statesman who had at various times served as Prime Minister, Foreign Minister, and Ambassador to Moscow, to probe the possibilities with Malik, the Soviet Ambassador in Tokyo.

This was as far as the Japanese government was able to go at the end of May when Grew was hopefully urging the President to issue a statement of our intentions before the struggle grew grimmer and the destruction worse.

Hirota's presentation to Malik (on June 3rd and 4th) was guarded. He hinted that Japan was seeking to assure sustained friendly relations between the two countries by accord, and asked how this might be arranged. Malik's answer was indifferent; the Soviet government would need time to think over what was being proposed. This reply does not seem to have been interpreted to be what it was: an evasive refusal.[8] The controlling Japanese military figures continued to argue that there was no extreme hurry to seek Soviet mediation.

The Army staff had been working on a formulation of basic war policy. This was shaped by its rigid refusal to acknowledge the certainty of defeat. It looked beyond the daily disasters toward victory in the ultimate battle in defense of the Homeland. Do or die. As well described by Butow, "Here was nothing less than the army's final, comprehensive demand that the nation engage the enemy on Japan's own shores, for only thus . . . could the imperial land be preserved and the national polity maintained."[4]

The statement of policy adopted by the Supreme War Council on June 6th, in face of the state of Japan's war strength and prospects, in

---

[8] Whether Hirota's reports were misleading, or whether Togo misjudged them, is unclear. But Togo in his later account wrote, "Hirota reported to me that opinions were exchanged on the fundamental problems involved in relations between the two countries; he said that the atmosphere of the talks was friendly, that the Russian side responded satisfactorily and the conversations seemed hopeful, and that arrangements had been made for subsequent meetings." *The Cause of Japan*, page 289.
[4] *Japan's Decision to Surrender*, page 93.

saner minds would have crushed its three supporting suppositions. These were (1) that it was going to be possible to maintain a sufficient production of weapons, raw materials, and food to put up a strong defense, (2) that with these means the battle for the homeland could be won, or in any case sustained so hard and long that the enemy would offer acceptable terms rather than endure more loss and suffering, and (3) that the Soviet government could be persuaded to stay out of the war. Togo alone challenged the validity of the assumptions and the connected course of action. The aged Prime Minister, Suzuki, turned aside the Foreign Minister's criticisms and persuaded him to glide along with the others.

The decision of the Supreme Council having been ratified by the Cabinet, the approval of the Emperor was sought at an Imperial Conference on June 8th. The routine of this conference, having been set in advance, was rigidly formal. All the military leaders present expressed confidence that the policy could succeed. The Army High Command vowed that it could. The Chief of Staff of the Navy, Admiral Toyoda, estimated that in the event of an early assault on Japan almost half of the enemy invasion force could be destroyed on the water, and even more if the assault was delayed, provided Japanese war production was maintained. Togo spoke gloomily of the prospect, but he did not renew his outspoken opposition. The statement, called "The Fundamental Policy to be Followed Henceforth in the Conduct of the War," was approved with a show of unity which smoothed over the depth of desperation. The Emperor remained silent throughout.

The Japanese Diet had been called in special session with the thought of stimulating the spirit of resistance and the production effort. In his opening speech, Suzuki spoke as one deeply imbued with the conviction that it was essential to continue the war. The enemy, he averred, threaten the very existence, the basic polity and the national aim of the Japanese empire. Unconditional surrender would result in the "destruction" of the state and the "ruin" of the Japanese race. There was only one path Japan could follow and that was to "fight to the very end."[5]

But on the same day, June 9th, Kido, Lord Keeper of the Privy Seal, aware that the Emperor was distressed at the outcome of the Imperial

---

[5] After the war was over, Prime Minister Suzuki explained this avowal as a deliberate disguise of his real purpose. He claimed to have made this defiant utterance because he thought it was necessary to avoid assassination and to leave the way open for the use of the dual technique which he intended to employ; that is, simultaneously, to try to increase the Japanese war effort and strengthen the will to fight, while using diplomatic channels for the purpose of arriving at a negotiated peace.

Conference, submitted to him a plan aimed to invalidate the decisions that had just been sanctioned. This plan contemplated the use of imperial influence to get the government to seek an end to the war on some broad terms of compromise—that is, to use the Emperor's influence against the Army and all others who remained opposed to an attempt to bring the war to an end before Japan was invaded.

Kido explained that he thought it essential that a more resolute move be made to end the war, that if the government continued to wait for a better chance Japan would share the fate of Germany and be unable to secure even its minimum demands: "the safeguarding of the imperial family and the preservation of the national polity." He recognized that it would be best that the Emperor should wait for the Army and Navy to admit that it could not continue the war, propose that talks about peace be started, and for the government then to submit its prospectus for the negotiations. But the Army and Navy were not willing to come forward. Therefore the Emperor was called on to intervene for the sake of the people and take steps to end the war. Kido's thought was that in pursuance of a personal message from the Emperor, the Soviet government should be asked to mediate for peace.

He described the penalties to which he thought the Japanese people could submit, if need be, in order to escape complete ruin of the country and nation. Its two telling paragraphs were:

"Honorable peace (it may be inevitable that this will be the minimum term). In view of the object of Japan's declaration of war, if a guarantee is obtained that the Pacific will be made true to its name, Japan will renounce her right of occupation and claim to leadership over those areas now under her occupation, provided only that the nations and peoples of these areas attain independence. Japan, on her own initiative, will withdraw her armed forces from the occupied areas. (In this case, some Japanese forces may be compelled to abandon their arms on the spot, but this question may be left to future negotiations.)

"Japan must be prepared to carry out a heavy reduction of armaments, which will be demanded of her. There will be no alternative but to be content with the minimum armament required for national defense."

How hesitant still the civilian members of the government were to brave the reckless anger of the men in Army uniform is revealed by this obscure sketch of Kido's. True, the failure of the long war in China would be acknowledged; and the Soviet Union would be rewarded for its mediation. But the rest of the Japanese empire would be left intact. Furthermore, Japan was to be spared the humiliation of foreign occupation and control. Who can know whether Kido appreciated that once negotiations with its enemies were started, the Japanese government would find itself compelled to accept more severe terms, but avoided saying so in order to minimize opposition at the moment.[6]

The Emperor approved Kido's initiative and instructed him to enter into immediate consultation with the leaders of the government. Within a week, Kido had gained the consent of all members of the inner circle except Anami. While at last granting that the situation was serious, the Minister of War continued to insist that it was essential to wage the homeland battle and inflict heavy losses on the enemy before seeking peace.

On June 18th, Kido's proposal was discussed in another tense meeting of the Supreme War Direction Council. Anami was supported by the Chiefs of the Army and Navy General Staff. They also affirmed their conviction that the invasion battle ought to be risked, since if it was won, better terms could be secured. The consulting group again preserved a semblance of unity by taking refuge in ambiguity; it was understood that the Japanese government should go ahead in its attempt to get the Soviet government to act as mediator in the negotiations of a peace on *acceptable* terms, terms more favorable than unconditional surrender.

Kido, fearing that even this guarded step forward might be frustrated by the military men, persuaded the Emperor to make known that he wanted it taken. The Emperor was the more willing to do so because he had just received two special and convincing reports to the effect that the preparations underway both in Japan and China to resist further allied attacks were inadequate and that resistance would fail.

Neither Kido nor the Emperor, of course, knew—as has been related in an earlier chapter—that in Washington on this same morning Grew was urging President Truman to let the Japanese know how they would fare if they surrendered; and the President was answering that while he

---

[6] Butow, in his book, *Japan's Decision to Surrender*, page 114, tends to interpret this statement as a disguise. To quote him: "As Kido saw it, Japan's outstanding requirement would be a 'peace with honor.' But he realized that this high-sounding phrase might merely signify the termination of the war on a basis *only very slightly removed from unconditional surrender.* Japan would thus have to be prepared to relinquish her role of leadership in and control over the occupied areas of the Pacific. She would also have to withdraw her armed forces from those areas and would have to reduce her own armaments to a standard which would provide only the minimum requirements for defense. In Kido's eyes, these were the fundamentals; the detailed terms around which any specific negotiations would eventually revolve would have to be drafted by the experts."
Butow bases this interpretation of Kido's intention on various statements made by Kido himself with some corroboration by Marquis Yasumasa Matsudaira.

liked the text of the statement which Grew put before him, he had decided to wait for the chance to discuss it with Churchill and Stalin in July; and that later on that morning, after listening to the presentation of the Joint Chiefs of Staff, the President had approved their plan for the invasion of Kyushu.

On the 22nd the American government announced the end of the campaign of Okinawa. The Emperor met again with the six members of the Supreme Council. This time he spoke up. He said that they ought not to limit their efforts to preparations for the defense of the homeland. He urged all possible effort to bring the war to an acceptable conclusion by negotiation. But all still sought to avoid the act of directly asking the Western enemies for peace terms. Togo said that while there was danger in approaching the Russian government, and that in order to get its aid Japan might have to make substantial concessions to it, he thought this was the only way of avoiding unconditional surrender. General Umezu, speaking for the Army High Command, advised caution in phrases which implied that extremist elements in the Army might refuse to countenance any attempt to arrange a negotiated peace, and try to take control of the government by force. But when he was asked directly by the Emperor whether he was opposed to any attempt to make peace without waiting for invasion, he said he was not.

This declaration of the Emperor's wish cleared the way for a less veiled effort to seek to end the war by mediation. Almost at once (on June 24th) the Japanese government renewed its addresses to the Soviet government. Hirota tried once more to get an answer from Malik about the possibility of a new pact, but the Soviet Ambassador would say no more than that he would transmit any definite proposal for a new Soviet-Japanese pact to Moscow. When Hirota voiced hope for an early peace in the Far East, Malik's reply was so curt that Hirota did not venture to broach the idea of having the Soviet government act as mediator.

Confronted with this negative passivism the Japanese government came out in the open. A few days later (on June 29th) Hirota submitted to Malik a definite proposal. The Japanese government bid high for a pact of nonaggression and mutual assistance with the Soviet Union. It stated it was willing in return to grant Manchurian independence, give up the Japanese fishing concessions in Soviet Far Eastern waters in return for aid from the Soviet Union; and it was not adverse to considering any other conditions which the Soviet government might want to advance. Malik confined his answer to a promise to inform Moscow of this proposal and to resume talks with Hirota when advised of its reception. What he did was to send the Japanese offer to Moscow by overland courier. During the days when the courier was on his way he evaded Hirota's inquiries on the excuse of illness, and the Soviet Foreign Office similarly evaded Sato's attempts to extract an answer.

Stalin, it may be recalled, was at this time expecting Soong, who was serving both as Prime Minister and Foreign Minister in the Chinese National Government, to arrive in Moscow shortly. He was confident that the Chinese government could be induced to assent to the rewards which were to be conferred on the Soviet Union for entering the war against Japan. Concurrently, the movement of Soviet ground divisions, armored units, and air forces in the Far East was being accelerated.

Such, in summary sketch, was the state of anguished judgment within the Japanese government in regard to asking for peace during these two months after the defeat of Germany. It is clear that up to mid-June, no exposition of the way in which we intended to act that honestly corresponded to ideas that prevailed within the American government would have been well received in Tokyo—even if it had left open the possibility that Japan could retain the Emperor.

But when the speculating historian travels toward the end of June and early July, *before Potsdam*, he cannot be so sure about the unrealized possibilities, for the effort to reach a conclusion runs into a mesh of elusive queries. One is whether the American government would have decided it was advisable or necessary to ask the Soviet government to concur in the statement of peace terms. If so, what would the Soviet government have done? Would it have agreed on condition that the advantages promised it at Yalta would be confirmed? Or would it have objected, and if so, would the American government have dropped the initiative? And if the American government had not consulted it, would the Soviet government have hastened to inform the Japanese government that it would remain out of the war at a price, and in that event would not the Japanese government have rejected the American offer?

Despite these and many other conceivable variations in circumstance, I think it may be concluded that even if the American government had made known that it would not insist upon removing the Emperor, the *first* Japanese response would have been only a preface to an effort to negotiate over other conditions of surrender; that the fighting would have continued well into July at the least, *unless*, and here we enter an even more misty field of conjecture, the American and Soviet governments together had let it be known that unless Japan laid down its arms at once, the Soviet Union was going to enter the war. That, along with a promise to spare the Emperor, might well have made an earlier bid for surrender effective. But it is improbable that the Soviet government could have been prevailed on to reveal its intention and so enable the Japanese better to prepare for the assault.

Even if these inferential conclusions are correct, the curious mind lingers over the reasons why the American government waited so long before offering the Japanese those various assurances which it did extend later. In his decision to postpone that step the President was influenced by the advice of the Joint Chiefs of Staff, the Secretary of State (Stettinius), and the Secretary of War. Each had his own reasons. The Joint Chiefs thought that the Japanese could be brought to surrender unconditionally only after they had been more thoroughly whipped in battle; they did not want to risk the chance that the American government might be induced to reduce its demand that Japan be occupied and its military power permanently broken.[7] The Secretary of State wanted to strengthen the bonds between the victors that he thought were being forged at San Francisco by having them act together. The Secretary of War wanted to wait until the atomic bomb had been tested, so that our call to Japan to surrender could be quickly supported in an irresistible way.

The President found it easier to follow than to reject this advice, for any statement of terms that could be construed as a renunciation of the principle of unconditional surrender would have aroused some opposition at home. Discussion of peace terms might have encouraged the Japanese to maintain their resistance; or it might have attracted so much popular support at home that the American government would have been pressed to make undue concessions to Japan, or to give assurances which the

---

[7] As expressed in a memo of June 9th by Marshall to Stimson on Basic Objectives of the Pacific War: "We must be careful to avoid giving any impression that we are growing soft."

Extract from a report of the Combined Intelligence Committee to the Joint Chiefs of Staff in early July: "Since the Japanese Army is the principal repository of the Japanese military tradition, it follows that the Army leaders must, with a sufficient degree of unanimity, acknowledge defeat before Japan can be induced to surrender. This might be brought about either by the defeat of the main Japanese Armies in the Inner Zone or through a desire on the part of the Army leaders to salvage something from the wreck with a view of maintaining military tradition. For a surrender to be acceptable to the Japanese Army, it would be necessary for the military leaders to believe that it would not entail discrediting warrior tradition and that it would permit the ultimate resurgence of a military Japan."

Japanese might claim later were broken, as had Germany after the First World War. Such cautionary thoughts would have led to the conclusion that the earlier action would involve avoidable risks for an unpromising cause.

Other components also entered the decision: the impetus of the combat effort and plans, the impulse to punish, the inclination to demonstrate how supreme was our power, the dramatic tension of the new promised weapon as the imposer of surrender.

We are left with the troubling question of what the effect would have been had the American government and its allies affirmed definitely in the Potsdam Declaration of July 26th that they would allow the Japanese people to retain, if they wished, the Emperor and their form of national polity. In that event would Prime Minister Suzuki still have made his mistaken and scornful rejection? Would the crisis of argument around the Throne have come to its climax before the bomb was used, terminated by the expressed will of the Emperor? Or would the Japanese authorities have continued to try to get release from other elements of the surrender terms? And if so, would they have gone on trying to do so until the bomb fell, or the Soviet Union entered the war—to the dismay of the Japanese Army leaders and the unmerited inflation of the Soviet part in its termination? To these speculative inquiries I can contribute no more by way of answer than I have in earlier pages.

It is time for the historian to leave this misty and alluring land of what might have happened had the American government acted otherwise than it did. In fairness, three assumptions which influenced the American course should be again recalled. One was that since Stalin was deemed to have restricted Soviet aims in the Far East reasonably in the statements he made to Hopkins, there was no sound reason for trying to avert Soviet entry into the war. Another was that the China upon which we were bestowing many benefits would be a faithful friend and ally in the Far East. The third was that there was no good reason to refrain from the use of the atomic bomb, like any other weapon, against Japan.

As later experiences upset these assumptions, they exposed to criticism the American decisions not to bid for an earlier surrender by a relaxation of our terms.

17. Comments and Conjectures on the Use of the Atomic Bomb against Japan

At the time of the event, only some contributing scientists protested the use of the atomic bomb against a vulnerable live target. The peoples fighting Japan looked upon its employment against the enemy as a natural act of war, and rejoiced at the swift ending it brought about. Any qualms they might have had over the cruel suffering of the victims were routed by the thought that if Germans or Japanese had developed this weapon they would surely have used it. Subsequently, however, as the blast and radiation effects of this new projectile were more fully appreciated, and as more and more powerful kinds were spawned, the precedent act has been regarded by many with rue.

Whether, if the United States had pledged itself as soon as the war ended to destroy the other bombs it had and dismantle the factories in which they were made other countries would have been willing to join with it in a trustworthy system of control of atomic energy, must remain forever a provocation to the speculative historian. But most probably the dismal failure to reach any restraining agreement was an inexpugnable accompaniment to the suspicions, animosities, fears and hatred that have been so rampant after the war. Unable to arrive at genuine peace with each other through mutual good will, respect and understanding, they live under the common canopy of mutual terror. Little wonder then that foreboding dominates the memory of the laboratory triumphs of the physicists, the achievements of the engineers, the test at Alamogordo and the display at Hiroshima.

In the evolving discussion about the decision to use the bomb, several related but separable questions have been commingled. One of these, and by far the easiest to answer conclusively, is whether it was *essential* to do so in order to compel Japan to surrender on our terms before it was invaded.

Some of the decision-makers were confident that the invasion of the main islands of Japan would not be necessary to compel surrender quickly and unconditionally. Japan's ability to fend off our tremendous naval and air assaults was shattered. It seemed to them that the Japanese people, crowded in their small islands, with insufficient and destructible supplies of food and oil, would have to give in soon—unless bent on national suicide. Among those were Secretary of the Navy Forrestal and Under-Secretary Bard and Admiral Leahy and General Spaatz, the Commander of our Strategic Air Force.

But others, especially those in the Army, remained convinced that final victory on our own terms could only be achieved on land, as it had been in the Philippines, Iwo Jima, Okinawa. Had not their military histories taught them that a hopelessly beaten Confederate Army had battled on? Had they not witnessed the refusal of the Germans under the fanatic Hitler to give up long after any chance of winning was gone, and how that people rallied from the shattering air attacks on their cities? Would the war in Europe continue many months longer, they argued, except for the combined crushing assaults of large land armies from the East, the West, the South?

To the historian, taught by the accumulated records and testimony, the answer is obvious. There cannot be a well-grounded dissent from the conclusion reached as early as 1945 by members of the U.S. Strategic Bombing Survey. After inspection of the condition to which Japan was reduced, by studies of the military position and the trend of Japanese popular and official opinion, they estimated ". . . that certainly prior to 31 December 1945, and in all probability prior to 1 November 1945, Japan would have surrendered even if the atomic bombs had not been dropped, even if Russia had not entered the war, and even if no invasion had been planned or contemplated."[1]

If then the use of the bomb was not essential, was it justified—justified, that is, as the surest way in combination with other measures to bring about the earliest surrender? That is a harder question to answer, and a more troubling one than it was thought to be at the time of decision.

It may be contended with the grim support by history that no exceptional justification for the use of the bomb need be sought or given. For the prevalent rule of nations—except when "knighthood was in flower" —has allowed the use of any and all weapons in war except any banned by explicit agreement; and this was the prevailing view at the time, qualified only by revulsion against use of weapons and methods deemed needlessly inhuman such as poisoning of wells and torture. Did not, it should be borne in mind, every one of the contending nations strive its utmost to invent and produce more deadly weapons, faster planes of greater bomb capacity, new types of mines, rockets and buzz-bombs? And was not

[1] A well-qualified group sent to Japan right after the war to ascertain and appraise the performance of the U.S. air assaults and their effectiveness.

each and every improved sort of killing weapon brought into action without ado or reproach? For this reason alone, almost all professional military men, and those in uniform in 1945, would then have denied that any special justification for the use of the bomb was needed, and would still dispose of the subject in this way.

The more thoughtful might add that the decision to use the bomb was not really important; that the measures of permanent significance to mankind had been taken when physicists learned how to split the atom, and when scientists and engineers and builders succeeded in encasing the energy of the fissured atom in a bomb; and that after these were achieved, it made little or no difference if this novel weapon was used against Japan, since it would certainly be used in the future time unless nations renounced war. Or if it were not, other equally dreadful threats would remain; chemical and biological ways of bringing death; and these were already in the secret arsenals of nations.

The source of restraint lies in fear of consequences; fear of the fact that the enemy will use the same terrible weapon. This was, for example, why neither side used poison gas in the war. When humane feeling is allied to such fear, it may command respect, and even those striving to win a war may recognize that "virtue it is to abstain even from that which is lawful."

These considerations seem to me conclusive defenses of our right, legal and historical, for the use of the atomic bomb against Japan. Those who made the decision took them for granted. They thus felt free to make it without scruples on these scores.

Their reckoning, I believe the record clearly indicates, was governed by one reason deemed paramount: that by using the bomb the agony of war might be ended most quickly and lives be saved. It was believed with deep apprehension that many thousands, probably tens of thousands, of lives of Allied combatants would have to be spent in the continuation of our air and sea bombardment and blockade, victims mainly of Japanese suicide planes. In spite of its confidence in ultimate success, our assailant naval force felt vulnerable, because of grim and agonizing experience. Since the desperate kamikaze attacks began, suicide planes had sunk 34 American ships, including 3 aircraft carriers, and damaged 285 (including 36 carriers of all sizes and sorts, 15 battleships, 15 cruisers and 87 destroyers). During the Okinawa campaign alone, 16 of our ships had been sunk and 185 damaged (including 7 carriers, 10 battleships and 5 cruisers).[2]

---

[2] These figures are derived from the official U.S. reports of losses definitely attributable to kamikaze attack. *The Divine Wind* by Captain R. Inoguchi and Commander T. Nakajima, with Roger Pineau, page 160.

It was reliably known that the Japanese were assembling thousands of planes, of all kinds and conditions, to fling against the invasion fleet and the troop-carrying ships.[3] Thus, should it prove necessary to carry out the plans for invasion, not only of Kyushu but also of the Tokyo Plain, it was feared by Stimson and Marshall that the American casualties alone might mount to hundreds of thousands.[4] Our allies, it was reckoned, would suffer corresponding losses.

But the people who would have suffered most, had the war gone on much longer and their country been invaded, were the Japanese. One American incendiary air raid on the Tokyo area in March 1945 did more damage and killed and injured more Japanese than the bomb on Hiroshima. Even greater groups of American bombing planes would have hovered over Japan, consuming the land, its people and its food, with blast and fire, leaving them no place to hide, no chance to rest, no hope of reprieve. A glance at the chart kept in the Headquarters of the U.S. Strategic Air Force at Guam, with its steeply ascending record of bombing flights during the summer of 1945 and scheduled for the next month or two, leaves visions of horror of which Hiroshima is only a local illustration. Observation of the plight of the country and its people made soon after the war ended left me appalled at what those would have had to endure had the war gone on.

But the same official forecasts of what it was thought would occur if we had to fight on, gave sharper shape to the impelling reason for the development of the bomb—to end the war victoriously. Thus the decision to use the bomb seemed to be the natural culminating act for the achievement of a settled purpose as attested by its leading sponsors:

General Groves: "My mission as given to me by Secretary of War Stimson [in October 1942] was to produce this [the atomic bomb] at the earliest possible date so as to bring the war to a conclusion."[5]

---

[3] The U.S. Strategic Bombing Survey did their utmost to get a reliable estimate of the potential strength of the Japanese air power at the end of the war. They encountered various inconsistencies in the records from which they reconstructed their resultant estimate. This reckoned that the Japanese had 5,350 planes ready for suicide use, of which about half were just primary trainers; and a roughly equal number of planes ready for orthodox use. They were to be dispersed on small grass fields and in "underground hangars," most of which were merely caves in hillsides. They would have had enough pilots for the suicide missions though many of them would have had only enough training and experience for this type of flying. *U.S. Strategic Bombing Survey, Report 62, "Japanese Air Power."*

[4] As noted in the footnote on page 9—when Truman's approval for the invasion of Kyushu was sought on June 18th, the figures presented to him indicated an expectation of smaller losses.

[5] Groves' testimony, Oppenheimer Hearings, page 171.

Truman: "I regarded the bomb as a military weapon and never had any doubt that it should be used."[6]

Churchill: "The historic fact remains . . . that the decision whether or not to use the atomic bomb to compel the surrender of Japan was never even an issue. There was unanimous, automatic, unquestioned agreement around our table; nor did I ever hear the slightest suggestion that we should do otherwise."[7]

Stimson: "Stimson believed, both at the time and later, that the dominant fact of 1945 was war, and that therefore, necessarily, the dominant objective was victory. If victory could be speeded by using the bomb, it should be used; if victory must be delayed in order to use the bomb, it should *not* be used. So far as he knew, this general view was fully shared by the President and all his associates."[8]

Some of those men who concurred in the decision to use the bomb discerned other advantages and justifications. It is likely that Churchill, and probably also Truman, conceived that besides bringing the war to a quick end, it would improve the chances of arranging a satisfactory peace both in Europe and in the Far East. Stimson and Byrnes certainly had that thought in mind. For would not the same dramatic proof of western power that shocked Japan into surrender impress the Russians also? Might it not influence them to be more restrained? Might it not make more effective the resistance of the western allies to excessive Soviet pretensions and ventures, such as the Soviet bid for a military base in the Black Sea Straits, and a foreseen demand for a part in the occupation and control of Japan akin to that which it had in Germany? In short, the bomb, it may have been thought or hoped, would not only subdue the Japanese aggressors, but perhaps also monitor Russian behavior.

Recognition of this element in official thinking must not be distorted into an accusation that the American government engaged in what Soviet

[6] *Year of Decisions*, page 419.

[7] *Triumph and Tragedy*, page 639. The Prime Minister certainly knew of Bohr's misgivings and proposals, and that they were shared by some of his closest advisers. The British official history recounts that Sir John Anderson had written—in consultation and in agreement with Lord Cherwell—a long memo to Mr. Churchill on the subject at the end of March [1944]. In a formal sense the statement in the British official history (Gowing, *Britain and Atomic Energy*, page 371) that "whatever doubts there were among the British did not receive expression at the highest level" is no doubt correct; no voice was raised in topmost official circles against the use of the bomb. But some clear indications of misgiving among some British scientists and officials did come to Churchill's attention.

[8] *On Active Service in Peace and War*, page 629.

propagandists and historians have called "atomic blackmail."[9] To the contrary, even after the American government knew that it would have the supreme weapon, it keenly sought to preserve the friendly connection with the Soviet Union. It rebuffed Churchill's proposals that the Western allies face down the Soviet government in some climactic confrontation over the outward thrust of Soviet power. After the testing of the bomb, at the Potsdam Conference, it patiently sought compromise solutions for situations in dispute. While knowledge of the successful test may have somewhat stiffened Truman's resistance to some of the furthest-reaching Soviet wishes, it did not cause him to alter American aims or terms as previously defined. In brief, and obviously, the men who determined American policy strove to achieve a stable international order by peaceful ways. They were not swayed by an excited wish to impose our will on the rest of the world by keeping atomic bombs poised over their lives. Even as the American government proceeded to use the bomb against Japan, it was brewing proposals for controlling its production and banning its use, except possibly as an international measure to enforce peace.

Had—the query continues to haunt the historian—the American government, *before* using the bomb, informed Stalin candidly of its nature and potential, and solicited his cooperation in some system of international control, might the Soviet government have reacted differently? Might it have been deflected from making the utmost effort to master the task of producing like weapons and accumulating them as a national atomic force. It is highly improbable, I think, considering Stalin's determination, as evidenced at Potsdam, to wear down Western resistance to Soviet claims, his suspicions and soaring assurance, and his belief that nations respected only strength. It would have been like him, in fact, to regard our confidential briefing as a subtle way of threatening the Soviet government, of trying to frighten it to accede to our wishes.

My best surmise is that while openness would have disarmed some foreign critics and improved the reception abroad of our later proposals for control, it would not really have influenced the Soviet policy. Never-

---

[9] An example of this type of accusation made by professional Soviet historians is the study by L. N. Ivanov, *Essays on International Relations in the Period of the Second World War, 1939-1945* (in Russian: *Ocherki Mezhdunarodnykh Otnoshenii v Period Vtoroi Mirovoi Coiny 1939-1945.* Izdatel 'stvo Akademii Nauk SSSR, Moskva, 1958). Among the many misstatements which mark the Soviet literature in this field is one to the effect that MacArthur demanded that the Emperor of Japan in his rescript and in his order to the Japanese armed forces to surrender, compelled the Emperor to mention the bomb in order to distort the real cause of the capitulation of Japan.

Professor Patrick Blackett has been the leading exponent in Great Britain of a similar interpretation, and his rendition of history has made an impression on various Western students of the subject, including a few Americans. (*Continued on page 202*).

theless, it is regrettable that we did not take Stalin into at least the outer regions of our confidence, thereby indicating to the world that we were not intent on keeping unto ourselves a secret means of domination. After all, our secrecy and our elaborate security measures in the end were ineffectual and suffused the atmosphere with the scent of enmity.

This train of inference about other reasons for using the bomb—confluent with the wish to end the war quickly and with minimum loss of life—that may also have figured in the minds of those who made the decision, can be carried further. The scientists who served on the Scientific Panel, as the narrative has told, were gravely aware of the lasting and supreme significance of the achievement. Stimson, sharing their perception of its bearing upon human destiny, was impelled, despite age and fatigue, to write memo after memo expounding his conviction that every effort must be exerted to get the nations to cooperate to prevent impending mutual destruction.

These official parents of this new form of force verged toward the conclusion that it would confront the whole world with a crucial and ultimate choice: to renounce war or perish. But would the nations defer to that reality unless the horrifying power of this new weapon to destroy human life was proven by human sacrifice? Would they realize otherwise that it was imperative that they subordinate themselves to the new international security organization that had just been created in San Francisco? Would they submit to the necessary restraints unless convinced that if they did not, they would all be consumed together in the vengeful bursts of atomic explosions? Thus, even men genuinely regretful about the deaths and suffering that would be caused by the use of the bomb, could think of the act as an essential step toward the creation of a peaceful political order. And connectedly, that undeniable proof of the destructive power of atomic energy would foster a willingness to subject its development to the collectivity of nations; for unless it was so controlled, any one country with a great atomic force could defy the rest.

As recounted, there were those who believed all these purposes would be better served if the bomb was introduced in some other way. They urged that before using it against Japan its immense destructive power should be displayed to the world by dropping it in some remote, uninhabited or emptied spot—an isolated island perhaps, or over a dense forest area, or on a mountain top, or in the sea near land. All suggestions of this sort were judged impractical, ineffective and/or risky.

A genuine fear of failure persisted despite accumulated evidence that the weapon was going to bear out the scientists' prediction. It will be remembered that as early as December 1944, Groves had been sure enough that one of the two types of bomb being produced (the type that was dropped on Hiroshima) would work satisfactorily, to report to Stimson that he and presumably his technical advisers did not think a preliminary full test essential. This confidence mounted as the effort neared fruition. The physicist, Smyth, who wrote up the authorized explanation of the undertaking, entered in his notes that "the end of June [1945] finds us expecting from day to day to hear of the explosion of the first atomic bomb devised by man. All the problems are believed to have been solved at least well enough to make a bomb practicable. A sustained neutron chain reaction resulting from nuclear fission has been demonstrated; the conditions necessary to cause such a reaction to occur explosively have been established and can be achieved. . . ."[10]

But the responsible officials and military men still had nervous fears of failure. As recalled summarily by Stimson, in explanation of the decision not to warn Japan in advance of the nature and destructive power of the weapon, "Even the New Mexico test would not give final proof that any given bomb was certain to explode when dropped from an airplane. Quite apart from the generally unfamiliar nature of atomic explosives, there was the whole problem of exploding a bomb at a predetermined height in the air by a complicated mechanism which could not be tested in the static test of New Mexico."[11]

This uncertainty remained despite the numerous varied trials that had been made in flight with a simulated bomb casing and components. For many precautions had been conceived and taken against each and every one of these hazards; many rehearsals to enable trained mechanics and bombing crews to detect any causes of failure beforehand and to correct them.

Then there were chances of human error or accident. What if the heavily laden plane carrying the bomb and fuel needed for the long flight to the point selected for the demonstration crashed? What if the individuals entrusted with the task of turning the containing tube (in the U-235 gun type bomb that was first available for use in Japan) into an atomic weapon, faulted?[12]

[10] Henry deWolf Smyth, *Atomic Energy for Military Purposes*, page 223.
[11] *On Active Service in Peace and War*, page 617.
[12] General Farrell decided at Tinian, in view of the tragic consequences if the plane carrying the bomb should crash on take-off, that this final step should be performed in the plane on the way to Hiroshima—a bold decision which Groves might not have approved

Then, also, there were chances of physical defects. Some part of the mechanism of any single specimen might turn out to be defective and malfunction.

Still another opposed reason was that the American government had so few of the new bombs. One would be consumed by the New Mexico test; another (of a different type) was promised in time for use after July 31; and it was reckoned a third by August 6th; and no others according to the schedule given to the decision-makers in June, until about August 20th.[13] By using all—two or three—with utmost effectiveness, the desired quick end of the war might well be brought about. If one of these was misspent in a demonstration that went awry for any reason, could the trial be justified to the men in uniform whose lives were in hazard every day the war went on?

Suppose an announced demonstration had failed. Would the consequences have been serious? Stimson, and even more decidedly Byrnes and Groves, thought so. They believed that if it did not come off "as advertised," the Japanese would take fresh heart and fight on harder and longer. They feared, also, that an uproar would ensue in Congress if the demonstration fizzled or failed to budge the Japanese. They had accepted the unavoidable risks of condemnation if the project on which such vast sums had been spent turned out to be a mistaken venture. But they were not willing to widen the margin of exposure for any other purpose. They tried to dismiss their worries as did the experienced construction engineer whom Robert Patterson, the Under Secretary of War, asked to size up the operation at Oak Ridge. On his return he assured Patterson, "You have really nothing to worry about. If the project succeeds, no one will investigate what was done, and if it does not succeed, every one will investigate nothing else the rest of your life."

Such were the grave apprehensions of the decision-makers of the consequences of a failure in an attempted demonstration. I cannot refrain from remarking that I do not think they would have been as upsetting or

---

had he been there. The job was done by Captain William S. Parsons, by whose advice Farrell was persuaded.

[13] *On Active Service in Peace and War*, page 630; the interview with General Marshall printed in *U.S. News and World Report*, November 1959; Wesley Craven and James Lea Cate, Editors, *The Army Air Forces in World War II*, Vol. 5. *The Pacific Matterhorn to Nagasaki, June 1944 to August 1945*, page 718; and testimony of General Groves in *Hearings before the Special Committee on Atomic Energy, U.S. Senate, Seventy-ninth Congress. First Session, S.R. 179*, Part I, Washington, 1945, page 40.

However, because of an unforeseen increase in the rate of production of plutonium, all ingredients and components for the third bomb made for use against Japan were in hand in the United States by about August 10, and could have been dropped some days before August 20.

harmful as imagined. The stimulant to Japanese military morale would have been very brief. In the United States, criticism would have faded as soon as the bomb was successfully proven—leaving admiration for a noble purpose.

However, speculation on this subject may be regarded as a professional indulgence. For, in fact, even if the decision-makers had not feared a possible failure in demonstration, they would not have tried it. For they deemed it most unlikely that a demonstration could end the war as quickly and surely as hurling the bomb on Japan; and that was their duty as they saw it. No matter what the place and setting for the demonstration, they were sure it would not give an adequate impression of its appalling destructive power, would not register its full meaning in human lives. The desired explosive impression on the Japanese, it was concluded, could be produced only by the actual awful experience. Such precursory opinion was in accord with Stimson's subsequent interpretation of why its use was so effective.

"But the atomic bomb was more than a weapon of terrible destruction; it was a psychological weapon. In March, 1945, our Air Force had launched the first incendiary raid on the Tokyo area. In this raid more damage was done and more casualties were inflicted than was the case at Hiroshima. Hundreds of bombers took part and hundreds of tons of incendiaries were dropped. Similar successive raids burned out a great part of the urban areas of Japan, but the Japanese fought on. On August 6th a B-29 dropped a single atomic bomb on Hiroshima. Three days later a second bomb was dropped on Nagasaki and the war was over."[14]

It has since been contended, and with perseverance, that even if the drop on Hiroshima was justified by its purpose and results, that the second drop on Nagasaki was not. For the exponents of this opinion think that if right after Hiroshima the American government had made it clear, as they did later, that the Japanese authorities could retain the Emperor, they would have surrendered; and hence the destruction of Nagasaki was unnecessary.

This is a tenable judgment. But the records of happenings within Japanese ruling circles during the few days between Hiroshima and Nagasaki foster the impression that if the second bomb had not been dropped, the Japanese rulers would have delayed, perhaps for some weeks, the response which was preliminary to capitulation. The military heads would have been so firm in opposition that the Emperor would probably

[14] *On Active Service in Peace and War*, page 630.

have waited until the situation became more hopeless before overruling them.

The first reports which the military investigating group that the Japanese Chief of Staff hurried to Hiroshima gave out minimized the awfulness of the effects of the bomb, describing the burns suffered from the blast by persons clothed in white and those in shelters as relatively light. Military headquarters started to issue announcements of counter measures which could be effective against the new bomb. The truth about its nature and effects, as estimated by a group of physicists after their inspection, was only made known to the Cabinet on the morning of the 9th while the mushroom cloud was over Nagasaki. Even thereafter, the Army heads accepted the decision to surrender only because the Emperor's openly declared conclusion relieved them of shame and humiliation, and lessened their fear of disobedience by their subordinates.

Thus, to repeat, it is probable that by intensifying the dread of the new weapon—of which, so far as the Japanese knew, we might have many more—the strike against Nagasaki hastened the surrender. But whether merely by a few days or few weeks is not to be known.

In summary it can be concluded that the decision to drop the bombs upon Hiroshima and Nagasaki ought not to be censured. The reasons were—under the circumstances of the time—weighty and valid enough. But a cluster of worrisome queries remain which the passage of time has coated with greater political, ethical and historical interest.

One of these—whether or not the desired quick surrender could have been induced if the American government had been more explicit in its explanations of how the Japanese people and Emperor would fare after surrender—was considered in the preceding chapter.

Another, which has often been asked, is why ten days were allowed to pass between the receipt of information regarding the results of the test of the bomb and the issuance of our final warning. I think the delay was due to an intent to be sure that if the warning was at first unheeded, it could be driven quickly and deeply home by the bombs. Thus we waited until we knew all was in readiness to drop them. These tactics worked. But I wonder whether it might not have been wiser to issue the warning sooner, and thus to have allowed the Japanese authorities more time to ponder its meaning and acceptability. I think it not out of the question that if allowed, say, another fortnight, the Emperor might have imposed his final decision before the bomb was set for use. However, because of the blinding fury and pride of the fighting men, it is unlikely. He hardly would have dared to do so until the explosion of the atomic bomb destroyed the argument that Japan could secure a better peace if it continued to refuse to surrender unconditionally.

But what if the American government had fully revealed the results of the New Mexico test to the Japanese (and the whole world)? Could that have induced the desired quick surrender? The most promising time for such revelations would have been in connection with the issuance of the Potsdam Declaration; for by then the American air assaults and naval bombardments were spreading havoc everywhere, and most Japanese were aware they had no way of countering them, no good idea of how to survive them. Suppose, to be more precise, the American government had published the reports on the test which were sent by General Groves to Potsdam for Stimson and the President, such photographs of the explosion and of the mushroom cloud and the testimony of scientists about the destructive power of the weapon that were available. Might not that broadcast knowledge, prefaced by an explanation that one of our purposes was to spare the Japanese, have had enough shock effect to cause the Emperor to overrule the resistant Japanese military leaders?

Perhaps. But in order to make the disclosure as impressive as possible, it might have been necessary to postpone the issuance of the final warning—perhaps until the end of the Potsdam Conference. The test was July 16th; it would have taken time to assemble convincing accounts and photographs, and explanation. This postponement might have prolonged slightly the period of combat.

However, in retrospect, I believe that the risk should have been taken and the cost endured; for by so doing this we might have been spared the need to introduce atomic weapons into war. In the likely event that the Japanese would not have been swayed by this explicit warning of what would happen to them if they rejected our ultimatum, we as a people would be freer of any regret—I will not say remorse—at the necessity of enrolling Hiroshima and Nagasaki in the annals of history.

But the mind, circling upon itself, returns to the point of wondering whether, if the exterminating power of the bomb had not been actually displayed, the nations would have been impelled to make even as faltering an effort as they have to agree on measures to save themselves from mutual extinction by this ultimate weapon. In a novel published in 1914, H. G. Wells prophesied that nations would not recognize the impossibility of war "until the atomic bomb burst in their fumbling hands." Now, two great wars later, it remains entirely uncertain whether they will bow before its imperative.

Footnote 9, continued from page 195: Recently this interpretation has been revived by members of the revisionist group of historians, sometimes called the New Left. A condensed summary of their argument is contained in the long review of this book written by Mr. Gar Alperovitz in the *New York Review of Books* of June 15, 1967. The conclusion is reached by ignoring the total pertinent historical circumstance and concentrating on diverse fragments in memoirs and diaries which can be read to fit preconceptions.

Main Sources Cited

Anderson, Oscar E., Jr. with Richard C. Hewlett, *The New World 1939/ 1946 Volume 1 A History of the United States Atomic Energy Commission* (1962)

Attlee, Lord, "The Hiroshima Choice," in *Observer* (London) (September 6, 1959)

Bailey, Charles W., II, *see* Knebel

Bundy, McGeorge, *see* Stimson

Butow, Robert J. C., *Japan's Decision to Surrender* (1954)

Byrnes, James F., *All in One Lifetime* (1958)

Byrnes, James F., *Speaking Frankly* (1947)

Churchill, Winston S., *The Second World War*, Vol. 6, *Triumph and Tragedy* (1953)

Compton, Arthur Holly, *Atomic Quest: A Personal Narrative* (1956)

Craven and Cate, *see* U.S. Air Force

Ehrman, John, *see* U.K.

Feis, Herbert, *Between War and Peace: The Potsdam Conference* (1960)

Feis, Herbert, *The China Tangle: The American Effort in China from Pearl Harbor to the Marshall Mission* (1953)

Feis, Herbert, Letter in *American Historical Review* (October 1962)

Forrestal, James, *The Forrestal Diaries*, ed. by Walter Millis (1951)

Freed, Fred, joint author with Len Giovannitti of *The Decision to Drop the Bomb* (1965)

Giovannitti, Len, joint author with Fred Freed of *The Decision to Drop the Bomb* (1965)

Goodrich, Leland M., *Korea, A Study of U. S. Policy in the United Nations* (1956)

Gowing, Margaret, *Britain and Atomic Energy 1939-1945* (1964)

Grew, Joseph C., *Turbulent Era, A Diplomatic Record of Forty Years, 1904-1945*, ed. by Walter Johnson (1952)

Grey, Arthur L., Jr., "The Thirty-Eighth Parallel," in *Foreign Affairs* (April 1951)

Groves, Leslie R., Letter in *Science Magazine* (December 4, 1959)

Groves, Leslie R., *Now It Can Be Told* (1964)

Haskins, Caryl P., "Atomic Energy and American Foreign Policy" in *Foreign Affairs* (July 1946)

Hewlett, Richard C., *see* Anderson

Hull, Cordell, *Memoirs*, Vol. 2 (1948)

Inoguchi, Captain Rikihei, and Commander Tashash Nakajima, *The Divine Wind, Japan's Kamikaze Force in World War II* (1958)

Ivanov, L. N., *Essays on International Relations in the Period of the Second World War, 1939-1945* (1958)

Jungk, Robert, *Brighter Than a Thousand Suns* (1958)

Kase, Toshikazu, *Journey to the Missouri* (1950)

Kawai, Kazuo, *Japan's American Interlude* (1960)

King, Ernest J., and Walter Muir Whitehill, *Fleet Admiral King* (1952)

Knebel, Fletcher, and Charles W. Bailey, II, *No High Ground* (1960)

Laurence, William L., *Dawn Over Zero: The Story of the Atomic Bomb* (1960)

Leahy, William D., *I Was There: The Personal Story of the Chief of Staff to Presidents Roosevelt and Truman, Based on his Notes and Diaries Made at the Time* (1950)

Lilienthal, David E., *The Journals of David E. Lilienthal, Volume Two, The Atomic Energy Years 1945-1950* (1962)

Meade, E. Grant, *American Military Government in Korea* (1951)

Morison, Elting E., *Turmoil and Tradition: A Study of the Life and Times of Henry L. Stimson* (1960)

Morison, Samuel Eliot, *History of U.S. Naval Operations in the Pacific*, Vol. XIV

Morison, Samuel Eliot. Review of *Japan Subdued* in *America Historical Review* (October 1961)

National Broadcasting Company, Transcripts of interviews with various American, British, and Japanese participants in the historic event (1964-65)

Oppenheimer Hearings, *see* U.S. Atomic Energy Committee

Oppenheimer, J. Robert, letter in *Science Magazine* (December 4, 1959)

Potsdam Papers, *see* U. S. Department of State

Romanus, Charles F., *see* U.S. Department of the Army

Royal Institute of International Affairs, *Survey of International Affairs, 1939-1946: The Far East, 1942-1946*, by F. C. Jones, Hugh Borton, and B. R. Pearn (1955)

Sherwood, Robert E., *Roosevelt and Hopkins, An Intimate History* (1948)

Shigemitsu, Mamoru, *Showa: Years of Upheaval* (1958)

Smith, Alice Kimball, "The Decision to Use the Atomic Bomb, 1944-45," in *Bulletin of the Atomic Scientists* (October 1958)

Smyth, Henry DeWolf, *Atomic Energy for Military Purposes; the Official Report on the Development of the Atomic Bomb under the Auspices of the United States Government, 1940-1945* (1945)

Stimson, Henry L., "The Decision to Use the Atomic Bomb," in *Harper's Magazine* (February 1947)

Stimson, Henry L., Diary

Stimson, Henry L., and McGeorge Bundy, *On Active Service in Peace and War* (1947)

Sunderland and Romanus, *see* U.S. Department of the Army

Sutherland, John P., "The Story General Marshall Told Me," in *U.S. News and World Report* (November 2, 1959)

Togo, Shigenori, *The Cause of Japan* (1956)

Truman, Harry S., Memoirs, Vol. I, *Year of Decisions* (1955)

U.K., History of the Second World War, United Kingdom Series, *Grand Strategy*, Vol. VI, by John Ehrman (1956)

U.S. Air Force, Historical Division of Research Studies, The Army Air Forces in World War II, Vol. 5, *The Pacific: Matterhorn to Nagasaki,*

June 1944 to August 1945, ed. by Wesley Frank Craven and James Lea Cate (1953)

U.S. Atomic Energy Committee, Transcript of Hearing before Personnel Security Board, *In the Matter of J. Robert Oppenheimer* (1954)

U.S. Department of the Army, United States Army in World War II, *China-Burma-India Theater: Time Runs Out in CBI* by Riley Sunderland and Charles F. Romanus (1959)

U.S. Department of Defense, *The Entry of the Soviet into the War Against Japan: Military Plans, 1941-1945* (1955)

U.S., 79th Congress, First Session *Hearings* before the Special Committee on Atomic Energy, U.S. Senate, S.R. 179, Part I

U.S., 81st Congress, First Session, House Committee on Foreign Affairs, *Korean Aid*, Testimony of General Helmick, Hearings on H.R. 5330, June 9, 1949

U.S. Department of State, *Bulletin*

U.S. Department of State, Potsdam Papers: Collection of papers and documents concerning the Potsdam Conference, assembled by the State Department for publication

U.S. Department of State, Publication No. 2671, *Occupation of Japan: Policy and Progress.* Appendix 16. *Authority of General MacArthur as Supreme Commander for the Allied Powers*

U.S. Department of State, Foreign Relations of the United States, Diplomatic Papers, Publication 6199, *The Conferences at Malta and Yalta, 1945* (1955)

U.S. Military Section, Headquarters Army Forces Far East.
> Japanese Monograph No. 45, *Imperial General Headquarters Army High Command Record*
> Japanese Monograph No. 138, *Record of Operations Against Soviet Russia (Japanese Preparations for Operations in Manchuria Jan. 1943-Aug. 1945)*
> Japanese Monograph No. 154, *Record of Operations Against Soviet Russia, Eastern Front (August 1945)*
> Japanese Monograph No. 155, *Record of Operations Against Soviet Russia on Northern and Western Fronts of Manchuria and in Northern Korea (August 1945)*

U.S. Senate Sub-Committee to Investigate the Internal Security Act, Hearing, *Nuclear Physicist Defects to the United States*, (*December 15, 1964*)

U.S. Strategic Bombing Survey, Report No. 62, *Japanese Air Power*

Whitehill, Walter Muir, *see* King, Ernest J.

Index